The Mysterious Past

By the Same Author

ONE HUNDRED THOUSAND YEARS
OF MAN'S UNKNOWN HISTORY
THE GODS UNKNOWN
THE LEGACY OF THE GODS
MASTERS OF THE WORLD

The Mysterious Past

Robert Charroux

A BERKLEY MEDALLION BOOK
published by
BERKLEY PUBLISHING CORPORATION

He who eagerly searches for truth should ask it of the one who knows, not imposters.

Original French title: LE LIVRE DU PASSE MYSTERIEUX

Published by arrangement with Robert Laffont, Inc.

SBN 425-02741-4

*BERKLEY MEDALLION BOOKS are published by
Berkley Publishing Corporation
200 Madison Avenue
New York, N.Y. 10016*

BERKLEY MEDALLION BOOKS ® TM 757,375

Printed in the United States of America

Berkley Medallion Edition, MARCH, 1975

CONTENTS

PREFACE

The history of civilization has been recorded, as historians intended, either to benefit or to influence people. We thought it would be both useful and reasonable, therefore, to divulge some strange facts which more orthodox thinkers have consciously ignored or distorted.

Our ensuing history is purely a series of anecdotes, occasionally adventurous but always factual. The principles which we set out might be challenged or even brushed aside, but it is possible that they can be accepted as occult phenomena or the "Mysterious Unknown." *The Mysterious Past*, like our preceding books, proposes to fling open the door to the mysteries and heresies that intensify curiosity in those who are not satisfied with standard doctrine.

We shall deal with lost civilizations, Christopher Columbus, magic portraits, and with Agpaoa, the surgeon who acted as if human flesh were as fluid as water, and the laws of science no more than imaginative fabrications imposed by sorcerers.

We shall cover numerous topics that would not be included in a conformist book: sorcery, mysterious space adventures, and incredible powers passed on to humans by ancestors from another plane. Secrets will be revealed and, to set the tone of the book, we shall begin with the mysterious words heard on the moon by the cosmonaut Worden.

Mysterious words heard on the moon

On Tuesday, August 3, 1971, at exactly 8:00 A.M., the newscaster on France-Inter,* René D was interviewing Lucien B, the science journalist who had come to comment on the moon landing of Apollo XV.

We were listening and can certify that the following conversation took place at the moment of contact:

"Good morning, Lucien B! No doubt you can translate for us the mysterious words heard by Worden when he was on our satellite."

René D then distinctly spoke eight to ten words and Lucien B, a little nonplussed, replied nevertheless:

"Alas, I cannot translate them for you."

That was the end of the incident, but all the same, those mysterious words, which came directly from the moon, were something to excite public opinion and arouse the curiosity of journalists. Surely the press must have seized on information which was such an unexpected windfall! But no. The press seemed to have joined a conspiracy of silence. The many approaches made to René D, Lucien B, and other science journalists from the ORTF (the French broadcasting network) met with noncooperation. No one had heard the fateful sentence. Lucien B no longer remembered it and René D gave way like a house of cards.

*A French broadcasting service.

A transmission of unknown origin

By chance, our colleague Alain Ayache had also listened to France-Inter on August 3 at 8:00 A.M., and in the weekly magazine *Le Meilleur* (edition 33, page 4) he published an article seven columns long, headed "Why has *no one* spoken of the mysterious message heard on the moon—twenty untranslatable words which really sow the seeds of panic? Perhaps it proves that other men exist—something NASA wished to hide." The full-page article, augmented by a photograph of Worden, related in detail the extraordinary incident which took place on the moon.

Everything was going very well that day on our satellite and then at 11:15 an extraordinary fading occurred and contact with Houston was lost. Worden, who was in charge of telecommunications, had his attention drawn by a strange noise coming through his receiver. It was a breathing sound which changed into a long whistle. His receiver was picking up a transmission whose origin was impossible to trace.

Stifled murmurs were followed by vague sounds resembling words, then a sentence constantly repeated on one note, varying from a small to a shrill tone, and from lightly stressed sounds to raucous exclamations.

Luckily, the transmission was recorded on Lem's tape recorder, and Worden transmitted it to NASA.

"After a few seconds of confusion," we read in *Le Meilleur*, "the conversation between Houston and Apollo XV was played back through a loudspeaker in a private office. The conversation and the reception of the mysterious message were pursued 'in camera.' " Following that, as we have said, there was a total blackout on the affair, in the USA as well as throughout the rest of the world.

How *Le Meilleur* came to know these details (and they are correct) we do not know, but one fact has been established: a conspiracy forbade the divulgence of the "moon" sentence.

The forbidden sentence

It has taken us a great deal of time and trouble to finally discover, by means which journalists describe as a breach of the professional code, some of the words of this enigma.

We thought we had remembered two words from the text: "*lamma,*" which was among the last words spoken by Jesus on the cross (*Eli, Eli, lama sabacthani*) and "*rabbi,*" which is easy to identify. This leads us to believe that the sentence which was reported to us phonetically is consistent with the original. Here are the eight separate words:

Mara rabbi allardi dini endavour esa couns alim.*

It seems as if some Hebrew words are mixed with others of uncertain origin. In Hebrew, "*mar*" means "mister," and "*mara*" means "bitter"; "*rabbi*" means "master" or "rabbi," and "*dim*" means "law" or "judgment." If "*endavour*" is from the English, it could refer to endeavor. *Allardi, esa, couns,* and *alim* remain a complete mystery. Perhaps some philosophers will find the key to the puzzle.

A preface is always tedious to read, but if ours has not proved too discouraging we invite you to take an unusual journey with us.

*It is possible we misheard the first word of the sentence, which could be "*mara*" and not "*lamma.*"

PART I

Primohistory

CHAPTER ONE

THE UNKNOWN WORLD

Since time immemorial, our ancestors have believed in fairylands, planets similar to Earth, and supernatural beings such as elves, giants, and genies. Nowadays men consider themselves enlightened and no longer believe those myths. Nevertheless, they speak of Atlantis, of a transmartian planet gravitating far out in the cosmos, and they believe in prophets, astrologers, the baby Jesus, and St. Anthony, who finds lost objects. What is more, they say they can perceive invisible worlds, merging with each other to form parallel universes.

In fact, although the beliefs are given new names, their nature changes very little; perhaps as time goes by they have become a bit more irreverent and scientific, but they are certainly no more reasonable. Nor, we should add, are they *less* reasonable!

Mysterious staircases

Traveling around the world is exciting and offers plenty of scope for the amateur archaeologist to make significant discoveries. The *pistas*, or giant drawings, of the pampas of Nazca in Peru are a typical example of the archaeology unknown to the very people who are paid to know. Why, and for whom were the routes marked out and the trails and paths constructed?

It is not only Nazca that presents this kind of problem: In England, Ireland, France, Czechoslovakia, Ceylon, and other places, there are other unexplained traces which are not mentioned in classical textbooks.

Before 1973, who was interested in those little staircases cut into the rock of the mountains? They climb, intercross, scale sheer cliffs, and twist and turn on the sandstone hillocks, sometimes stopping in front of the outline of a door, a sort of landing or a hollow carved in the rock, but sometimes not leading anywhere at all or just ending at a fault in the rock. In Czechoslovakia, some professional archaeologists concluded that the staircases were the result of natural erosion, a theory which does not even merit discussion. Obviously these staircases were carved by man. Their dimensions vary according to the places they are found. In Ceylon, where they are more numerous, their surface or "giron," is about 20 x 15 centimeters and the height of one step is only 10 centimeters. Occasionally two or three flights of steps are carved in the rock; sometimes they are parallel, sometimes not, for no apparent reason. One flight of steps might stop abruptly, another continues, and a third joins the first. The general plan appears to be incoherent and one can ascertain that the stairs would not be any particular use to men. Besides, the human foot would find it difficult to gain a hold on each tread, as they are so close together.

Paths to the beyond

As for the *pistas* of Nazca, one cannot really give a rational explanation for something which does not belong to our realm of reasoning. One can only imagine builders in ancient times, motivated by thoughts which were very different from our own, combining the elements of our world with those of a supernatural plane.

In Celtic mythology, one finds examples of marvelous physical and intellectual feats in the "perilous castles" whose walls open and close to allow their heroes to enter a universe governed by unknown dimensions, where space-time has no common measure with our science. That is why we think that the staircases of Ceylon must have been cut for people from another world, for ghosts, gods, or strange entities who knew how to skirt the precipices and pass through the rock doors —who knew how to communicate with other worlds as well as our own. The rough-hewn doors, sketched on the rocky walls, perhaps open into an enchanted country, forbidden to humans unless, by special favor, they are invited to go in.

In France such doors can be found in the Dordogne region; in Peru we saw wide and well-built staircases that stopped in front of a mountain, or, in some cases, at the tops of mounds not more than a meter high. In Petra, in the Hor Mountains on the western frontier of modern Jordan, there is a real city which opens onto an amphitheater of mountains. In the south of Areguipa, in Peru, the rock of d'Ylo bears the inscription, THE DOOR OF THE SECRET ENTRANCE OF THE SOCOBAN [TUNNEL] LEADING TO THE MYSTERIES AND THE GOLD OF THE ANCIENT LOST WORLD, IS HIDDEN BEHIND ONE OF THESE THREE SUMMITS, AND IS FORBIDDEN TO MORTALS.

Men of today are no longer psychologically prepared to believe in a parallel universe of this nature. It is perhaps the secret of the Ancients, lost with the spoken word, the drink of initiation, and the ability to enter a supernatural world.

On certain rocks in Ceylon, at Sigirya, the staircases climbing sheer cliffs are nothing more than grooves, like the rungs of a ladder, hollowed out of the rock. Sometimes the rock staircases are scattered with square holes 15 x 15 centimeters, set out like the squares of a chessboard. Again, the logical mind is incapable of finding an explanation, but there is no doubt that these staircases are the work of an ancient civilization, all traces of which have vanished in the mists of time.

The door with a cross

In bygone days, the Initiated knew how to bypass the physical laws which try to keep us within our concept of reality. Pythagoras knew how to pass the barriers and travel through time, but he did so by means of geometry, rather than cars, airplanes, or rockets.

According to tradition, some Yogis in the Himalayas occasionally see a drawing representing a closed door, symbolized in our alphabet by the letter *A*. The words "Come and join us" are included in the message. The Yogi knows how to become absorbed in his "self," how to become letter, number, and equation. He detaches his superior inner self from his body and all terrestrial and universal laws, thus becoming "another." His imponderable "self" climbs the staircases of the chosen mountain, opens the door sketched in the rock, and passes through the solid granite. Behind the Yogis, the doors of the mountain are barred with a cross.

The Book of the Dead of the ancient Egyptians says that the cross is the sign forbidding entry. It is also a sign of forgetfulness to place a cross on someone or something. Like the first, the cross symbolizes death, and it also indicates conspiracies and evil. The sign of truth is a circle, a triangle, or a rectangle.

The key to open the forbidden doors

It is on the exploration and analysis of the unusual in the world that the logical observer bases his theories, however haphazard they may appear. To this method of investigation we add a confrontation with the phenomena of the present day, for we think that the mysterious unknown human has a center of information, a sort of coordinator where all past experiences are recorded. In other words, the whole history of man since his creation is engraved on its chromosome-memories, as the genetic code is for each species.

An oak follows the long tradition of the tree through the knowledge acquired and retained by its ancestors; a cat, a swallow, a plant, all have in their chromosomes, or in the messengers of their evolution, the qualities, the taboos, and the manifestations of life and of survival which constitute their character as living things. It is by this process that one can, perhaps, explain the hippie movement and the Jesus cult. One can confront it with the phenomenon of Jesus 2,000 years ago.

All the same, the mystery of the pyramids of Egypt cannot be explained except by the study of the pyramids of France, Ireland, Peru, and China and by investigating the use of cryogen. The actual freezing of the dead in nitrogen liquid at −169°, to permit future resurrection, is the explanation of the immortal chambers which are the pyramids of Gizeh, where the mummy had to remain intact while waiting for resurrection by the grace of Osiris.

In carrying out as complete an exploration as possible of the unknown terrains, we can try to open the forbidden doors of the Mysterious Unknown. In France, the enigma of the Rock of Footprints is perhaps correlated with that of the staircases for the ghosts of Sigirya in Ceylon.

The Rock of Footprints

This rock, near Lanslevillard in Savoy, is an enormous block of stone, bearing the prints to which it owes its name. Our friends and collaborators of the Study Group of the Friends of the Unknown, and fellow readers of Robert Charroux went to the site, leaving La Madeleine pass at an altitude of 1,750 meters, and following the path marked GR5. The journey took three and a half hours. The Rock of Footprints is situated between the Great Black Rock and the Pisselerand Rock. It is like a slab of granite resting on the mountainside at an angle, so that climbing it is easy.

It is oval in shape, and about five meters in diameter, the steepest face being two and a half to three meters high and dominating the valley towards the west. About fifty footprints are perfectly visible on the stone, and most of them seem to have been shaped with a tool, following the outline of shoes. These three-dimensional prints are 16, 20, and 25 centimeters long, corresponding to shoe sizes 6 (children), 12 (children), and 3. The depressions are about 2 or 3 centimeters deep.

"With one exception, they all point in the same direction," said Gilbert Bovard, "toward the sun and the valley. There are numerous stones with cupules [cup-shaped indentations] in the region, and when we were twenty minutes' journey from the shelter of Vallonbrun, someone showed us a rock with a sun engraved on it."

Marks denoting ownership

An explanation of this has not yet been found. One might imagine that short men of an unknown race climbed the rock, traced the shapes of their feet, and then carved out the stone within the outlines. Most of these beings wore shoes, although a few had bare feet, as some of the prints indicate.

Taking into account the area and one's concept of the ancient religious rites, the Rock of Footprints, in its unusual situation, must have been the foundation of a belief or superstition. A tribe of sun worshipers had the idea of making an observation post for the sunset, perhaps in the form of an altar or temple, but pilgrimages would have been difficult in all seasons and impossible in winter, because of the position. This resulted in the idea of substituting this symbol for their actual presence.

In the prehistoric caves at Glozel and at numerous other sites around the world, men have made marks or signs with their hands. Often, these were to show their sovereignty over a particular area and to indicate their strength and number. At the Great Rock, the tribe must have traced and hollowed out the footprints of each believer, which accounts for the different sizes and shapes of the feet. In this way, the owner of each print was always supposed to be in adoration or standing guard, represented by his mark. This is usual in ancient magical rites, and even nowadays. According to the tracings, there is a connection between the cupules and the myth of sacred water, which no doubt was thought to contain marvelous properties.

The two prints of the chief are on the extreme edge of the rock, but two others, lying sideways, imply an intention of sacrilege or desecration and were perhaps the work of an enemy. Admittedly, these are only hypotheses, but then, the Rock of Footprints is a fairly rare case in known archaeology.

The magazine *Phenomenes Inconnus* mentions the existence of prints of this kind in Catateni and Slon, Rumania, and in Yugoslavia, Spain, and Scandinavia, but nowhere are the marks so clear and so numerous as on the Great Rock.

Chapter Two

Islands And Countries From Another World

Some of the early civilizations disappeared, leaving only puzzling traces of their existence, which rational 20th century man often chooses to deny.

Now, however, gigantic structures and submerged foundations have been found near the island of Bimini, about 80 kilometers to the east of Miami, Florida, and this discovery has lent further weight to the argument for the existence of Atlantis. Many people believe that Bimini is the remainder of the great island described by Plato. Others, notably Professor Doru Todericiu, believe it is just the site of an Atlantic colony.

Irrespective of these conflicting views, we feel confident that future discoveries will finally confirm the reality of Atlantis. The documents that we shall quote in support of our cause deserve to be included because they indicate that the last islands of Atlantis did not disappear until the 15th century.

In 1971 Professor Manson Valentin discovered large stone tables, and columns which are presumably the foundations of a temple. A pyramid and a fresh water fountain, fifteen feet in depth, were also discovered.

Jean Ponce de Leon, a Spanish captain (1460-1521) and Governor of Puerto Rico, visited Bimini in the 15th century, in hopes of finding a fountain whose water, according to the locals, had rejuvenating properties. It is a curious coincidence that Bimini should have this source of fresh water and that the Fountain of Youth of Atlantis had always been sought in that same area.

According to the encyclopedia *La Mer* no. 16, April, 1972, the Soviet geologist N. Zirov took a ton of limestone disks from the submerged Atlantis mountain. They were fifteen centimeters in diameter and four centimeters thick, smooth on one side and rough on the other. One survey shows that 12,000 years ago, these disks must have been exposed to open air.

The Mirage of Saint Brendan

The vision of the Fortunate Islands that inspired the adventurous travelers of the Middle Ages was in fact a reality! Despite previous misunderstandings, errors, and approximations, one can in all probability identify the famous Isle of St. Brendan as Madeira or one of the Canaries.

The Madeira Islands are noted as the Fortunate Islands of St. Brendan on the Venetian map of 1367 belonging to the Pizzigani brothers. They are referred to in the same way on another map (of which the name is defaced) which can be found in the Weimar library, dated 1424, and on the chart dated 1435 of the Genoan, Beccaria. Admittedly, the geographers of the Middle Ages did sometimes place St. Brendan to the west of Ireland, and even as far away as the West Indies.

Many sailors landed on the island, including three Portuguese from Setúbal, among whom was Pero Velho, the pilot who made several trips to Brazil. Even more voyagers sighted St. Brendan and some were able to draw it from memory. But the overriding question is whether they actually saw Madeira, or just the reflection of the island of Palma, created through a chance cloud formation to the northwest.

The Mystery of the Island of Antilia

In the case of Antilia, the situation is completely different, and there is good reason to believe that at the beginning of the fifteenth century these last remains of Atlantis still survived in the middle of "the Western Ocean" at about the 28th parallel.

Madeira, the Azores, and the Canaries are the remains of the continent of Atlantis, but the earth has been reformed as a result of volcanic eruptions, so it has completely lost its Atlantean history.

Tradition has it that in the 8th century, Spanish Christians, chased by the invading Arabs, sought refuge in the middle of the ocean, "in a place whose position was not revealed to the world before 1500." The famous globe constructed in 1492 by Martin Behaim for the town of Nuremberg has the following notation inscribed in Old German.

"In the year 734 A.D., when all of Spain was invaded by the devils of Africa, the island of Antilia, known as the Seven Cities, as noted hereunder, was populated by an archbishop of Porto,* six bishops and Christian men and women who had escaped from Spain in ships and had arrived there with their beasts and goods. It was by chance that in 1414 a Spanish ship should pass close by."

The Florentine professor, Paulo Toscanelli, mentioned that

*Porto was at this time in Lusitania. The Kingdom of Portugal did not exist until the time of Alphonse I, 1114-1185, son of Henry the Younger.

Antilia was situated in the middle of the Atlantic Ocean, between Japan to the east and St. Brendan to the west, below the mythical island of Man Satanaxia. He even tried to give some idea of the distances involved by saying that one must count twenty-six "spaces" between Lisbon and China and ten spaces between Antilia and Cipangu (Japan). One space was 250 nautical miles, or 5 degrees. Martin Behaim's globe, doubtless inspired by Toscanelli's map, showed Antilia at 330° and Lisbon at 15°.

M. d'Avezac tells us that Antilia was known and visited in the fifteenth century. Toscanelli, he adds, wrote to the royal court of Portugal, "This island, which you know of, and which you call the Seven Cities. . . ."

Ferdinand, the son of Christopher Columbus, is more precise in *The Life of My Father*:* "Several Portuguese have noted it on their maps, giving it the name Antilia, even though the position of the island does not tally with that given by Aristotle. No one has placed it at more than 200 leagues directly to the west of the Azores and the Canaries.

"It is accepted that the island of Seven Cities was populated by the Portuguese in 714 A.D. when Spain, under King Roderick, was overrun by the Moors. Seven bishops founded seven cities there and, so as not to harbor thoughts of returning to Spain, they burned their boats and all their navigational equipment."

Ferdinand Columbus states that a boat landed at Antilia and the sailors entered a church to verify that the Catholic faith was being observed.

It would seem then that the island really did exist and that it

*The exact title is *F. Colombo, Historia del almirante Chr. Colomb suo padre*, etc. Italian translation by Ulloa, Venice, 1571; French translation by Cotolendi (1681).

was not far from Madeira, a fact supported by Peter of Medina, the sixteenth-century author of the well-known *Treatise on the Art of Navigation.*

"Not far from the island of Madeira," he wrote, "there is another island, called Antilia, which one can no longer see nowadays. In a Ptolemy*, which was read to Popu Urbain [Pope Urban VI], I found this island, shown with the following legend relating to it. 'This island, Antilia was once discovered by the Portuguese, but today one cannot find it; the people spoke Spanish, and reputedly sought shelter there when fleeing from the barbarians who invaded Spain during the reign of King Roderick, the last governor of Spain in the Gothic Era. There was an archbishop with three bishops, and each one had his own city; this is why it is often known as the island of Seven Cities. The people followed a very Christian way of life, surrounded by the riches of the world.' "

In this Ptolemy, Antilia is eighty-seven leagues long (on its north-south axis) and twenty-eight leagues wide. This island is situated at latitude 36-1/2° on a parallel with Gibraltar. It was known, therefore, back in the 2nd century A.D. and it is likely that it really did exist, but it was engulfed in the wake of earthquakes that were registered in Portugal during the 15th century. Such cataclysms do occur in the Atlantic, and on several occasions volcanic islands have appeared, the most recent being in 1956, at the tip of Fayal, in the Azores, to which it is still linked.

If the Spanish bishops could have constructed seven cities so quickly on a deserted island, they must have found all the materials already prepared, perhaps the last remains of the

†Peter of Medina refers to the work of a famous second-century Greek geographer and astronomer, Claude Ptolemy, as a Ptolemy.

towns and villages of the powerful Poseidon (Atlantis or Atlanta). Let us consider the decision that the Spanish took regarding the burning of their boats. It could have been an indication that they had found what they thought to be paradise, or the land of the First Fathers.*

These indications, which are so unconvincing to demanding rationalists, give us cause to believe that Antilia was a small part of Atlantis that had miraculously survived the universal upheaval for 12,000 years before it finally disappeared around 1550.

Antilia-Atlanta

The fantasies concerning The Fortunate Islands are rich in surprises and phenomena which forge a link with the Mysterious Unknown.

Well before the time of Christopher Columbus and Cabral, there is mention of a Brazilian island situated either to the northwest of St. Brendan, or between Antilia and the Island of Sheep.

The continent discovered by Vincent Pinson and Cabral was originally called the Land of the Holy Cross, and then became known as Brazil, which is a corruption of the word *''braza''* (braised), indicating a similarity in color to the *''bresillet''* wood which proliferates in that part of the world. Brazil also signifies ''red,'' and this country was in fact the fatherland of the Indians.

The etymology of Antilia becomes more and more curious. The name comes from *''ante-ilia,''* which means the island before (the then still unknown continent) or the anterior island, *i.e.*, the oldest island, or Atlantis. This is the most likely

*Curiously, it is at the point where Antilia emerges, the last remains of Atlantis, that mysterious phenomena occur. These range from the disappearance of boats to the eruption of islands.

interpretation, especially as one can read the following inscription on a map dated 1445: "This island was called 'the island of Antiliis.' Plato, a great and knowledgeable philosopher, notes that it was almost as vast as Africa." The naval charts of the Middle Ages plot Antilia in the group of islands called *"Insulae de novo repertoe"* or "the newly discovered islands," which also included Royllo, Man Satanaxia, and Tanmar.

The archipelago had nothing in common with the Azores, Madeira, or the Canaries, which were well known. These islands were therefore either mythical or else they had been swallowed up by the ocean, individually or as a whole.

Those who study words and the Mysterious Unknown still attempt to discover the origin of the name "Man Satanaxis," or the Island of Satan's Hand. The Venetian geographer Dominic Mauro Negro called it the "Island of Mana"; Beccaria knew it as "Satanagro," and Bianco called it "Satanxio." These names suggest the magical power of *mana,* the word *"man,"* which denotes "human," and imparts the idea of an evil hand emerging from the sea.

Was it a magical island? Perhaps, but more likely it was an island of charms, where men could exercise extraordinary powers, or an island of "the original man" and the center of the world, as the Isle of Man was for the Celts. So we come back to Atlantis, the country of the First Fathers!

The Green Children

In the Middle Ages, there was a strong tendency toward religion and belief in the occult. In fact, these quite often merge in tales of angels, which remind us of the land of fairies and the depths of hell, thus conjuring up thoughts of underground worlds. In this respect Antilia was both the earthly paradise and the forbidden city in the depths of the seas or the bowels of the earth. Even these days, strange happenings can lead one to believe that these old myths are not entirely without foundation.

On August 29, 1911, at midnight, the employers at a slaughterhouse in a small California town discovered a naked man, half dead from exposure. His language bore no resemblance to any of the aboriginal dialects known at the time, and no one ever found out where he had come from, although anthropologists asserted that he was one of the last wild Indians.

Still more extraordinary was the appearance in Spain, during the last century, of two children, belonging to an unknown race. The story was recounted by George Langelaan, in *La Vie Claire* in February, 1972, but one might perhaps doubt its authenticity, since our research in conjunction with the journalist Sergio Berrocal did not result in the location of the village of Banjos, near Gerona in Catalonia, where the event is supposed to have taken place.

It is claimed that one bright afternoon in August, 1887, the villagers were taking their siesta in the shade of some olive trees, when they noticed two young children crying bitterly.

The Catalans were stupefied and somewhat horrified to see that the children, a boy and a girl, were half naked and that their skin was completely green, similar in hue to the fruit of their olive trees. The strange little beings ran away shrieking, but they were soon caught and taken to the house of Señor Ricardo da Calno, mayor of Banjos, who tried to find out more about them.

When he tried to calm them down and persuade them that no one meant them any harm, they spoke for the first time, using words from a completely unknown language. Then Señora Calno washed the bodies of the two children, as the green color closely resembled decomposing flesh and it disgusted her. But the hue did not change at all. The mayor became more and more perplexed, and eventually decided to ask the opinion of a doctor and the authorities of Gerona, who established the verbal method of examination which, according to George Langelaan, exists at Banjos.

A country under the mountains

It was evident from their pigmentation and their behavior that the two little creatures did not belong to the human race. Their features were somewhat negroid, they had slits of eyes, and although they accepted water to drink, they refused point-blank all the usual food such as bread, meat, potatoes, carrots, olives, figs, raisins, etc. After five days, when the locals despaired of finding anything for the children to eat, the pair saw some shelled beans which they ate raw.

The little boy, who was the younger and also the more delicate, was only able to survive for a month. He passed away quietly and was buried in the village cemetery, but the little girl, who appeared to be thirteen or fourteen, slowly grew accustomed to her new way of life. Gradually she learned enough Spanish to be able to recount a story that defies all credibility and, it would appear, exceeds the limit of possibility.

''My brother and I,'' she said, ''left the hill through a grotto which opens into our world.* We lived with our family and our people in a country where there is night all the time. Sometimes we would see a great light, far away on the horizon, beyond a great lake. One day when I was with my brother, there was a deafening noise all around us like the explosion of a mountain, and without knowing how it all happened, we suddenly found ourselves in the cave near the village.''

*This story resembles the mystery of the staircase hewn out of the mountain. The children seem to have come out of a rock as if they were expelled from a parallel universe.

The mayor of Banjos and some amateur archaeologists returned to the cave, explored it thoroughly and sounded the rocks, but they could not find a fissure, a gap, or any hint of a passage into the depths of the earth. Even a snake would not have been able to hide there.

The green girl, who came from the "world beyond," lived for five years with the da Calne family, with whom she had completely integrated. She died peacefully, like her brother, and was buried next to him, taking with her the secret of her life, her color, her race, and perhaps her universe.

Green beings from outer space

Since 1887, man's knowledge has expanded considerably in certain ways, and isolated events have made it possible to put forward a plausible explanation regarding the "green children."

In the first place, assuming that George Langelaan's story is accurate, one might be forgiven for doubting the young girl's story. Those scholars who put forward the theories of extraterrestial beings would not hesitate to point out that the color green is traditionally associated with the planet Venus and that, everything taken into consideration, it would be more acceptable if the children had landed in an intergalactic ship rather than being ejected from an underworld.

One could postulate that an extraplanetary race had made an attempt at acclimatization on earth. More interesting, however, is the theory of Doctor Dominic Recoldin, of London University, who has dedicated himself to the study of the physiological and morphological changes that occur in the human being as a result of photosynthesis. This is a process carried out by plants to transform the radiant energy of the sun into chemical energy, such as sugar and proteins.

In the 19th century, the doctors of Gerona probably did not approach their examinations in this way, but it would be interesting to know whether the children of Banjos possessed an organ capable of photosynthesizing by itself by means of chlorophyll, thus explaining their green appearance.

Chapter Three

Our Superior Ancestors

In their speculations prehistorians have always underestimated the event of 12,000 years ago which was actually of the utmost importance: the Great Flood! Practically the whole of the human species perished, by water, fire, or a universal epidemic, and was resurrected by a handful of individuals who had forgotten what occurred in antediluvian times. We certainly had ancestors before the Flood, but opinions differ as to how advanced they were.

An island for the Initiators

In our opinion, antediluvian man of Atlantis (and perhaps also of the World of Mu and Thule) had great scientific knowledge of a level that is difficult to evaluate in comparison with ours. It is not impossible, though, that this prehistoric knowledge will one day be revealed through some revelation of our complex biology.

Our very important genetic legacy, one which perhaps goes

back to the first man, is probably stored in the unused areas of our brain. As our knowledge increases, the unused areas will gradually become unblocked. The phenomenon could continue until man has completely recovered his past knowledge.* The learning process cannot be compared with the physical evolution. It takes place much more rapidly and involved not only the mind's development, but also an ability to remember things deeply embedded in the past. This last aspect of the theory implies, therefore, that man did have superior ancestors.

Certainly one does not come across "locomotives and bicycles" that might have been made by these great ancestors, as our colleague Jacques Bergier mentioned, but then it is unlikely that one would find steel from a locomotive that has been rotting for dozens of centuries or more. On the other hand, even if locomotives or bicycles did exist on other planets, it would be difficult to prove. For the superior ancestors were not necessarily earth beings, or might only have been so in recent times.

In mythology gods and goddesses always seem to come from a lost island. This is in keeping with the idea that the Thulians, Cabires or other Initiators disguised themselves because of their extraterrestrial origins and began their teachings on an island. Chinese mythology refers to the island as Saints, while the Japanese name it Oraisan and others suggest Delos, Samothrace, Man, Avalon, Thule, Titicaca, Dieu, etc.

The real name of the Isle of Yeu in the Vendee is "Dieu," under which name it appears in all the old manuals. The name is probably derived from *ogia* (*Insula ogia* and not *insula ova*),

*Man is a being endowed with immortality. He reproduces by fission, but the original man, Adam, persists throughout this vast process of reincarnation. The two and a half billion individuals on our planet are only reflections, in distorting mirrors, of a single primordial man.

which reminds one of Ogham or Ogmius, the god of knowledge. Ogmius, according to the Gauls, was the inventor of writing and the one who taught man wisdom. Oannes is believed to have done the same in Chaldee, Apollo in Delos, and the Cabires, Orejona and Quetsalcoatl, were dressed strangely according to those who saw them and perhaps they were also physically different from people on Earth. This is doubtless the origin of carnival disguises.

One might suppose that if the Initiators came from outer space, or especially from the oceans of Venus, they would have been looking for the type of place which, on their own planet, they associated with spreading the knowledge of science. An island, of course, offers the particular advantage of minimizing the possibility of possible contamination of poorly adapted organisms. On this basis, if we are to believe world mythology, the original superior ancestors, First Fathers, or saints, were extraterrestial beings.

Man as a solely terrestial being

Certain flying-saucer fanatics and astrophysicists like to claim that "mathematically" life and civilization must exist on other planets. The view that there must be more than one inhabited world is based on the same principle as Darwin's theory of evolution: the virus, the amoeba, the earthworm, the serpent, the crocodile, the cow, the monkey, man.

It is an idea which bears thinking about. Man might be a product of the normal cycle of evolution of the living. The same thing could have occurred on other planets, either by accident or for some unknown reason.

One does not find any obvious links between the monkey, with its 950 cc cranium and man with his 1,550 cc. There is an enormous gap between a gibbon in the zoo and a learned atomic scientist. The argument simply does not hold. Several theorists regard man as a special animal that has probably resulted from a sudden and miraculous mutation. The same could apply to the dolphin and the sea lion, whose intelligence and mysterious attraction toward man are outstanding in the reputedly inferior animal kingdom. The dolphin, like man, gives the impression of being a breed apart. This implies that it was not created in the normal pattern.

Under these circumstances it seems unlikely that a similar miracle could have occurred on other planets, even if they were identical to Earth. Other planets have given or will give birth to viruses, worms, snakes, crocodiles, etc., right up to gibbons. Gibbons would probably evolve into more superior gibbons, then by the successive steps into an animal more intelligent and more perfect than us, but not identical to us. The laws of probability make it highly unlikely that fortuitous mutations could repeat themselves in exactly the same way, purely by chance, on two separate planets, even if these planets were identical. Only the rational processes—physical and chemical—could reproduce themselves.

For all those who believe, and we do, that man is a being belonging to the evolutionary chain, but who has benefited from a mutation or from exceptional luck, it is difficult to believe that other men somewhere in the universe could possibly resemble him!* On the contrary, if man does exist in several places, then man, the unique specimen, was "exported" there.

*The human species seems to be well established; it does not seem to tend back to an original source, or wish to return to a primitive type (the monkey for example). The most backward primitives seem to be fallen men, with a tendency toward a climbing back, rather than men in "normal" evolution toward higher things.

Attempts at acclimatization

Given the hypothesis of a plurality of inhabited planets and the exportation of the human species, on which planet would the first man have seen the light of day?

That is a question to which there is probably no answer. Perhaps on Earth, but it is unlikely, and we are inclined to think that he was transported to our globe, "sown" in some fashion, and the acclimatization has more or less succeeded. We suggest there were several such "importations," the first taking place millions of years ago. The conditions were not favorable, the imported subjects did not succeed in acclimatizing themselves, and they did not found a civilization.

This theory has no scientific foundation in the usual sense of the phrase. It supposes the existence and intercession of entities similar to God or gods. It is from this angle that it loses a certain rationalism, but, in fact, the laws of science are at fault, since only total knowledge can be rigorous, which is not the case with human science. God or gods which, in our simple way, we believe to be spirits, may perhaps have a reality unknown to us, a consistency or a nature which we cannot conceive. It is for this reason that we call our theories, our hypotheses, and our various speculations "games." In this present study, one must imagine man as having been brought here and sown on our globe by men from another planet.

One can imagine, without having proof, that several futile attempts were made, probably with more and more elaborate "subjects." It is obvious that these "men" were not very developed, but more likely the more aggressive among them, that is, those who had the greater chance of adapting themselves to the conditions of the difficult and precarious environment.

In our time, man has sent other men into space, technically for the futherance of science, but also out of curiosity and perhaps because in the subconscious they are being called to by their memory chromosomes. In fact, the conquest of space will basically be a return to our origins; a pilgrimage to the lands of the First Fathers. If our civilization still exists in a hundred years' time, it is certain that the astronauts will have visited the nearest planets and that these explorations will take them toward distant horizons where they will perhaps have the possibility of finding a small planet identical to the Earth. If this is so, they will find there animal life and flora almost identical to the ones we know; but probably not our exceptional species: man and the dolphin.

The biologists of Earth, because it is part of human nature to propagate civilization, will try to introduce men there, choosing the most primitive and the most likely to survive: the equivalent of the Baloubas and the Papuans of our era. The First Fathers, in their colonization attempts, must have done it this way, conditioning their "subjects" by modifying their blood and respiratory systems; perhaps even attempting hybrids with animals and plants, who, on that distant planet resembled us the closest.

A Cosmic Initiation Center

Reliable tradition has it that acclimatization, or hybridization, succeeded 15,000 to 20,000 years ago, for we know that we had ancestors at least as advanced as we are, in the age of Atlantis. Those men who were imported or conditioned could easily have spread over the Earth a great civilization with the aid of demigods, whom we call the "First Fathers," some of whom came and installed themselves on our globe.

This theory, just as rational as the Darwinian evolutionary theory, presupposes the existence, somewhere in the cosmos, of an initiating center from whence our superior ancestors were exported—those who populated Atlantis and the Hyperboreans, as well as the people of Mu. We have a logical explanation:

1. Of the lack of links between monkey and man.
2. Of the monsters or fantastic beings, half-man, half-animal, who, according to tradition, fought with man for the supremacy of the Earth.
3. Of those first prehistoric creatures (the subjects incapable of evolving, or badly hybridized).
4. Of the Superior Ancestors who, by the side of this failed humanity, came to colonize our planet.

In this way, one can explain the mysterious empathy which still exists between the exported humans who have succeeded on land, and the exported dolphins whose marine experiment proved abortive.

The Hardy Initiates

The Great Flood put an end to this fantastic operation, just as a similar cataclysm will one day put an end to our civilization. However, the myths claim that a group of Initiates were established in the polar regions before the great flood: the Hyperborians. They have often been called "The Great White Ancestors," the "First Fathers," mentors and supreme chiefs of Atlantis.

Hyperborea, their capital, situated somewhere between Iceland and Greenland, was surrounded by mountains of ice, but enjoyed such a temperate climate that the countryside was lush and green, with great trees, and wheat grew in abundance.* The capital of this small kingdom was, they say, Thule, though other tales mention Thule as an island in the North Atlantic (perhaps Iceland). Whatever it was, Hyperboria, with or without Thule, seemed to be the initiatic center of Atlantis, the great headquarters from which orders were sent out.

Much has been written about the Hyperborians since Hesiode and Homer, but no author has ever expressed surprise that the Initiators, directors of the science and conscience of a vast civilization, deliberately chose to install themselves in a polar region, even supposing that by a miracle of nature or of their own making, they managed to create a temperate climate.

The Great White Ancestors

We know that the Great North was once warmer, due to the fact that the Earth, before the Flood, turned on a perpendicular axis and on an ecliptical plane, thus abolishing the seasons. Sweden and Norway once had tropical climates, which explains the formation of amber, whose origin is from a resin found on the shores of the Baltic. Even so, it is probable that the choice of the geographical position of Hyperboria was motivated by reasons far more rational than fantasy or chance.

The Hyperborians were reputedly very large, very white, and had very clear blue eyes and blond hair, thus typifying our present notion of the Nordic type, as opposed to the darker-skinned people who live in tropical areas. It is therefore logical to believe that the white-skinned Hyperborians had purposefully chosen the least warm area of the Earth because it corresponded more closely to their own climate on the planet from which they originated.

*The history of Herodotus (Paris, 1909), says: "Our globe became colder and colder or passed in cycles from very cold spells to warm

In brief, if the First Fathers were extraterrestrial, we must conclude that their planet is farther from the sun than our own. If they belong to our solar system, they could come from a zone near the orbit of Mars, or the asteroids, where the temperature is considerably lower than on Earth. These extraterrestrial Hyperborians were, according to the original verbal transmissions, the ancestors of the white race.

We assume that the blood of these First Fathers was not red like ours, but perhaps tinged with blue, the reason for this would have been due to the concentration of carbon on their original planet. From this detail, comes the expression "to have blue blood": namely to be noble, to have descended from a superior race.

---

ones. The geologists believe that in two centuries the mean temperature of the globe will have dropped by 10 degrees. A new glacier age will then follow, replaced millions of years later by a tropical period. During an earlier tropical cycle, the advanced civilizations made their way north, where new species of animal developed. Conversely, during the colder times, civilizations, species of animals and vegetation, disappeared from the North.

Chapter Four

LOST CIVILIZATIONS

Almost every year chance discoveries, together with planned excavations, push back the date of the first appearance of man on Earth. In the same way, ruins and the remains of civilizations which no one knew existed come to light, throwing prehistorians into confusion.*

The *"Zinjanthrope"* (East African Man), for instance, has recently been ousted by an even more ancient hominid, given the barbaric name *Paraustralopithecus Aethiopicus,* found in Ethiopia. In the process the theories of our orthodox palaentologists have been badly shaken. Incredibly, they still teach that prehistoric man lived in caves and that his bronze tools (made before those of iron)† were invented a mere 4,000 years

*We refer mainly to French prehistorians and more precisely to the prehistorians of the "old school." Their views are not accepted outside France, fortunately for science.

†In consequence we are presumably expected to believe that the prehistoric men of Saint-Acheul (Somme), of Chelles, and of Grand-Pressigny, where there are no caves, went all the way to Eyzies each evening in order to bed down!

ago! That is 6,000 years *after* he was manufacturing fourteen different alloys of bronze at Medzamore, Soviet Armenia.

What bad luck for the conspiracy—this *official* discovery of a prehistoric factory at Medzamor!

What bad luck too that the Musée de l'Homme in Paris finally consented, in 1937, to take out of their cellars the engraved stones from Lussac leś Châteaux, on which can be seen a woman wearing a hat, shoes, jacket, and trousers!

What is to become of the prehistorians' sacrosanct theories; their assurance that Stone Age man dressed only in animal skins?

Now, Russian archaeologists have unearthed a burial ground 35,000 years old near Vladimir, USSR: the largest Stone Age burial ground so far discovered. From this, evidence has come to light very early clothes; a king of crude, trouserlike garment, its seams decorated with bones.

On nearly all aspects of prehistory the orthodox "experts" have been proved wrong: on Bimini and the rediscovered Atlantis; on the site of the world of Mu where inexplicable beds of metal have been found; in Greenland and Siberia, where the remains of unknown civilizations have been discovered in the Sahara, where, according to Dr. Faibridge, a geologist from the University of Columbia, the south pole was situated, 450 million years ago; in Iran, where a 6,000-year-old industrial city has been unearthed, Shahr-I-Soktch, which is estimated to have had 100,000 inhabitants, skilled in working precious stones and metals in actual factories!

In 1923, a Russian expedition discovered in Laponia, Kola Peninsula, the remains of an extremely ancient civilization, believed by Professor Bartjenko to be earlier than that of the Egyptians. Tombs constructed with huge quantities of stone, similar to the pyramids of Egypt, were described. With this sort of evidence how can open minds refuse to accept the existence of superior ancestors and unknown civilizations, some of which were probably more advanced than our own?

The maverick archaeologists

The maverick, or freelance, archaeologists do not claim to refute orthodox science, and they themselves often make mistakes, through lack of funds or because of technical shortcomings, but despite their errors—often excusable—they bring something precious and stimulating to official research.

Accepted science itself is not always free from error, exaggeration, and even outright misrepresentation. Statements from even the most authoritative quarters are not always beyond criticism, as seems to be the case with Madame Kouleshova, the Russian woman who "sees with her fingers."

It took seven years of research by Russian experts to expose what must surely be some sort of trick.

The magazine *Literaturnaya Gazetta*, reporting these happenings, claimed that during the official experiments made in 1963, the spectroscope emitted a special sound each time the colors of the light rays changed. Madame Kouleshova must have based her colored visions on these sound changes, which were almost imperceptible to a normal ear.

However, the mystery is far from solved: Biologists assure us that *all* the body cells are to some extent capable of *all* the sensory functions.

The Pillar of Ashoka

There have been many claims that the famous Pillar of Ashoka, made of iron which does not rust, is 4,000 years old. This is an exaggeration, as can be proved from a minute examination of the monument.

It stands in the court of a temple in New Delhi, India, in front of a huge archway with an Arabic inspiration. It is about 7 meters high; its diameter varies from 42 centimeters at its base to 32 centimeters at the top, and it weights six tons. Even a preliminary examination of the pillar shows that it cannot be as old as is sometimes claimed: The ornamentation at the top is of an easily identifiable style. It is usually known as the "Pillar of Ashoka," after a king, grandson of Bindusara, who from 260 B.C. to 227 B.C. erected columns around the borders of his empire on which his edicts were often engraved.

As its architectural style proves, the pillar was not erected by Ashoka, but by the Emperor Candrugupts II, surnamed Vikramaditya, who reigned from 380 to 413 A.D., and was the originator of the Golden Age of Indian Civilization.

Louis Renou, a great French Orientalist is adamant on this dating. The pillar is therefore about 1,550 years old, not 4,000.

It is nonetheless a curiosity, for despite the humidity and the Indian monsoons, the iron of which it is made has never shown the slightest sign of rust.

Made of iron

In a well-documented study in the magazine *Inforespace*, Jacques Scornaux writes that "an exceptional purity, beyond the reach of our most advanced technology has been attributed to the iron to account for its resistance to rust." If this feat could be repeated today it would only be as a result of very recent advances, and then only in very small quantities and at an exorbitant cost.

The Pillar of Ashoka, or rather of Vikramaditya, must therefore be made of an unknown alloy, derived, some people claim, from an extraterrestrial source, or from some secret method, now lost. An extreme hypothesis, but one that is tenable in the absence of a more convincing explanation.

Specialists in corrosion assure us that the pillar consists of several sheets of iron, hammered until fused together. Analysis of samples, however, has revealed considerable heterogeneity, *i.e.*, particles of impurity: carbon (0.1 to 1.2 percent) phosphorus (0.11 to 0.18 percent), silicon, copper, nickel, and an external layer consisting of 80 percent iron oxide (Fe O and Fe 03).

This iron is therefore impure, writes Scornaux, and the enigma of its resistance to deterioration still remains—unless it is due to the fact that over the centuries the Indian faithful have smeared it with ritual animal and vegetable fats, which may, in penetrating the metal, have protected it.

It is notable that the metal of altars and other objects worshiped in the same way in India and Nepal enjoy a similar miraculous immunity.

The Valley of Marvels

In a deserted and not easily accessible area of the mountains of Provence, in France, the Valley of Marvels offers to those archaeologists who are not discouraged by the difficulties of reaching it an incomparable site, rich in rock drawings.

Who drew them? What civilization once existed in these gorges and valleys, high among the mountains? Very little is known about it.

The best route for reaching this enormous site, stretching over many kilometers, starts from Tende and goes to Saint-Dalmas, from where one can climb as far as Mesces. From there one goes through the Valley of La Minière, arriving after six kilometers of hard walking, at the edge of the Valley of Marvels.

The region is dominated to the northeast by Mount Bego, which from its height of 2,873 meters reigns over a chaos of rocks, whose shapes, when the light is behind them, evoke zoomorphic images which grip the imagination.

Etymologists have suggested that the name ''Bego'' comes from the Provençal ''begon,'' meaning ''sorcerer,'' or from ''beg'' meaning lord,'' but there seems in fact to be an association of ideas with ''beugh'' or the bellowing of a bull or ox. In addition, almost 16,000 drawings, out of a total of about 45,000, depict these animals.

The altitude of the site varies from 2,100 to 2,600 meters, and two neighboring peaks carry the names the ''Bull's Horn'' and the ''Peak of the Billy-Goat's Horn,'' which seems to indicate that the Valley of Marvels was once consecrated to agriculture; to the rearing of bulls and their magic cult.

One searches through a labyrinth of rocks to discover the drawings, engraved in the stone with a pointed instrument; or traced geometrically, possibly in more recent times. In some areas they abound on the polished slabs of reddish sandstone, laminated shales or petrosilicons, some of which are a greenish color, some violet, and some orange. The most frequently depicted objects are bulls (or oxen), two-pronged forks, checkered rectangles, knives, weapons, human silhouettes, spears which are strongly reminiscent of certain letters of the Phoenecian, Carian, Roman, Cretan, Aramaic, and Sabine alphabets, and even more to the drawings on Easter Island.

The checkered engravings, or ''enclosures,'' represent plans of houses or agricultural divisions; they can be found virtually throughout the world, notably in Peru (the Plateau of Marcahuassi) and in the region of the Snake River in the United States. Other drawings are stylized sorcerers, dancers, bulls, and men driving pairs of oxen.

It should be noted that next to these petroglyphs, one finds graffiti, the names of visiting vandals, intent on recording their identity on indestructible stone. On the Grand Table, writes André Verdet, "totem signs vie with alphabetic signs."

Everywhere the scenery is grandiose, titanic, desolate, empty—yet somehow peopled with invisible inhabitants.

The Men of Bego

It would seem that the men of Bego wanted to fill this eroded area, chiseled by the winds, ice, and rain, this natural city of fortresses, roads, and amphitheaters, with ghosts and animals engraved on the rock slabs; ghosts which, according to their beliefs, would by some strong magic take on real life on certain sacred days fixed by the Grand Sorcerer.

Approximate estimations date these drawings to the 5th century B.C., but the archaeologist Carlo Conti considers them to be 4,000 or even 5,000 years old.

There is some hesitation in defining what is sometimes called the Civilization of Bego, or the Civilization of the Valley of Marvels: It could be the work of a race driven from the coasts of the northeast by an invasion, and which settled round the Bego mountain to cultivate a soil which was known to be fertile, at the end of the Neolithic Age.

However, basing their theories on the magical character of many drawings, some historians believe that the men of Bego formed a nomadic civilization of which traces can be found in the region of Hesse in Germany, around Lake Iseo, in the north of Brescia and in the Camonica Valley, Italy.

The legend of Valmasque

André Verdet reports two legends which represent one popular explanation of the mystery of the Bego mountain.

The men of Entraque, he writes, wanted to ravish the virgins who once lived in the valley. They forced the maidens to flee, but the latter placed a curse on the whole area, from the lake of Agnel in the north, to the lake of Enfer (Hell) in the south.

The second legend offers a better explanation of the rock drawings depicting sorcerers, clenched fists, and scenes which are believed to have magical connotations.

In the Middle Ages the Count of Tende controlled the then fertile region of valleys surrounding the Bego mountain. Then, one day, he went off to the Crusades and was absent for several years; years of great calamities and declining prosperity throughout the country.

"It is the Sorcerer who has sent us such misfortunes," said the people of Tende.

A poor woman who lived in a cottage on the outskirts of the village was reviled by everyone, and the local children threw stones at her.

After seven years the count returned, thinner, older, embittered, and escorted by the handful of men still capable of dragging their bones back from the Holy Land.

The population begged the count to find a remedy to the catastrophes, and to the appalling weather.

"There is nothing I can do, my good people, against the infernal powers which make us undergo so many miseries," said the count. "In vain have I prayed to the saints and done penitence in the Holy Land—the Devil has us firmly in his hands."

So it was decided to exorcise the "witch." They forced her to move out with her goats and then burned down her house.

Each in turn—the count, the justice of the peace, and the priest pronounced their curse on her:

"Go to the Lake of Hell, to the Devil's Mount, to the Valley of the Mask, where your master, Satan, rules among the evil-shaped rocks, and never return to Tende!"

The witch departed with her herd, her charms, her book of spells, and her evil potions. Everything that she had touched with her impure hands: her house, her furniture, the wood enclosing the house, were burned, sprinkled with holy water, and brine.

Then, says the legend, peace returned to the bodies and souls of the people of Tende, and sterility struck the Valley of Marvels, as if the curse had been transferred there.

Since then, claims Verdet, the inhabitants of Tende, of Saint-Dalmas and La Brique, do not venture into the Valley of the Mask and of Hell.

The White Horses of the Downs

Before man learned to write, he was forced to use drawing to record his impressions, his feelings, his needs, his enthusiasms, and his fears.

It is probable that the Man of Lascaux knew how to write, but he has only left witness of his qualities as an artist.

In England, on the slopes of the chalky hills of the south—the downs—particularly in Dorset, can be seen gigantic figures, cut out of the chalk, usually depicting horses.

It is the message of an ancient, perhaps prehistoric people, but one which survived into relatively recent times, since certain drawings are less than 1,000 years old.

The White Horse of Uffington dates, according to one tradition, from Alfred the Great, an Anglo-Saxon king who was crowned in 811, after defeating the Danes. The work, cut into the chalky hillside in order to commemorate his victories, was to have shown him mounted on a horse, but only the animal was finished, raising doubts as to the authenticity of this explanation.

Archaeologists believe, on the other hand, that the very

stylized horse which overlooks the Berkshire countryside really is the work of prehistoric man.

In the county of Wiltshire, one can count six white horses, drawn in the same way; the one near Westbury being the most typical example of this titanic art form. Other examples exist at Cherhill, Wiltshire, on the side of a hill, at Alton Barnes, Wiltshire, at Kilbura, Yorkshire, and at Osmington, Dorset, although this last only dates from the 18th century and honors George III.

Even more recent is the Lion of Bedfordshire, carved to draw attention to the proximity of Whipsnade Zoo.

The human representations at Trendle Mill in Dorset are in the same artistic style: as are the Giant with the Club, and the Giant of Wilmington at Eastbourne in Sussex.

The former measures fifty-five meters long, the latter eighty meters. They are drawn in meadows, tracing deep furrows, which seem to have some relationship with the *pistas* of Nazca.

Legend has it that the Giant with the Club was an ogre who was killed by the people of the Blackmore Valley, from whom he had stolen sheep with which he stuffed himself until he could not stand up, weighed down by his gluttony!

Forgotten cities of the forest

Our friend and correspondent in Rio de Janeiro, Mrs. J. Renout da Cunha, has recently sent us a report of the latest developments in Brazilian archaeology.

An unknown city has been discovered at Inga.

In 1753 another city was explored and monuments and sculptures reported. It was never found again.

At Pirarucura, in the state of Piauhy, the archaeologists are not certain whether they have discovered a real town or some sort of phenomenon of erosion. The place is called the Sete Ciudades (the Seven Cities); on the rocks are to be found inscriptions and an unknown script traced in red. It is reported that sphinxes are carved in the stone.

The uncertainty is similar to that which attaches to a series of pillars and lines of parallel walls, a kilometer long, near what appears to be the ruins of a vanished civilization in the region of Monte Alto.

In 1743 a Portuguese, Francisco Raposo, accompanied by some adventurers, wandered for several years in the forest of the Mato Grosso, searching for the "gold mines of Muribeca," the site of which had been lost for more than a century.

Raposo sent a detailed report of his expedition to the Viceroy of Brazil, Don Luis Peregrino de Carvalho Menezes de Athayde, and this report was discovered by Lieutenant Colonel Percy Fawcett, an ex-Indian Army officer, when he was examining the archives of Rio in 1923.

Fawcett, rightly or wrongly, like so many before him,* claimed that it described lost cities, their names redolent of adventure: the city of Great Paititi, Manoa, Americanas, the City of Los Cesares, etc. He called the one he set out in search of "City Z," and after numerous crosschecks, fixed its location in the region of the Xingu River, a large tributary of the Amazon, between the Serra Formosa and the Serra do Cachimbo, at about the 10th parallel, Greenwich meridian.

In May, 1925, Colonel Fawcett, his son Jack, their friend Raleigh Rimel, and an escort of Indian guides plunged into the Amazon forests.

*Mysterious cities, lost in the forest, were sought in vain in 1902 by the Krupps von Essen and in 1913 by President Theodore Roosevelt, who was accompanied by General Candido Mariano de Silva Rondon.

The writer Henri Vernes searched for this expedition, which came to a tragic end: none of the explorers were ever seen again.

Vernes notes in his book, *Sur la Piste de Fawcett (On the Trail of Fawcett)* a letter dated April 20 in which Fawcett, piecing together things an Indian guide had told them, writes of a lost city in the forest, where houses with enormous doors were lit inside by a light which shone from a great crystal placed on the top of a pillar.

On May 29, he is supposed to have sent another message—the authenticity is extremely doubtful—giving his position as northeast of the Serra Formosa, fifty kilometers from the junction of the Ronuro and Xingu Rivers.

A good many rumors reached Rio, some claiming that Fawcett had become king of a tribe of white men, others reporting that he had died in the forest.

One report claims that the expedition rediscovered the secret city mentioned in the report of 1743. A gigantic archway marked the entrance.

In one square there was said to be a statue with raised arms, seeming to point in a northerly direction. It was the capital of the great Muribeca, the son of a Portuguese explorer, who had married a native woman and worked the fabulous gold mines.

Several expeditions which went in search of Fawcett and his "City Z" returned, having come no nearer to the solution of the mystery.

IMAGINARY KINGDOMS

As in adventures of romance, folklore always gives rise to exaggeration which bestows on it a fairy-tale aspect. But there is always truth to be found in the original versions.

We do not believe as do some people that the moons of Mars and the other planets are artificial structures or interplanetary machines, but we accept that they may be hollow. We have doubts about the existence of Agartha, that mysterious empire beneath the Himalayas, but are inclined to accept the authenticity of Antilia, the possible remains of Atlantis.

As for the fantastic kingdoms which the Conquistadores of the 16th century sought in the three Americas, we reluctantly believe them to be imaginary, although behind the tales of wonder told by the Indians and the Spanish chroniclers, there must be an element of truth.

No matter what your views, the American Eldorado which moved so many adventurers, from Pizarro to Fawcett, was a fantastic, marvelous, terrible, fatal dream, worthy of the centuries-old legends of the New World, which again, in our time, is reopening the dossier on the "lost cities."

The subterranean city

According to "Professor" Henrique José de Souza, president of the Theosophical Society of Sao Lourenço, Brazil, Fawcett and his son remain prisoners of a subterranean people of the Mato Crosso.

The explorers, after following a long passage plunging into the depth of the earth, are said to have entered the city of a brilliant civilization beneath the earth's surface.

"The inhabitants of this kingdom descend from an antediluvian race which originated in Lemuria and Atlantis, continents which were swallowed up by the oceans."*

*According to Haeckel, the great German naturalist, the human race began on a continent now submerged under the Pacific Ocean: Lemurie, named in the Pouranas "Shalmali." This continent was the cradle of the third human race, the first fully developed one. Its

José de Souza thus echos the traditionalist writer Ferdinand Ossendowski, who asserts the existence of such peoples. "I heard a Chinese lama scholar say to Bogdo-Khan that all the subterranean caves of America are inhabited by an ancient people who vanished underground. These people and their subterranean kingdoms are governed by chiefs who in turn recognize the sovereignty of the King of the World."

Once more it is a question of Mueans and Atlantans saved from the flood, who inhabit caves lit by a peculiar light, suitable for the growth of vegetation.

These people are said to live almost eternally, completely free from disease.

According to Ossendowski, most of the old civilizations before disappearing designated a group of the Initiated, close to the King of the World, for survival. From these the subterranean people, who "have attained the highest knowledge," are descended, and inhabit the sub-himalayan kingdom of Agartha.

More than 6,000 years ago a holy man and his people "disappeared into the ground." This must be what happened to the two so-called Lost Tribes of Israel.

The entrance to Agartha is situated either in Afghanistan or in Tibet, between Chigatse and Shamballah.

The man with two tongues

Prince Choultoun Beyli had himself given the description of the Agartha Kingdom to Ossendowski, who reports it without the slightest indication of skepticism.

What is one to make of it?

---

destruction by fire and water "was accompanied by the appearance of another continent, Atlantis, called Kusha, where the powerful and magnificent civilization of the fourth Initiating race flourished." (According to Theosophical tradition.)

An old Brahmin from Nepal once met a fisherman in Siam, the prince claims, who took him on a sea voyage.

"On the third day they reached an island where a race of men with two tongues lived, who could speak different languages at one and the same time.

"They showed him strange animals; enormous serpents whose flesh was good to eat, birds with teeth which caught fish for their masters. These people told him that they had come from the subterranean Kingdom and described certain regions to him."

Manoa

We are very skeptical about these reports, most of which appear to be pure fantasy. Nevertheless, it is intriguing to note that they tally remarkably with folklore, which mentions the existence of mysterious "*soccabons*" (caves) which abound in South America, particularly in Brazil.

According to the American writer Raymond Bernard, one of them, the Road of the Incas, hundreds of kilometers long, had an entrance south of Lima, passed through Cuzco, Tiahuanaco, and came up in the desert of Atacambo. It was by this tunnel that the Incas escaped with their gold when the Conquistadores conquered Peru.

Colonel Fawcett and his son Jack are said to have disappeared into a *soccabon* in the Roncador Sierra, to the northeast of the Mato Grosso.

These legends, which become exaggerated through the centuries, were important ingredients in those fantastic dreams which inspired the Conquistadores at the time that Pizarro entered the Inca Empire.

One magic country (in fact probably no more than a man's name) especially captivated them: the fabulous Eldorado.

The Spaniards believed it to be in what is now Colombia, or even in North America. Voltaire places it in Paraguay; an anonymous explorer claims that Eldorado was on the banks of the Parana river, with the magnificent city of Manoa as its capital.

It is thought by some that the legend owes its existence to wily Indians or Incas who wanted to send the Conquistadores off on a hopeless and possibly fatal quest.

Indians and Incas were constantly referring to Manoa, its silver roofs, and its people who dressed in gold cloth.

Sir Walter Raleigh searched for the sparkling domes of Eldorado, which "shone in a vast plain."

Ferdinand Denis suggested in 1843 that the fabulous city was possibly Palenque in Mexico, "that sister of the Egyptian Thebes, the great, empty city, abandoned in the middle of the forest, with her porticos, her temples ornamented with bas-reliefs and mysterious hieroglyphics."

On the other hand, the Conquistadores seemed to believe that Eldorado was the king of a fabulous land. "Pontif and king, it was him who the city of Manoa obeyed, and to whom the hommage of an immense people was continuously paid. Philippe de Utre saw his fantastic palace as created in the savanna from a ray that had escaped from the sun."

Americanas

In Brazil they talked of the *"Mai das aguas,"* a siren who guards the treasures of a great lake, and above all of the country of "Americanas, a country which is said to be situated either in Minas (Uruguay) or in the Mato Grosso."

In Americanas, gold is everywhere, together with topaz, and palaces are built with stones which sparkle in the sunlight.

"In the eighteenth century, Bartholomeu Buenno traveled

through unknown forests, crossed nameless deserts, and returned laden with enough gold and precious stones to dazzle even the richest of sovereigns. His route was sought in vain: it is lost like that which once led to the treasures of Cebora or of Paititi.'' Tradition has it that Paititi was built on the tops of the mountains which surround the Gulf of Darien, from Maracaibo Bay to the Isthus of Panama. In this region there could still be seen in the last century the gigantic ruins of the cities of the Cares, as well as the ruins of the forges where the cyclops of Central America forged the gold armor of the kings and princes of the area.

Yet to this day one can hear rumored in the inns from Lima to Rio that the desert of Americanas is strewn with gold, emeralds, crystal, and acquamarines in almost indecent abundance, among ordinary stones.

But to find them one has to risk terrible beasts and natural disasters: only by braving the flash of lightning and the rumble of thunder can one reap the riches of the deserts and mountains!

The town of Los Cesares

Pedro de Angelis's book, *Derroteros y Viages de la Ciudad Encantada o' de los Cesares*, published in Buenos Aires in 1836, reveals a rival to Americanas and Manoa.

According to the author the Spaniards who escaped from Osorno and other *pueblos* (villages), founded in 1599 three towns which were destroyed toward the end of the 17th century. One of them, the richest, was ''Ciudad de los Cesares.'' It was built in the middle of Lake Payegue, its temples covered in solid silver. All the household utensils, right down to the cooking pots, were made of that metal, as were the very ploughs.

Finally, to enhance this enticing story, it is worth knowing that the inhabitants' chairs were of solid gold, as were the bells in the temples, which could be seen gleaming from ten leagues away.*

The original Eldorado

Eldorado was invented around 1536 by Lieutenant General Sebastian de Belalcaçar, and by his soldiers then garrisoned at Quito.

The information came from an Indian who told that in the Santa Fe or Bogota valley "a nobleman plunged into a lake in the middle of a balsam forest, his naked body annointed with gum, and was astonished to find particles of gold adhering to his body."

Balacaçar gave this country the name of Eldorado. It is believed that the lake in question was Lake Guatavita, twenty-eight kilometers north of Bogota, but some people also situate this land of milk and honey between the Amazon and the Orinoco.

Some chroniclers, on the other hand, claim that Eldorado was dreamed up by one of Pizarro's lieutenants, named Orellana.

A certain Martinez claimed that he had lived for seven months in the town of Eldorado, and as proof of his claim he produced a map of the region, easily identifiable by the three mountains surrounding it. The first was of gold, the second of silver, and the third of salt.

Martinez went much further in his description. The Emperor's palace was supported by magnificent columns of porphyry and alabaster, and encircled with galleries of ebony and cedar encrusted with precious stones. Situated in the center

*One can understand the explorer's fantasies, says the great Larousse Encyclopedia; where the peak of Calitamini in Guyana is struck diagonally by the rays of the setting sun, it shines as if encrusted with gold, or crowned with diamonds.

of a green island, it was reflected in water of unrivaled transparency. Two towers guarded the entrance to this palace, each supported by a column twenty-five feet high, whose capitals were decorated with silver moons. Two live lions were tied to these columns with chains of solid gold. Fountains played into silver basins from golden pipes. In the heart of the palace a vast silver altar supported a huge golden sun in front of which four lamps burned perpetually. The master of all these riches was El Dorado.

The capital of this imaginary kingdom was Manoa, and its king was called Great Paytiti or Great Moxo or Great Paru or Enim, or, more fittingly, the Golden King (El Dorado in Spanish).

This capital was also called the city of the Omeguas or Omaguas, but it was in fact Eldorado or Manoa, these names being as yet uncoined.

At a later period a different explanation of the fable was given: The young brother of Atahualpa, the Inca reigning in Cuzco, fled with stolen treasure into the depths of the earth, where he founded a new empire.

Nowadays it can be accepted that these tales, contradictory though they are, are based on real events: The last of the sovereigns of Peru, the Inca Manco, retreated into the secret city of Machu-Pichu, a city which was not discovered until 1911.

It is probable that immense treasures are hidden in this city, lost in the Altiplano.

Dreams, delirium, and death

The myth of Eldorado was gradually transferred to the mysterious interior of Brazil.

The chronicler Magalhaeus Gandavo reported this astonishing piece of information:

"Indians from the region of Santa Cruz [Bolivia?], finding themselves unhappy in their own country, plunged into the vast wilderness of the interior, a great number of them to perish from exhaustion and misery. Those who survived reached a country full of large villages, thickly populated and so rich that they claimed to have seen long streets inhabited by people whose sole occupation was the working of gold and precious stones.

"The inhabitants, seeing their iron tools, and hearing them speak of white, bearded Portuguese or Spaniards from Peru, gave them presents of gold shields, asking them to take them back to their own country and to announce that they were prepared to exchange such things for iron tools."

Then Eldorado moved to North America, to Quivira in California.

Myths, dreams, the fantasies of the human imagination . . . everything which gold fever, greed, and thirst for adventure can inspire in a man, the New World kept alive for more than three centuries—indeed right up to the present day.

Vasquez de Cornado claims to have found Prester John in Cibola, about 400 leagues north of Mexico, and Alexander von Humboldt described the discovery of the remains of ships from Cathay (China) in this region.

Paititi

Nuno de Guzman, President of New Spain, assembled an army of 400 Spaniards and 20,000 Indians to go in search of Cibola or Cibora (now California), the capital of the country of Seven Towns, "where gold was as abundant as pebbles."

He found seven poor little villages!

But so strong was the passionate belief in the religion of the golden calf that another Cibola was dreamed up; this time the real one, naturally!

"It is said to be in the region of Tiguer. A king was having a siesta under a large tree, from which golden bells had been hung, the breeze causing them to sound softly . . . a large golden eagle decorated the prow of the royal boat. . . ."

Yet another fantasy pulled the Conquistadores into the search for "the most beautiful empire," that of Waipite or Paititi, which at first took the place of Cibola, making use of the same legend of Manco Capac II, but placing it in Peru, in the sandy region of Apurimac and Ucayale.

"It was a powerful kingdom," wrote Juan de Velasco, "founded by the Incas, but those once powerful kings knew how to confuse the Spaniards with powerful spells. Therefore all Lima was ready to believe him when Benito de Ribera, a priest of the Franciscan Order, who had worked in the missions at Guanuco, told how he had visited Paititi, and gave an enthusiastic description of it. A kingdom of millions, where nothing was more common than gold."

Several gentlemen of Lima raised an army at their own expense and set off, in 1670, under the guidance of the Franciscan, in search of Paititi. The expedition was a fiasco, but still the legend was not destroyed.

In 1681 Father Juan Lucero claimed that he had been to the country of the Piros, and had held in his hands "plates, crosses, earrings, and other jewels mounted in gold, made by the Indians."

In these legendary tales, incredible in their exaggerated details and descriptions of fantastic treasures, one nevertheless finds elements which make one pause. This "country of the Piros" described by Father Juan Lucero very probably did exist, although all trace of it appears to have been lost.

"Montesimos, who about the year 1652 collected the fables still preserved by the Amautas, a college of Peruvian priests and astronomers, reports that the Inca civilization had only relatively recently succeeded a period of barbarism, which in turn was preceded by the ancient civilization of 'Pyr-Huas' [the Piros of Father Lucero], which had developed after a catostrophic flood, and which possessed mysterious hieroglyphics, like all the peoples who had links with the engulfed Atlantis."*

The country of the Piros was perhaps Tiahuanaco, Bolivia, Machu-Pichu, or one of the cities found on the Altiplano, or in the region of the Peruvian Amazonas. However, we are inclined to see its remains in the ruins of Caballo Muerto, Peru where the American Michael Moseley, of Harvard University, discovered the ruins of a temple and a colossal stone head more than 3,000 years old.

Such were the lost cities of the 16th and 17th centuries, and the myths which sent the adventurers into forests, deserts, and mountains, where more often than not they found death rather than fortune.

Fountain of Youth

Yet another myth and another unknown land formed part of the dreams of the explorers of the New World: the Fountain of Youth and the Isle of Bimini.

Arriving in the Antilles, the Spanish heard from the Indians of Cuba and Haiti that to the north of these islands there was a fountain whose water had rejuvenating powers.

In 1514 the Protestant theologian Pierre Martyr repeated this rumor to Pope Leo X, and added, "Your Holiness should not dismiss these stories as jokes or idle tales."

Lucas Vasques d'Ayllon, the first explorer of Florida,

*Extract from *Un Continent Disparu, l'Atlantide*, by Roger Dévigne.

reported that the aged father of his Lucayan maid, wishing to prolong his life, went to the Fountain of Youth. He stayed there several days, bathing and drinking the water and taking the remedies prescribed. He returned home having recovered his strength, remarried, and sired many sons.

The fountain was said to be in the Florida region, in Bimini, "A powerful island-state inhabited by a mixture of races, whose skin was paler and finer than that of the Cubans." The women "were so beautiful that the men of the mainland and Florida went to live with them."

Juan Ponce de Leon, ex-governor of the Island of Boriquen, "armed two caravels and went in search of the Island of Boyuca [Bimini?] where the indians believed the fountain to be which transformed old men into youths. He entered Bimini, and discovered Florida in 1512, but did not find the Fountain of Youth."

It is nevertheless interesting to note that Bimini, whose location was discovered in 1970, preserves in its watery depths the remains of a vanished civilization, and the divers who discovered it tell of a spring of sweet water still flowing in the submerged ruins.

The Fountain of Youth was also reputed to be located in Egypt, as well as in India, where Alexander the Great searched for it.

Gilgamesh, the hero of Assyrian mythology, undertook his journey to the country of the Great Ancestors at the borders of the East, to search for the plant that rejuvenated the old.

The wise man Um-Napishti (the Assyrian Noah) revealed to him that it grew under water. Gilgamesh, weighed down with stones, dived like a pearl diver, and picked up a plant from the botton of the fountain, called *"kishkanu"* or *"sihlu"* (our watercress?).

The most astonishing thing about this legend, however, is that Gilgamesh went to look for this watercress in a Fountain of Youth, which, according to reputable mythologists, *was situated in America, and probably in Flordia or Bimini.*

It is difficult not to be impressed by this strange coincidence, so unlikely that there seems no doubt that it rests on historical fact.

Thousands of years ago, the Fountain of Youth existed somewhere in the region of Bimini, and our Superior Ancestors handed down the story, which was still remembered and told in detail 5,000 years later.

Chapter Five

Mysterious Civilizations: Scotland, France, Sardinia, and Malta

We know very little about the dolmens, menhirs, and various megaliths scattered all over Europe.

Our knowledge of the Druids and the Gauls is also scanty, and we still do not know who was the first King of France.

Then what do we know of the mysterious civilization which flourished in France, Scotland, and other countries of Europe, and the numerous forts of glazed brick that can still be found there?

It is true that they are not mentioned in European "history" books, and for good reasons (we prefer not to go into them here), but these glazed forts do exist, and pose questions for those who dare take a serious interest in Europe's real past.

The vengeance of Azuria

These "forts" are more accurately described as elliptical

enclosures. They were built on hills or around naturally steep promontories.

The walls are formed of granite, which on the lower parts, sometimes on one side only, sometimes on both sides, appear to have been glazed, presenting archaeologists with an almost insoluble enigma.

In those cases where the walls are protected by ramparts, these too bear signs of vitrification.

One's first reaction is that great fires must have been lit at the foot of the walls. But this is not very convincing in those cases where only the inside was glazed, while the outside surfaces, sometimes one or two meters thick, were built of perfectly natural stone.

It becomes even more unconvincing when one considers the 1,300 degrees of heat needed to fuse such rocks.

The English archaeologist James Anderson, in a book published in 1777, was apparently the first to report glazed forts in Scotland. He believed that ferruginous earth served to harden the stone, which was then fired to achieve a glaze.

Charles Hoy Fort, in *The Book of the Damned*, puts forward an even stranger theory: Because the Britons did not want to paint their skin blue, the gold Azuria "poured his electricity on all their forts, whose glazed and molten stones still exist today."

The major glazed forts in Scotland are: Craig Phoedrick, Ord Hill of Kissock, Barry Hill, Castle-Spynie in Invernesshire, Top-o-North in the county of Aberdeen, and the glazed cairns of Orcades (Isle of Sanday). Other forts of this kind exist in Bohemia.

Craig Phoedrick

The two most typical constructions are Craig Phoedrick and Ord Hill, which rise like two great pillars on the slopes, separated by three miles, and situated at the edge of the Moray Firth, near Inverness, defending its access from the sea.

The archaeologist Jules Marion describes these fortifications as being like an acropolis, with regular features, their top parts flattened to form oval terraces, in the middle of which is a hole of about two to three meters in depth, resembling a volcanic crater.

The surrounding earthworks are covered in gigantic glazed blocks of stone which must have been part of the building.

They dominate the Ness Valley on the eastern side, where the slope is steeper. The dark-colored stones of the forts are huge, held together by mortar, the whole forming a very compact solid mass, impossible to pry apart.

Certain blocks which have been subjected to even greater extremes of heat look like volcanic debris, and if broken open reveal large globules of melted material, similar in color and consistency to bottle glass, rather like the material called lunar tectite, which the astronauts have since shown is not to be found on the moon after all!

It is not certain that Craig Phoedrick and Ord Hill were actual forts, and it has been suggested that they were beacons or observation posts dating back to the Vikings.

In fact, we do not know for certain either their functions or their origin.

The glazed forts of the Creuse

We still do not know the age of the glazed forts which are to be found in France.

Items that have been excavated from them have been dated to the 5th century, but we believe the constructions are often much older, as witnessed by the Irish manuscripts which speak of the flaming tower of Tory.

Futhermore, historians would surely have mentioned these forts if they had been constructed only 1,500 years ago.

At the Gueret museum there is a melted granite block containing a Roman tile, thus complicating the matter still further.

The principal glazed forts of France are in the Creuse area: at Châteauvieux, at Ribandells, facing Châteauvieux, on the opposite side of the Creuse, at Thauron, at Saint-Georges-de-Nigremont; in Brittany: at Peran; in Vienne, perhaps at Thorus, near Château-Larcher, where a fortified promontory dominates the valley of Clouère.

The walls at Châteauvieux are oval in shape and 128 meters long; the rampart is terraced, 7 meters wide at the base and 3 meters wide at the top.

On the substructures a wall had been built with granite partitions.

"The space between two partitions," writes de Nadaillac, is filled with a cover of melted granite, 4 meters wide and 60 centimeters thick, resting on a bed of calcified rock. Nowhere can one find the use of mortar, as in Scotland."

The interior of the wall is completely glazed, while the outside is of natural stone.

The old fortress of Ribandelle-du-Puy-de-Gaudy, which was occupied by the Celts, then successively by the Romans and the Visigoths, is of a similar construction.

The inside walls of glazed granite are separated from the outer walls by beds of heather. The glazing is only superficial, no more than two centimeters thick.

There are indications that the construction work was finished when the molten granite was poured into the walls, or when the fire which melted the stones was lit.

Another point: The glazed mass is divided into portions approximately three meters long, as if the work were carried out over some period of time, rather than in a single operation.

At Thauron, near Bourganeuf, the stones of the fort were subjected to such heat that they have become a sort of lava. Some arches are still standing.

The scorched stones

Prosper Mérimée wrote that the walls at Péran seemed to have been cemented with some sort of melted glass.

The camp of Peran, in the area of Pledran (côtes-du-Nord) is 134 meters long and 110 meters wide, and is called locally "The Scorched Stones."

These stones are not so much cemented as fused together, however fantastic this may seem.

The history of Camp Peran extends well before the Roman conquest of Gaul as testified by the findings which have been made there, thus proving that glazed forts date back at least 3,000 years.

What unknown civilization built these fortresses in France, Scotland, and Bohemia?

Probably the Celts—confounding the historians and prehistorians who, to please the Conspiracy, have deliberately belittled a people who as early as the Bronze Age, could melt rock as hard as granite at heat of 1,300 or 1,500 degrees!

Their methods are still unknown, but one can only assume that their prehistoric chemists made use of soda and potassium to create a sort of Greek fire.

We also know, although not by what means, that the people of Leinster, in the early days of the Irish Celts, knew how to "build a red wall." Was this a wall of fire or glaze?

In any case it formed part of some impenetrable taboo. The same source speaks of a Druid fire of intense heat.

De Cessac, who has studied the old forts at Creuse, has managed to actually bring down a wall of granite and wood, but his experiment was not conclusive as far as the strength of large surfaces is concerned.

The hypothesis of Druid E. Coarer-Kalondan

In their fascinating work *The Celts and the Extra-Terrestrials*, the blind Druid E. Coarer-Kalonden and Gwezenn-Dana give a possible explanation of the mystery of the glazed forts.

The flamethrowers that Burned Tara

In *Gods and Heroes of the Celts*, by Sjoestedt, another scientific weapon is stated to have been used at this time. Each year at the feast of Saman (November 1) a warrior came alone to challenge the town of Tara in Ireland. This warrior, called Ailenn Mac Neidhna, went into the terrorized city, spitting fire and burning down the various districts one by one.

Finn, Ossian's real father, put an end to this by killing the fire-raiser.

The flamethrowers used during the two world wars give a possible explanation of how Ailenn Mac Neidhna burned down the ramparts and houses of Tara.

This report would seem to show that the Celts had sufficient knowledge of chemistry to make use of inflammable liquids and gasses.

TORINIZ, THE GLAZED TOWER

The ruins of the tower on the island of Toriniz, today known as the Isle of Tory, still existed in the last century, and archaeolgists were amazed to note that the remnants of the tower were of glazed stone.

There are three possible explanations:

1. The tower which belonged to Fomore was atomized by the Tuatha* at the end of the second battle of Mag Tured. The incredible heat given off by their scientific weapons (flame-throwers? atomic fallout?) glazed the granite of the fortress.

2. The fort was coated with some kind of glazed material, which protected it against the radiation from any attacking weapons.

3. Only the base of the building was built from rock. Beneath a sublayer of granite rose the actual body of the tower, completely constructed of glazed material. A strong beam of solar energy could then create this remarkable phenomenon.

Such are the mysteries of the glazed forts of France, Scotland, and the civilization, probably Celtic, which built them, to the bafflement of 20th century archaeologists—that is if they really are seriously concerned to understand our heritage.

The brochs

The brochs of Scotland, on the islands of Shetland and the Orkneys, are made from very hard stone, shaped like giant thimbles. They are entered through a long, narrow corridor.

It is believed that these dwellings, with their difficult access, served the islanders for defense against the Vikings in the 11th century.

More plausible is the theory that their history goes back even farther, to the first migrations of the Western Celts, that of the Picts (and the Pictones of Poitou), but this is as yet unproved.

The Picts came to Scotland over 4,000 years ago and perhaps

*The Tuatha de Danaan were a mysterious people, expert in magic, who had invaded Ireland. They came from the land of Tertres, situated "beyond the Sea of Shadows." They were the Initiators of the Celtic world, about 4,000 years ago.

it is to them that one should attribute this civilization of Shetland and the Orkneys.

The brochs usually have the same sort of interior as the glazed forts of Dun Angus.

Dun Angus

Built on a jutting cliff, and commanding the sea from a height of about 150 feet, Dun Angus, on the Isle of Aran, to the west of Ireland,* is one of the most beautiful and enigmatic forts of Western Europe.

Its three defensive ramparts are semicircular, the smallest of them supporting a road and houses.

Outside the fort the ground is littered with a chaotic collection of great raised stones, whose purpose was to make access difficult and dangerous for invaders.

The archaeologist Peter Harbison, who is a specialist, believes that Dun Angus dates back several centuries before our era, but that it was used as a bastion up until the 17th century.

One legend attributes the building of the strange "Babylon" to the Firbolgs* a pre-Celtic people. The structure when built 3,000 years ago was probably very different from what it is now, since it is estimated that erosion by sea and landslide may have destroyed about half of the fort.

Other, more daring theories suggest that Dun Angus may have been a Phoenician port on their tin route (but then why a fort?), or perhaps part of the defensive system of the ancient peoples of Ireland against powerful enemies—the Atlantans!

Dun Angus is on Innishmore, one of the three Isles of Aran, close to Galway.

*The Firbolgs or Bolgs Men, according to the *Livre des Invasions*, invaded Ireland about 2,400 years before our era. Their origin is unknown.

No doubt this is stretching the evidence, but turning to Celtic mythology, one might think that the fort, dominating the "Western Seas," the Dark Ocean of the ancients, was a strongpoint used against the Tuatha De Danann who invaded Ireland and brought civilization with them.

The Venus of Quinipily

The old French château of Quinipily formerly stood in the district of Baud, not far from Evel Brook and four kilometers from the left bank of the Blavet.

It was the residence of the squires of Langoueouez, a strange family whose history is very interesting, as it seems that they were deeply involved in the changing fortunes of the Venus of Quinipily.

This Venus now stands at the edge of a small wood on the château grounds, but is much altered from its original appearance, since it has been much reshaped, profaned by sacriligious hands.

The estate passed in the 15th century to the house of Lannion, and then to La Rochefoucauld-Liancourt.

Quinipily was a strange château, possibly a museum of ancient statuary or a sanctuary, perhaps even a secret temple for the refuge of the French national religion against the persecutions of Christianity.

Two sculptures which had formed part of the chimney stack were transported to the neighboring village of Botcoet. They depicted, it is said, a Gallic Hercules, or possibly the god Ogmios. These cariatides now ornament the entrance of the Château of Plessis (Ille-et-Vilâine).But much more interesting is the statue whose origin has excited the attention of the whole world.

It is roughly hewn out of stone and, according to certain archaeologists, depicts a Gallic goddess. Others claim that it is of Roman or Egyptian origin. For some people this Mater has a vaguely Egyptian outline. One legend says "that the Moorish(?) soldiers of the Roman occupation put it on the mount of Catennec." There is no doubt that it is in fact a Gallic goddess: "Baud," the etymology of which echoes the name of the Celtic god Belin, Balin, Belinus, was certainly a sacred high place 2,000 years ago.

Until the 17th century it stood at the top of Castennec Mountain, to the north of Baud.

The Guardian Witch

On the statue there is a celtic name: GROAC'H EN GOUARD (The Guardian Witch). She was an object of worship, and had the same role as the statues on Easter Island, according to Francis Mazière—to radiate health, happiness, and power over the surrounding country.

In recognition of its good services the country folk would bring offerings of wheat and flowers.

At the feet of the Guardian Witch is a large basin hewn out of a block of granite, which is always full of water. Women after their confinement would come here to bathe, thus ensuring a quick recovery and radiant skin. Finally, according to very old tradition, young lovers would go there to carry out their erotic rites at the feet of the statue. If they did this, they were sure to marry that year!

In 1661 missionaries passing through Baud went to ask Claude de Lannion, Lord of Quinipily, to use his authority to put an end to these immoral and nonsensical practices.

Religion was all-powerful at this time, and it was thought

praiseworthy to destroy the manuscripts and monuments of the Celts so as to show allegiance to Palestine and please the Conspiracy.

The Witch was thrown into the small river of Blavet in the presence of the authorities, both civil and religious. The curate gave a sermon and assured the faithful, who had come in great numbers to watch the spectacle, that "Our Lord Jesus and his venerated mother the Virgin Mary were so pleased with this holy act that forthwith the country would enjoy great peace, children would be born healthy and strong, the harvests would be plentiful, and the weather favorable for all undertakings."

The Gallic Mater versus the Holy Virgin

The peasants went home subconsciously perturbed, as if they had drowned a saint.

Missionaries and priests excelled themselves, singing hymns to the glory of the Almighty and preaching against the evil witch. It was even decided to replace the statue with one of the Holy Virgin!

But things did not turn out as the curate had forecast, and as had been promised in the name of Jesus and the Holy Virgin.

The stone statue must have indeed been blessed with "mana"; perhaps she represented the real Queen of the Sky, protector of men. A few days after her drowning in the Blavet it started to rain, it began to pour, as it had not rained since the Flood. The whole harvest disappeared in torrents of water and mud.

The peasants were incensed and decided that a trick had been played on them by the priests. They retrieved the statue from the river and replaced it on its former site.*

*According to *Les Cahiers du Pays de Baud* by Henri Maho, the

The weather immediately improved, and the people were convinced that the Gallic witch was more powerful than the Holy Family!

Religion was thus placed on trial. The affair created a crisis, and aroused great controversy. The King's police came to find the criminals and blasphemers who had dared to encourage the glorification of the Gallic goddess and defame the glorious Virgin and her infant Son.

Some of the peasants were captured and imprisoned; left to die. Once again the priest intoned hymns to the glory of the Trinity, and Claude de Lannion had the statue thrown to the bottom of the river. A semblance of order returned to the district of Baud.*

The indecent statue

In 1696 Pierre de Lannion, having inherited his father's estates, but not his stanch Catholicism, had the statue retrieved from the Blavet and transported to the Chateau of Quinipily, "as an interesting antique."

The Church was once more outraged. What will happen to the faith of the peasants and their belief in Our Lord, if a pagan statue is impudently displayed to mock them and their laws?

This time a really criminal act was carried out: M. de Lannion, no doubt under duress, had the statue resculptured "to rid it of its indecent aspects."

So she disappeared from public view and gradually her cult was forgotten.

---

statue was simply remounted on the bank. Although mutilated, she still attracted her faithful in the area. She remained in this place from 1660 to 1664 and the harvests were very bad during those years.

*In 1670, following a new episcopal intervention, the statue was again thrown into the Blavet.

Today we can only guess at the identity of the Venus of Quinipily and its "indecent aspects."

Whatever she was, she probably represented the "Mater," mother of humanity, or else a Celtic Isis.†

Today, the statue tops a monument 5 meters high, with a Norman arch, from which emerges a gargoyle which once served to channel water to a fountain. The water then ran into a large hole in a boulder, measuring 1 1/2 meters high, by 2 1/2 meters long, by about 2 meters wide, which was the swimming pool (now empty) where women who had recently given birth came to bathe.

The Venus measures 2 meters high. Her arms are crossed beneath her breasts. The whole statue is made of a very rough stone.

The "restoration" which M. de Lannion had ordered does not allow one to guess much about its original character. A sort of scarf starts at the neck and covers her stomach, continuing between her legs.

On a band round the forehead there are three letters which defy explanation: LIT

It has been suggested that they represent: *Lux Initiatrix. Terrae* (Light of Initiation into the Unknown World).

These initials were probably there before the "restoration."

Other inscriptions, in Latin, almost illegible and difficult to translate, adorn the base.

The Venus of the Celts, or of Quinipily, guards her secrets; magic, impenetrable, close to the fountain which no longer flows, but it is said that even today miracles are performed by her intercession.

†The prehistoric Venuses, those of Lespugne, Kostienki (USSR), of Laussel, and Willendorf (Austria), etc., all had enormous breasts, stomachs, and thighs and a very highly developed pubis.

The Civilization of the Nouraghes

Once more our ideas differ substantially from those of the orthodox archaeologists, in that we believe that a group of pre-Celtic peoples left the high mountain ranges of Persia, long before the dawn of history, and moved in a westerly direction, toward the Atlantic Ocean.

These people we shall call Aryans, though it is possible that they were known by another name which has not come down to us.

The Aryans, who formed the main branch of the Celtic race, went in search of their original land of origin—Atlantis—searching from Ireland to Senegal, leaving along their route great megaliths and ever more intriguing and complex structures, as they and their technology advanced and they penetrated farther and farther into new lands, encountering new peoples who had survived the Deluge.

There is a definite connection between the great megalithic structures of Stonehenge and those at Karnac and the much more advanced civilization of Filitosa in Corsica.

In Corsica, the Celtic Aryans became sailors—the Pelagos—and sailed to Italy, Sardinia, Greece, Malta, and Phoenicia, where their civilization was to crystallize and spread throughout the Mediterranean.

One group settled in Sardinia and developed forms of primitive art, of which indications still remain, particularly at Barumini.

The builders of Barumini were called the Torians, due to the circular nature of their dwellings and fortresses; their civilization is known as that of the "Nouraghes."

During this partially mythical period the Italian peninsula was still in a state of barbarism, as was the rest of the Western world.

The little-known Nouraghes civilization seems to have begun

about 3,500 years ago, and continued under the Punic and Roman empires, but we believe it to have been considerably older even than this.

Barumini has an imposing defense system, including a fortress with four towers connected by impressive ramparts. This inner system is in its turn surrounded by a rampart also strengthened by towers, the whole forming a formidable maze, bristling with obstacles.

The walls are made of great uncemented blocks, reminiscent of those at Sacsahuaman in Peru and at Dun Angus in Scotland.

A temple shaped like a hand

The largest prehistoric sites in Europe are not at Karnac or Stonehenge, as is generally believed, but in Malta and its neighboring island Gozo, where one can admire the most splendid assemblies of megaliths in the world.*

These sites are, naturally, well known to prehistorians, but their mystery and magic eludes them.

Officially nothing is known about the people who built these megalithic towns, whose names have Arabic origins: Hagar-Qim, Mnajdra, Ghar Dalam, Ggantija and called by the Greeks and Romans the Tarxian temples, Hypogeum etc.

We see here a natural progression of the forms and styles of the Northern Celts and the Nouraghes of Sardinia, although more stylized. In Ireland, England, Brittany, Filitosa, Sardinia, and Malta (as well as in Phoenicia) one finds numerous common denominators, seeming to point to a common origin: slabs of stone engraved with cupulas or spirals; megaliths; constructions

*In Phoenician times Malta was called Ogygie. Under the Greeks its name became Melite, and the island of Gozo was called Gaulos. It is the Island of Calypso, described in the Odyessy. Calypso was the Queen of Ogygie.

in the shape of towers in Sardinia and Malta; tumulis; the cult of the Mater, etc. Moreover it is certain that these megalithic peoples were considerable navigators, a quality passed down to their descendants or cousins, the Celts. Our friend, the writer Paul Almasy, wrote in the *Courrier de L'Unesco* that the most ancient potteries of Malta greatly resemble those of Stentinello, near Syracuse.

One of the more important temples, that of Hagar-Qim, ten kilometers from Valetta, is a Stonehenge-like structure, made of limestone, which, just as at Barumini, is built like a maze, with rooms on the inside, but oval in shape rather than round.

Hagar-Qim (or *Jadjar-Kim*) means "cult-stones," or monument-stones. Some are five meters high. The largest, at Ggantija, measures 5 x 8 x 4 meters.

Emile Isambert writes in *Orient, Malte, Egypte*: "It is a temple open to the sky, thus enabling it to receive the rays of the sun, the moon, and the stars, and prayers were offered up to these deities without being blocked by a roof."

Archaeologists believe however that the Maltese temples were originally covered with stone.

Seen from above, the layout of Hagar-Qim looks like a hand, although the first impression is of a slightly more sophisticated Stonehenge.

As a result of excavations, seven statues of obese persons have been found, which some archaeologists identify with the seven Cabires or the Seven Powers.

Inside the temple one can see throughout the labyrinths a number of "oracle holes," about which we shall say more later, and a sacred slab on which numerous cupulas and spirals are engraved in relief, in the center of which one can see an "omphalos" (sacred egg).

On the slab is a "sacred step" where the priests or priestesses officiated.

Hagar-Qim was originally in a tumulus, the apses being adorned with cupulas and the corridors protected on each side by long, horizontal slabs. This style is common both to the temples of Malta and those sites regarded as typically Celtic.

The Hypogeum of Hal-Saflieni

In 1902, while building a house at Paolo, about three kilometers from Valetta, workmen found the hypogeum of Hal-Saflieni, a great complex of underground grottoes, passages, and rooms, whose three floors showed many of the main characteristics of Aryan temples.

The layout of the hypogeum is interesting: If the one at Hagar-Qim is in the shape of a hand, the one at Paolo "represents the ideal construction of man, as conceived by the Esoterics; that is to say, it is composed of seven centers: sexual, motor, instinct, normal emotion, superior emotion, normal intellect, superior intellect."*

Hubert-Bonnal, who has made a particular study of the symbolism of Malta, sees in the general orientation of the hypogeum "the evolutionary development of man, from the primitive to the ideal of perfect equilibrium."

He claims that we witness here the concept of a religious civilization with a deep understanding of the laws of the cosmos.

The ground-plan of Hal-Saflieni does indeed resemble the human form, with head, trunk, legs, and the male genitals clearly indicated.

*According to a study by A. Hubert-Bonnal.

The largest hall, on the upper floor, represents the "holy of holies," with small altars for animal sacrifice.

On the lower floor, twelve meters below, the last step of the staircase is two meters high. Perhaps it was for hiding treasure or perhaps it tapped the water of the reservoir.

According to Maurice Deribere, the hypogeum can be dated about 6,000 years ago. About 7,000 incinerated bodies were found there, but are believed to date from more recent times.

Even more mysterious and laden with magic than the civilizations of Stonehenge, of Barumini, of Machu-Pichu, and of Chichen Itza, is that of Malta, the sacred island, which seems to have subscribed to the cult of a strange Mater, even fatter than the Mater of prehistoric times. Excavations have turned up several statues, all headless, appearing to be breastless women.

These remarkable fat figures, almost as broad as they are tall, have their arms crossed over their chests, like the Venus of Quinipily, or sometimes only one arm so crossed, the other hanging by the side.

Christia Sylf calls them "the three huge ladies" and is surprised to note that they do not boast the enormous breasts (symbolic of nourishment) usually found in such figures.

It would therefore appear that they are not Maters, but partially nonsexual creatures, designed in their physique and psyche for particular religious purposes. These purposes become clearer when one studies the architecture of the labyrinth of the hypogeum.

Everything here is designed in conformity with the laws of acoustics, with deep understanding of those laws.

Voices and sounds from one room are directed by scientifically designed channels to an echo chamber, amplified in the rectangular cavities, the ceiling and walls of which have been carefully smoothed, also passing through rectangular openings like resonance chambers.

On one wall, at a slightly higher level, is an oval window with concave sides, on which three disks appear, painted in ocre. If a man with a deep voice speaks into this opening, the words reverberate in a very arresting manner. (The female voice, or high voices in general, do not reverberate very well acoustically.)

Some believe that the breastless Maters, hidden in the transmission room, listened to the questions asked by the priests and replied in a hollow voice, so effectively that the faithful were convinced that they had heard the voices of the gods.

On one wall of this transmission room, near the ceiling, was found a small passage carved in the rock, the purpose of which was to carry the divine words by a second channel, thus producing a stereophonic effect.

In other words, the rooms, the antechambers, the corridors of the hypogeum, were designed by a gifted architect with an advanced knowledge of acoustics.

The three huge ladies

These facts, in helping us to understand the role of the temple, also enable us to envisage the nature of the "Three Huge Ladies."

They were probably pythonesses, acting as oracles. They lived in the underground rooms, never seeing the light of day, and becoming, in their immobility, so fat as to make walking impossible.

The statues show them without breasts because they had probably been removed, as part of the physical and psychic conditioning, which Sylf asserts took place to develop their inborn gifts of "seeing" and the extrasensory perceptiveness for which the priests had chosen them.

So they became enormous and at the same time developed their strange powers, acquiring through their changed physical condition the deep voice indispensable for a game of deceit, though probably not fully aware of this aspect of their activities.

They officiated at Hagar-Qim and at Mnajdra, where the "hole of the oracle" is still visible, cut into thick rock. They also officiated at all the temples of Gozo and Malta, but it seems certain that the Oracle of Hal-Saflieni had particular authority because of the masterful hoax perpetrated there.

There the crowds of faithful believed the gods really spoke, since the loud vibrant sound of their voices could be clearly heard!

The machine for bringing the dead to life

In all religions the greater the deceit the more easily it is accepted by the faithful.

The most curious aspect of this is the effect that mass faith has in producing positive results.

No miracle has ever been produced at Lourdes; no amputated finger has ever regrown, not by a fraction of a centimeter, but in this huge gathering of sheer faith, cures have been effected which, given dishonest interpretation, have been deemed miraculous.

This is what happened in Malta, notably at Hal-Saflieni, This is what happened at Delphi, Delos, at Dodone, where the forest of oaks reverberated with the rumblings of the bronze caldrons . . . and the priests' deceptions.

This is what happened in the temples of Egypt, where doors closed at the sound of a voice, where statues rose into the air as if by magic, where fire ''lit itself'' in the divine cavity.

The Oracle of the Dead of Acheron or ''Nekyomanteion,'' of which Homer and Herodotus spoke, and which was one of the most famous of antiquity, has just given material proof of the deceptions practiced by the ancient religions.

The site was thought to be in the ancient epirus of the Greeks across from Corfu, near the twin villages of Kastri-Mesopstamon and the former Acheron ''river,'' which is in fact a small stream.

The sages, the tyrants, the princes, the kings, all went to Nekyomanteion to consult the spirits of the dead, whom they believed they could see and hear.

The writer and archaeologist Henry N. Ignatieff, who has studied this phenomenon and taken part since 1961 in excavations led by Professor Dadakis, has revealed the remarkable tricks which were perpetrated to deceive the faithful.

They were subjected to rites and a form of conditioning which reduced them to a state of exhaustion, totally stripped of their critical faculties, then ushered into the room of apparitions.

Having wandered through endless labyrinths in the flickering and shadowy light of torches, and having drunk hallucinogenic drugs, the subjects were only too ready to see phantoms and hear them speak.

For it was not only a matter of hallucinations: Ghosts did appear to come out of the gloom of hell and voices emerged, supulchral, but discernible to the solicitant!

The voices were those of priests hidden in a crypt beneath the incantation room. As for the ghosts, they were the result of an ingenious system of cinematographic projection that Professor Dadakis discovered in a secret room adjoining the room of ghosts.

The machine consisted of a kind of wheel with bronze spokes, connected to an axle which went through the wall, the whole operated by a handle.

Ignatieff believes that this apparatus projected shadows, and perhaps huge images, onto a smoke screen by means of a complex system and colored lights.

The mechanism was found broken, but the pieces of bronze, still intact were reassembled. It had fooled people for almost 2,000 years. It was more or less the same with the oracles: At Delphi the pythoness was hypnotized by the priests or bribed by the notables; at Miletus the burbling, sacred spring was interpreted cleverly; at Claros the voices which emerged from the well owed nothing to the occult; the Sibyl of Cumea operated exactly as the priests of Nekomanteion.

However, it must not be thought that all the priests were frauds, that all the pythonesses and all the sibyls discoursed only to the sound of a purse filled with gold pieces.

Fear; clairvoyance, natural or supernatural; inspiration aided by drugs, certainly have the power to send a medium into a time-space which does not belong to our world.

Here then is the answer to the mystery of the hypogeum of Malta, which would have been revealed long ago if it had been known that on the other side of the Three Huge Ladies there was a real Mater, as fat as the others, but differentiated by her prominent breasts and her recumbent form. For there are good reasons for believing that the priests also kept and raised in the underground cells of Hal-Saflieni those women who were destined to bear their children, perhaps to be the future servants of the cult.

The Three Huge Ladies are headless, and there is a rod of iron attached to their bodies, through the neck. They were no doubt deified and for some reason, while their stone bodies were kept, the heads were interchangeable.

The mysterious paths of Malta

In southeast Malta, in the region of the Dingli cliffs, a strange site has been found, which in certain ways resembles the *pistas* of Nazca. In the rock which makes up the substratum of the island one can see deep parallel ruts, about 1.4 meters apart, which go toward the sea or simply appear to fade away.

Could they be the ruts of a chariot or ancient carriage roads?

These *pistas* form a veritable network of paths which cross each other and split in numerous places to go off at a tangent.

Their meeting places are San Pawl Tat-Targa, Bengemma, Babrija, Buskett, and Dingli.

These mysterious paths suggest the existence, in high antiquity, of a land or undersea connection between Malta and Sicily, or even more likely with Tunisia or Libya.

The theory may be bold, but these routes even suggest an aerial route, four or five millennia ago, before the subsidence into the Mediterranean of the empire of King Minos.

But the mysterious civilization of Malta yield little in comparison with those of Atlantis and the Brazilian *sertao*.

Part II

The Mysterious Unknown

Chapter Six

Christopher Columbus and Magic

Academic books, newspapers, and television create a deliberately distorted picture of history which can be at least partially enlarged upon through so-called heretical authors and apocryphal writings.

For example, there is the appearance of the angels in Genesis, which is described in just nine lines in the Bible, and yet commands 105 chapters in the Book of Enoch!

This is the case with most great events of political significance: the terror of the Viking invasion of Normandy in the year 1000, the Crusades, the French Revolution and the 1940-45 war . . . and it certainly applies to the astounding adventure in which Christopher Columbus emerged as the hero.

Many books have been written about Columbus and one would have thought that everything concerning his physical appearance, morals and ambitions had been told again and again. Like Galileo in 1633, however, a genuine historian, Salvador de Madariaga, set the cat among the pigeons when he published *The True History of Christopher Columbus.* It was history to make the cutthroats of the Conspiracy gasp, so of course they made sure that the heretical book was largely ignored. The Galileo syndrome recurred in 1968. Salvador de Madariaga had courted disaster—the stake—simply by having the effrontery to postulate a theory diametrically opposed to that of orthodox historians.

The earthly paradise

According to Madariaga, Columbus, or Colonus, had told Brother Juan Pérez that he had already been to the West Indies, by a sea route that a strange explorer had revealed to him.

In the 15th century, adventure seekers and poets dreamed of legendary islands: Antilia, or the Seven Cities, St. Brendan, Brazil, La Mano Santamaria, etc., which they thought were located in the Dark Sea, far beyond the Pillars of Hercules.* They were called the Fortunate Islands, and many Westerners, including Christopher Columbus, looked upon them as the

*In 743, an archbishop of Porto together with six bishops and worshipers carrying their worldly goods, fled from Spain (which had been invaded by the Moors) and landed on the Island of Seven Cities, which was also called Antilla or Sete Ribade. The chronicle says, "The bishop, who was a great scholar versed in the arts of necromancy, bewitched these same islands so that they should vanish from the sight of man until Spain was recalled to the good Catholic faith." (Foulche-Delbose)

In the 11th century, the Arab geographer El Edrisi wrote in his *Description of Africa and Spain,* "The expedition of adventurers who planned to discover the secrets and boundaries of the Ocean, left from Lisbon . . . after eleven days sailing they reached a sea whose cloudy waters emitted a fetid smell. . . . Then they sailed south for twelve days and arrived at the Island of Sheep whose flesh was rancid and inedible. Continuing south for twelve more days, they landed in a large town where they saw tall naked men, with red skin covered in hair and with long, plaited hair. The women were extremely beautiful."

earthly paradise described in the Bible and also as a treasury of beautiful jewels and gold nuggets.

It was in this era that *The Book of Marvels*, by John Mandeville, fired imaginations by claiming that scattered throughout the world one might find headless men, devils belching fire from mountain tops, winged monsters strong enough to lift an elephant in their talons, and seas so hot that the fish were boiled alive.

Did Columbus believe in these nonsensical visions? No one knows, but he undoubtedly hoped that the West Indies would yield what was most important as far as he was concerned: gold, precious stones, and glory. Perhaps he also believed in the existence of the earthly Paradise in the West, corroborated by the myths of Egypt, Ireland, and India. He wrote that the Earth was not round, but pear-shaped with a hump on one side like a woman's breast. Situated in the equatorial zone, the point of this breast was that part of the globe nearest the sky, and Columbus thought that here the Paradise described in Genesis could be found.

"No one may reach this earthly Paradise," he wrote, "save by the Divine will."

Señor *Glorioso*,* as he was then called, did not see himself as the first arrival!

This "convert," who was more or less committed to Christianity, possessed qualities and faults typical of his race. He was intelligent, greedy for profit, and considered himself superior to the rest of humanity. He wrote to his sovereigns, "Having expelled the Jews, you have sent me to India and made me a

*"Señor *Glorioso*" or "*Fabuloso*" alludes to Columbus' assertions, which were taken for the ravings of delirium, imagination, or make-believe.

great admiral. Having humiliated my race, you have exalted me."*

In fact, Columbus was as bad a Jew as he was a Christian, and, despite his greatness as an explorer,† he revealed himself as an embarrassingly avaricious hero, heartless, and sometimes dishonest.

Toscanelli's map

One gathers that Columbus set out on his voyage after stealing the map of a Florentine doctor, Paolo del Pezzo Toscanelli.

Here is the text of the first letter sent to Christopher Columbus by Toscanelli. It suggested that the Florentine had given Columbus a map and exact specifications for the journey to the West Indies. Historians do not believe in the authenticity of this letter: which could have been written by Columbus himself in order to vindicate his name from the charge of theft. First letter: "To Christopher Columbus, Paolo Fisico, Greetings. I know of your noble and great desire to go to the place where the spices grow. That is why, in response to one of your letters, I am sending you the copy of another letter which I wrote to a friend of mine a few days ago. This friend was a servant of the most serene King of Portugal before the Castile Wars, and the letter is a reply to another on the same subject which this friend had sent to me at His Highness' request. I am also sending you a navigation map like the one I sent him, which will meet your requirements. Here is the copy of the letter to which I refer."

On June 25, 1474, Toscanelli sent to a Portuguese Canon,

**Christopher Columbus*, Salvador de Madariaga, p. 268.

†It is clear that Christopher Columbus was not the discoverer of America; the Celts, Vikings, Irish, Basques, etc., had visited the continent long before him.

Fernao Martins (or de Roritz) "a geographical map" on which he had marked out the route "leading towards India via the Western Ocean," and indicated the locations, poles, Equator, and distances.

"It is possible to undertake the voyage to the West," wrote the Florentine, "and reach those parts of the world which are richest in all kinds of spices, jewels, and precious stones. . . . For anyone who sails westward in the southern hemisphere will find the said routes to the West, and anyone who sails in an easterly direction following the earth's circumference in the northern hemisphere will come across similar lands in the East."

The map and explanations finally came into the possession of Alfonso I who, on the strength of Toscanelli's theses, is believed to have sent explorers to Brazil on several occasions; apparently they brought him back gold and precious stones. These transatlantic mariners were obliged to take refuge on Madeira, the island farthest from the empire, where it so happened that in 1474 Columbus was destined to marry Señorita Perestrello or Palestrello, daughter of one of these explorers, and heiress to his maps and documents.

Shortly after he gained possession of the maps belonging to the deceased, Columbus abandoned his wife, Felipa Perestrello, and fled from Porto-Santo with his son Diego.

According to Pedro Vasquez de la Frontera, a Portuguese ship went to the unknown islands of Ponant. The only survivor to return went to die with Bartholomeu Perestrello's widow, to whom he told the story of his voyage and left his documents.

Moreover, it was thanks to Toscanelli's letter that in November, 1475, Fernao Telles was made governor of the Kingdom of Seven Cities which was supposed to exist somewhere in the direction of St. Brendan and Antilia!

It is probable, if not certain, that Columbus, the fortune-hunter and meddler obsessed by the idea of ocean voyages, read this famous letter and was inspired by it.

Salvador de Madariago wondered why Columbus fled from Portugal (in 1488, we think). "A man who has stolen an important document would have to flee!" he wrote. "Columbus fabricated the correspondence with Toscanelli (who was dead and thus could not repudiate it) . . . in order to provide plausible explanations to prevent its return to the Portuguese."

In support of n, Madariaga cited a letter from King John II, who assured "his especial friend, Christopher Colon" that if he returned to Portugal in the course of his journey he would not be arrested, detained, accused, deported, or summoned to answer any question of any kind, whether civil or criminal."

How does one explain this strange pledge? "Columbus was a thief," wrote Madariaga. "Do we not possess positive proof that he had stolen Toscanelli's letter? . . . He stole the means of reaching the New World."

The mirage of the Fortunate Islands

This is a very complex affair. The famous and rather dubious map of Piri Reis could be a copy of the maps drawn by Columbus and of those which were continually reproduced in Europe around 1550. It seems very probable that Christopher Columbus had seen the documents which, during the 15th century, circulated among sailors and adventurers interested in the mystery of the Dark Sea.

It was a true case of psychosis. Mandeville had written, "Some time ago, a courageous countryman of ours left home to explore the world. He went to India, then continued for more than 5,000 leagues beyond and circumnavigated the world for many seasons."

The chroniclers say that "Joano Cortereal," a representative of the Portuguese Crown, may have taken part in an expedition to the New World in 1473, and that on his return he was elected governor of the Azores, "As a reward for his discovery of the Country of the Mornes, which was either Newfoundland or Labrador, *i.e.*, the American continent.*

Columbus was well aware of these tales of discovery. He had read Duarte Pacheco Pereira's theories about the West Indies in *Esmeraldo Do Situ Orbio*, Ptolomy's *Cosmology*, and John Mandeville's *Book of Marvels.* He would also have been familiar with the writings of Philippe de Beauvais, which mention the existence of an unknown new world beyond the ocean, and with *The Book of Marco Polo*, the accounts of Henry the Navigator's voyages, etc.†

We should believe him in this matter, for he had studied everything to do with his project. He had seen and copied

*The man in question was in fact Gaspard Cortereal, to whom in 1500 Emmanuel the Fortunate of Portugal may have given command of an expedition to explore the northern coasts of North America. It is said that Cortereal brought fifty-seven Indians back from Canada and sold them as slaves when he arrived home. It is he who gave Canada the named Labrador (worker), a name which was later associated with the peninsula further north. The discovery of Canada, whether by Cabot, by Cortereal, or by Jacques Cartier, is as much disputed as that of America by Christopher Columbus.

†The Infante D. Pedro, brother of the Infante Henry, had spoken of a voyage to the East, and of a very valuable map and book entitled *The Voyages of the Venetian Marco Polo.*

In the remarkable *The conquest of Maritime Routes*, Carlos Pereyra writes, "Columbus' scheme was based on more than fifty maps and harbor plans. . . ."

Henricus Martelus Germanus' map of the world, the *Globe* of Laon, innumerable sea charts, and possibly also Martin Behaim's rough drafts giving the position of the Western islands of Cipango, Candia, Java, Mayor, Java Minor, Anguana, Ceylon, Antilia, and Brazil.

Vinland and Mexico before Columbus

Apart from Martin Behaim's Globe (1492), officially accepted harbor maps and charts were kept in the grand ducal libraries of Weimar, Parma, Geneva, Rome, Venice, and Lisbon, in the 15th century. In particular, people consulted the Venetian maps of the Pizzigani brothers (1367), André Bianco's atlas, and the charts of the Genoese Beccaria (1435), Bartholomew de Pareto (1455), and Andrea Benincasa d'Ancon.

The scholars of the time knew that a continent existed beyond the Dark Sea and that it was not the Grand Khan, but vinland, or the Country of the Vine.

"In about the year 1000," says the Larousse Encyclopaedia of 1872, "a colony was established in the country nicknamed Vinland, which, as far as we know, must have been part of North America." It is said that some fishermen had been shipwrecked during a storm on the island of Estotiland (?), where they found a civilized people who had developed a peculiar form of writing. Because the fishermen knew how to use the compass, they were entrusted to lead an expedition heading further south along the Drocco coast where they were taken prisoner by some anthropoid savages. One of them traveled the country as a slave and learned that further on there stretched rich, fertile and civilized land.

The anthropophagi of Drocco could have been the natives of Nova Scotia and Canada, and the civilized land was perhaps Mexico. Whatever the case, it is probable that these stories, known to Christopher Columbus (writes Larousse), only served to confirm his belief in the existence of land in the West.

Columbus was not the first to discover America. In ancient times, Aristotle had suspected the existence of what Columbus called the West Indies and one must remember the more recent journeys of the Scandinavians to Greenland and the island of Newfoundland, which were probably known in Italy during the 15th century.

Martin-Alonzo and Vincent Pinzon

Despite Columbus' virtues, the honest historian should mention the flaws which have tarnished the reputation of the illustrious Genoese sailor.

In the first place, one should emphasize that Columbus profited by the fact that the brothers Martin-Alonzo and Vincent Pinzon equipped the three ships for his expedition: the *Pinta,* the *Nina,* and the navigator Juan de la Cosa's *Santa Maria.*

Columbus would never have been able to set out for the West without Juan de la Cosa,* and the ships would never have crossed the Atlantic had the Pinzons not supervised their equipment.

The crossing was a long one. After covering the 700 leagues anticipated by "the admiral," Christopher Columbus, the sailors realized that he was an incompetent navigator. He was incapable of taking the ship's bearings, his maps were in-

*Martin-Alonzo Pinzon was on his way from Rome when he met Columbus. It is more or less certain that Pinzon had just been to the Pontifical library to consult the geographical charts and accounts of voyages to Vinland (North America) contributed by the Christian messengers from Greenland, who came to Rome in 1110. In 1327, Greenland still paid her tithe to the Crusades. It is difficult to believe that the missionaries from the Arctic would not have entertained the Pope with tales of voyages, expeditions, and conquests in the Land of the Vine, across the ocean.

accurate and, above all, he was incapable of giving orders that could reasonably be carried out. They grumbled continually and even spoke of throwing their ridiculous admiral overboard.

When mutiny broke out, Columbus was certainly ready to die bravely, and was perhaps on the point of turning back, but once again Martin Pinzon saved the situation.

"I pray God," he cried, "that the fleet of so great a Queen turn not back, either tonight, or at any time this year!"

According to Pierre Margry, author of *The French Navigators and the Maritime Revolution of 14-16 Centuries*, "Vincent Yanez Pinzon may have been second only to Jean Cousin whose ship discovered Brazil and circumnavigated the Cape of Good Hope in 1488—four years before Columbus' voyage."

Forerunners of Columbus

Jean Cousin was a native of Dieppe who, by following the directions of his fellow countryman, the learned hydrographer Descaliers, discovered the mouth of a large river. He called it Maragnon but it later became known as the River Amazon. Ten years before Vasco de Gama, he was also the first to reach the Point of Needles, which was renamed the Cape of Good Hope. According to tradition and ancient accounts, this is the chronological order of the known "discoverers" of America, from the Flood down to Columbus:

"9,000 to 10,000 years ago, some emigrant peoples from Europe crossed the ocean," states the Popol-Vuh, sacred book of the Mayas-Quiches, "and in gradual stages went from the lands of the North (Canada) to Mexico, via the United States. These same migratory peoples moved to Yucatan-Guatemala, then to Columbia, Peru, and Bolivia. Doubtless from there they went on to Polynesia and most notably to Easter Island."

In the days of King Minos, Cretan navigators may have landed in Mexico.

850 A.D.: Badezir, King of Phoenicia, may have gone to Brazil, if one can believe the inscription (in fact indecipherable) on the Stone of Gavea in Rio de Janeiro. The possible translation is "Badezir—high priest of Baal, King of Tyr and Phoenicia."

999: The Icelander Bjorn Asbrandson.*

1003: The Norwegian Leif Ericson (according to epic poem).

1029: The Icelander Gudlief Gudlangson.

Eleventh Century: The expedition of "adventurers" recorded by the Arab geographer, El Edrisi.

1121: Erik Gnupson, Bishop of Greenland, voyage to Vinland.

1362: Eight Swedes, twenty-two Norwegians, according to the runic inscription on the Kensington stone.†

1473: The Portuguese, Danes, and Norwegians in an expedi-

*A Scandinavian account states that in 985, while en route to Greenland, the Icelander Bjorn was blown by a storm far away to the southwest onto a fertile, wooded island.

†This stone was discovered in 1898 by Olaf Ohman, an American farmer from Douglas County, Minnesota. It was put in the bank in Kensington, hence its name. The following is the text of the runic inscription, as translated by the archaeologist Hjalmar R. Holand:

"There were eight of us from Gotland and twenty-two from Norway in an expedition bound for the country of Vinland. Our camp is near two rocks, a few days walk north of this stone.

"We had come here to fish. When we returned to camp, ten of our companions were lying soaked in blood. They had been murdered. A.V.M. save us from peril."

Three further lines engraved on the edge of the stone read, "Ten of our companions are on the seashore watching over our boats, fourteen days march from this island—the year 1362."

tion (very dubious, this!) led by the German captains Pining and Pothorst.

1488: Jean Cousin from Dieppe may have gone to Brazil and discovered the mouth of the Amazon.

1497: Jean Cabot set foot on Terra Firma before Columbus.

Cabot lands before Columbus

Jean Cabot, navigator and cosmographer, set foot on the American continent (then called Terra Firma) before Christopher Columbus, who, at the time of his first voyage had only touched at one of the Antilla islands (San Salvador).

Here, as written by his son Sebastian, is the story of the expedition.

> The year of Grace 1497, Jean Cabot, Venetian, and his son Sebastian, left Bristol with an English fleet, and discovered that land which no one had found before; this was the 24th June at 5 o'clock in the morning.
>
> They called it *Prima Vista* because it was the first land which they sighted from the sea.
>
> They gave the island which was situated off the continent the name *Saint John*, probably because they arrived on St. John the Baptist's day.
>
> The inhabitants of this island were dressed in animal skins and were very proud of their appearance. . . . They used longbows, crossbows, pikes, darts, wooden clubs, and slings as weapons.
>
> They found that in many places the land was barren and bore little fruit; that it was full of white bears and stags much larger than those in Europe, and that it produced

quantities of fish, including some of the larger varieties like seals and salmon.

They found sole three feet long, and plenty of the fish which the natives called *baccalaos*. They also noticed partridges, falcons, eagles, but one very odd thing about them was that they were all raven-black. [This account is not very convincing—Author.]

The first stretch of land that Jean Cabot discovered in 1497, was Labrador. He followed the coast as far as Florida, then returned to Bristol, bringing with him three live "savages" and a rich cargo.

Christopher Columbus did not set foot in the Americas until 1498, a year after Cabot and ten years after Jean Cousin who had discovered the mouth of the Amazon.

The true goal: to rebuild the Temple of Jerusalem

If one attempts to prove too much, one might end up proving nothing at all! Was Columbus a thief? It is anyone's guess. There is no doubt that he was not the real discoverer of the Americas, but he certainly provided Spain with an immense empire, and history with one of its finest ornaments.

The American adventure is so complex that it is almost impossible to unravel the threads. Was the Genoese explorer a crafty Jew or a cunning Christian? No one can say. He was certainly attracted above all by the lure of gold.

In his astonishing book, Salvador de Madariaga reveals that the secret objective in conquering the Americas was to amass enough wealth to rebuild the Temple of Solomon in Jerusalem. In Baza Columbus may have assured the King and Queen *that all the gifts he brought back from his enterprise would be dedicated to the liberation of the House of Zion and to the rebuilding of the Temple.*

The end of the world in 1656

Columbus sincerely believed that he had been sent by God to achieve great things, which proved a powerful, driving force throughout his venture.

In calculating the width of the sea he turned to Esdras and learnt that six portions of the Earth were dry and that there was one under water—and from the teachings of the Hebrew prophets he predicted the end of the world, which he set in the year 1656.

It was for this reason that he urged the King and Queen of Spain to plunge into the project to conquer the Indies. With reference to the mission which Columbus believed was his responsibility, Madariaga wrote:

"He was the Lord's agent, chosen not only to conquer a new world, which had hitherto existed only in his imagination, but also to meet the King and Queen who were oppressing half his people and preparing to send the other half into inhuman exile."

He invoked Abraham, Moses, Isaac, Sarah, and Isaiah, and after his triumph he compared himself with David. Intoxicated with ambition, he also longed to imitate the Biblical prophets. He groaned, considered himself oppressed, covered his head with ashes, and finally wrote a *Book of Prophecies*, which, unfortunately, has not survived, but which probably dealt with the problem of the restoration of Israel, either in Palestine or in the West Indies.

Some historians have said that the Jews wished to make Spain into a new land of Zion, so they monopolized official posts and titles, and even aspired to the throne. This theory is plausible, but one cannot accuse Columbus of being part of the conspiracy, since in order to make his trip to America he had previously petitioned the Kings of England, Portugal, and also, it is said, France.

Columbus, Grand Master of the Temple

One of the great mysteries about Christopher Columbus, apart from those of his birth and his discovery of America, is that of his signature reproduced here:

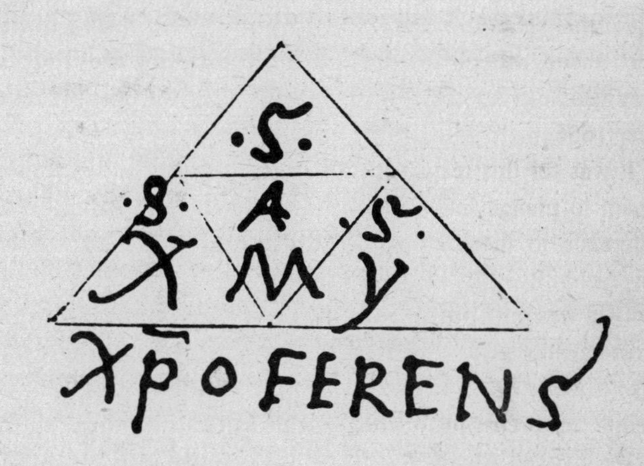

Maurice Privat and Joseph Hariz* believed that Columbus was a magician, and that his signature proves he belonged to the Order of the Temple, of which he may even have been Grand Master. This signature contains two triangles with dots.

"The last line, *xto ferens*, stands for Christoferens; this represents Columbus's motto, 'Christ's messenger,' which had become his Christian name.

**The Great Nostradamus*, No. 1, May, 1934. This publication ceased to appear in about 1936.

"The third line is an allusion to the fact that he fought the Moors beneath the walls of Granada, dressed as a Franciscan friar.* He was also dressed in a monk's robes when he landed after his second and fourth voyages. . . .

"*X, M, Y,* indicate Christ, Mary or Marian, and Joseph or Yousouf.

"It is now only a question of finding the key to the triangle thus formed. Let us climinate the central *A* [Privat quickly overcomes difficulties!] and we have the triple triangle, clearly recognizable as an allegorical representation of the Egyptian pyramids. Columbus thus unmistakably testifies to his Initiation."

A Templar mission

According to the Kabbala, Mr. Privat calculates that *S* repeated three times = 15 × 3 = 45, and 4 + 5 = 9, which is an abstract divine number. In arithmetic, 45 represents the inheritance or the legacy.

Columbus was thus assured of inheriting a Templar's mission. Besides, 15 divided by 3 makes 5, which is the number assigned to the great hierophant between the Pillars of Hercules and Solomon, or simply the Initiated.

"Columbus unequivocally reveals his titles through the letter *A*. 'I am the first of my order.'

"Thus he is the Grand Master of the brotherhood which aspired to conquer and rule the world, which was wiped out in 1307 by Philip the Fair, but whose power survived."

Such is the opinion of Maurice Privat. It is improbable but

*This is an allegation which we have been unable to trace anywhere.

does, nevertheless, suggest some possibilities which arouse one's curiosity.

Maybe the Templars were involved in this story in the same way as the Jews, for one cannot help observing that Columbus was a *convert*; he "discovered" America, where the most powerful state, the USA, was gradually to become the new land of Zion.

According to Louis Charpentier, the Templars had been kept informed of the reports made by the missionaries from Greenland, and that since the 12th century they had known that a maritime route to the western hemisphere existed.

Privat furthermore asserts, "The Templars had set up an immense empire in Mexico at the end of the thirteenth century.

"Thus Columbus was indebted to the Templars for their charts and maps which enabled him to go to the New World, and for the magnificent legacy that he inherited from them."

Those considering this theory should ask themselves why Columbus needed to steal Toscanelli's map and go to so much trouble to procure documents for himself.

Columbus as a Kabbalist

Examination of Columbus' signature does not lead me to the same conclusion as Maurice Privat, but I would agree that the "Genoese" was of Jewish origin and probably practiced magic.

"At the time of his fourth voyage," wrote Dr. J. Hariz, in *The Grand Nostradomus*, "Columbus practiced exorcism.

"During a terrible storm on the Venezuelan coast, when he was suffering from scurvy, he got up, put on his coat, belted on his sword, lit consecrated tapers in the ship's lanterns, and brandishing the Gospel according to St. John and the Gospel of the Holy Ghost, cut the air in four.

"Was it as a result of this ceremony that a gigantic waterspout shot up between the ships but did not suck them down?"

This ceremony is not recorded in the *Log Book of Christopher Columbus* at the time of the tempests on Wednesday the third and Thursday the fourteenth of February, 1493. On the contrary, the admiral and his crew lit candles and made thoroughly Christian vows.

One thing is clear, Columbus believed in the power of letters and numbers, and his signature was undoubtedly meant to have a talismanic appearance. What it really boiled down to was a Jewish, Kabbalistic pentacle! In effect, Columbus was of Jewish origin, as his temperment, versatility, and intellect show. Like all Jews, even the converts, he was a firm believer in mysterious powers which would help him to accomplish his mission.

"Even nowadays," writes Jean Marquès-Rivière, "some Jews use the pentacle called the *Shadai*, which all Israelite children wear for the Bar Mitzvah ceremony. It is a round medallion inscribed with the sacred name *Shadai*, and it has been used since time immemorial. This same sacred word also occurs in numerous magic and texts."

A talisman for the Master of the World

Columbus' signature can be divided into two distinct parts: the signature, *Christoferens*, at the bottom, with the pentacle set above to protect the name by seven magic letters and six dots which are reminiscent of the six points in the Seal of Solomon.

According to Kabbalistic tradition and Hebrew superstition, this is the meaning of the pentacle:

In the admiral's mind then, the purpose of this magic was (reading from right to left, as in Hebrew) to place him under the

. . S.amaël
(Prince of Demons)

.S.hamshiel Arets .S.ikiel
(Light or Sun) (the Earth) (the Storm)

X = C Metatron Yahvé
(Christopher Columbus or Christ) (Master of the World) (the Lord)

protection of Samael-Sathan to ward off storms and to discover a land toward the country where the sun sets. *May Yahvé, the Lord, make the undersigned Master of the World: Christopher Columbus.* If *X* refers to Christ, the sentence becomes, "May Yahve make Jesus Master of the world." Samael, Shamshiel, Arets, and Sikiel are often called upon in Jewish magic.

Columbus was puffed up with vanity, greed, and thick-skinned pride; for example, he had claimed to be a seer when he wrote his *Prophecies* and set the end of the world in 1656, What's more, he had demanded to be made a knight, grandee, grand admiral, and vice-regent before setting out across the ocean.

In about 1498, when his venture had succeeded, he wrote the Spanish sovereigns a delirious letter in which he called himself prince of the world and the true Metatron. "Did God do more for Moses or for David?" he asked, and speaking of himself he added,

"Since your birth He has always taken great care of you. He has made your name outstandingly famous on Earth."

In fact, the talisman, hidden in a small bag which Columbus must have worn next to his skin, seems to have played an effective role, for although he did not discover the Americas, and did not even dream up the western maritime route, Columbus did become a kind of Metatron: the most famous man in the world.

Samael, Sikiel, Arets, Shamshiel—Y—M and *X* (*X* your name, especially if it begins with a *C*), *there's a powerful, marvelous talisman which has proved its worth*!

Although apocryphal, the *mayorazgo** of 1498 is probably based on the vanished 1592 document, suggested Madariaga. It contains this curious clause about the signature.

"My son, Don Diego, or whoever inherits this estate, after inheriting it and obtaining possession, *will sign* the signature which I now use, consisting of an *X*, with an *S* above it, with the characters and the commas as I do now, and as will be seen from my previous signatures, and by the signature below.

"And he will sign himself only *The Admiral*, even though the King should give him, or he should earn, other titles."

A pact with Satan

If one wants to analyze the signature it means, "Christopher Columbus—light or sun—Master of the Earth—answerable to Samael—Lord—of the storm."

If the six dots were joined they would form two linked triangles. If one were to join them up from all possible angles one would have two geometrical pyramids (in the space), each one being four-sided.* By interpreting the triangles we get the seal of Solomon, which brings us back to the Hebrew magic pentacles.

From these specifications it transpires that the admiral had signed a pact with Satan which involved his direct descendants.

**Mayorazgo* means majorat or inalienable property. In this case it refers to the official document stating this majorat.

†Madariaga notes that the first *S* of the pseudo-monogram should only have one dot, on the left-hand side.

Of course, one does not believe that such a pact had any significance, any more than one believes in Satan, but it is interesting to note that Columbus' adventure followed exactly the pattern one might have expected had the Devil been involved. There was the collection of demons, talismans, and incantations; there were strange accidents, unexpected strokes of luck,** not to mention the providential assistance he received but did not always deserve; there was also an atmosphere of evil, intensified by the lure of gold, the horrors, chicanery, duplicity, and the bloodshed and atrocities in which the West Indian savages indulged.

Salvador de Madariaga draws attention to the triangular shape of Columbus' signature, and connects it with the Kabbala. He goes on to say that the arrangement of the dotted *S*'s almost exactly corresponds to the shape of the shield of David.

An Israeli Kabbalist, Mr. Maurice David, told Madariaga that as the son and grandson of a rabbi he had seen the inscription which appears in the top left-hand corner of all letters except one written by Columbus to his son Diego, and had recognized it as being the same sign his father and grandfather inevitably used to put in the same place on all their letters. It was an old Hebrew greeting, a blessing. Madariaga points out that Hebrew graphologists do not share this opinion.

According to J. R. Marcus, Jewish Professor of History at the Hebrew Union College of Cincinnati, Ohio, if one transcribed the letters of the charm into Latin one would get

Shadai
Shadai—Adonai—Shadai

**The patron saint of converts, San Angel, helped Columbus with his expedition because some treasure had been discovered in a lucky moment! This idea smacks rather of fire and brimstone!

YHWH—male—Chesed
Nose—Ovon—pesha—chata'ah

This is a Jewish incantation which is both magic and religious. The writer, Don Armando Alvarez Pedroso, suggests another interpretation:

S = Senor
S.A.A. = Su Alta Senoria
X.M.Y. = Excellent, Magnificent, Illustrious

The first explanation still seems more plausible.

Chapter Seven

Albert the Great's Black Book

The scholar is a simple sort of man, whereas the physicist, chemist, or mathematician tends to be more of a seeker whose knowledge, although out of the ordinary, is arbitrary, uncertain, and transitory.

The Mysterious Unknown is a collection of phenomena or facts which no one can explain, perhaps because they belong to the science of the future, perhaps because our thought processes and methods of investigation are not suited to their comprehension.

The stroke of luck

Mathematicians have done their best to explain luck, but their clever theories vanish in a haze of statistics.

Mr. M. L. de Moissac, for example, is an ardent racegoer. When he was filling in his betting card one Sunday in November, 1971, he wrote down the number 16, thinking he had put 18, but it was horse number 16 which came in first. The following Monday, he arbitrarily placed a bet on a number, and came up with the winner of the daily double. Whatever anyone may say, that is a disturbing record: a winner by mistake, and then a correct entry on the form produced exactly the same result. Does chance enjoy privileged options or, to put it another way, is there an unknown quantity which baffles the laws of reason?

A mistake once saved the life of my friend and correspondent, E. Bécouse. It was just a tiny blunder, but enough to make one stop and think very hard. Mr. Bécouse tells his own tale.

"It was October 1, 1918, in the middle of the Champagne offensive. I was then commanding 18th battery of 102nd Division Heavy Artillery. With the help of Levejac, my lieutenant, I was preparing for firing.

"We were sitting one on either side of a trestle table in the tent which served as HQ when I dropped my pencil. I bent down to pick it up, and at that precise moment a large piece of shrapnel flew through the canvas at the point which would have been level with my head had I not bent down. I ought to light an especially fine candle in gratitude for this coincidence, as the shell which had just exploded killed a driver, wounded a brigadier, and disemboweled three horses."

During that terrible 1914-18 war, when one needed as much luck as possible to save one's skin, each incident took on an extra dimension, and chance or luck were of the greatest significance. Mr. Bécouse was in a position to witness four extraordinary "coincidences" which led him to believe in an active Mysterious Unknown.

Strange facts

When Lorrell Wilhelm was born in Perth, Australia, a family

tradition was confirmed, for she was born on April 8, like her mother, her grandmother, and her great-grandmother.

A report dated March 17, 1972 reads as follows:

"A ten-year-old pupil at a primary school in Athens saved his friends and schoolmaster by telling them about a dream he had had the preceding night. In a tone of conviction which impressed his audience he said, 'The school roof collapsed.' The schoolmaster, who was undoubtedly exceptionally sensitive, then moved all the children into a part of the classroom where the ceiling looked stronger than the rest. A few minutes later, the roof collapsed at the spot which had just been evacuated."

In June, 1971, in Romans, France, a hen was kept which, since the last partial eclipse of the moon in February, had laid eggs that were flattened on one side and engraved with the picture of a sun represented by a circle and thirteen rays.

One of my readers told me of the following unusual occurrence that he had heard from his mother and from several other people of her age. In 1868, the postman in the village of Ignerande, France, let his chickens into the kitchen of his small farmhouse. Now, one of these hens had a habit of roosting in front of a clock, and one day she laid an egg engraved with a perfect replica of the clock face. Other eggs followed, but the image gradually grew fainter. The news soon got round the village and the postman, who was an astute man, charged everyone two cents to watch the egg-laying and inspect the first phenomenal egg. Then he had the idea of covering the dial with a portrait of Napoleon III, in the hopes that the hen would reproduce the picture and thus provide him with a new source of income. He was disappointed, however, because the hen laid an egg with only a very vague outline of the portrait.

The story is supposed to be true. No doubt a biologist could explain it as a phenomenon of psychic impregnation, but what would he say to the 500 swifts which, in June, 1969, gathered in the chimney of twenty-four-year-old Mrs. Girard to die. The flue was cleared out on three occasions, but each time the flock of birds came back and suffocated. Why they chose Mrs. Girard's chimney for this strange suicide remains a mystery.

What impulse prompted American film producers to give left and right their traditional significance in their Western movies? Invited to comment on the subject a film critic said,

"The Americans have formally established that the direction of certain movements, such as entrances, exits, and pursuits, is of considerable importance in films. Thus in most Westerns, if the good man pursues the bad, they ride from right to left. If the bad man chases the good, the pursuit goes from left to right."

No one knows why, but traditionally the left (the side of the heart, incidentally) is associated with evil and the right good.

The signal from the world beyond

In a competition, Ulrich Ronde, a six-year-old boy from the Naila Comprehensive School in Bavaria, drew the picture of a child knocked over by a car, stretched out on the ground beside his bicycle. The drawing also depicted another child in a telephone booth contacting the police. His picture was awarded a prize by the school authorities, but Ulrich did not know, because in the meantime he had died in exactly the same circumstances as those he had imagined—knocked over by a car while riding his bicycle.

Straton le Nimois, who writes in the *Dauphine Libéré*, tells a story of the extraordinary adventure which befell the Egyptian writer, Ibrahim Fahri. On June 12, 1942, Fahri's car broke down just approaching a corner on the desert road between Cairo and Alexandria. On the side of the road, there was a sign saying, in French, BEWARE, MIRAGE. Fahri was somewhat surprised so he looked more closely and saw that some dry sand had stuck to the sign in the form of two parallel lines on either side of the *V* of *Virage* (French for "bend"), making it read *Mirage*. Then a dilapidated old car came clattering by, and the Egyptian writer saw on its bodywork this strange inscription, still in French, AMRIA CEMETERY AND BEYOND. Haunted by these coincidences, a few days later he went to the Amria cemetery, which he had not previously known existed. He found, *as though it were by chance*, an ancient, cracked pillar, on which was a partially effaced name: IBRAHIM FAHRI.

Straton le Nimois also tells a story which is equally astounding, if it is true. Luigi Bianchi, a young factory worker from Naples, was recently going home on his scooter when he came across a girl thumbing a lift. He told her to climb on behind him, and when it began to drizzle lent her his coat to protect her from the rain. The girl gave him the address of her home, to which he duly took her. He enjoyed the encounter so much that he forgot to reclaim his jacket, but when he turned up at his passenger's home to get it back the next day, he was greeted by a couple who exhibited great surprise and asked, "What jacket and which girl do you mean?" Luigi described what had happened the evening before, and the father looked very upset as he replied, "Oh, our daughter has been dead for more than two years!" Stunned and incredulous, Bianchi went to the cemetery and found the girl's grave. On the railing surrounding it was hanging his jacket. . . .

The secrets of Albert the Great

Albert the Great was a book of mysteries based on the most childish superstition, albeit occasionally enlived by some sensible observations, which enjoyed enormous success in the 18th century. A sequel to this, entitled *Little Albert*, then came out; it was supposedly a translation of the works of a certain Albertus Parvus Lucius, who probably never existed.

Since the 16th century, and doubtless even before that, illicit pamphlets were secretly circulated. These added fuel to the fire in the dens of sorcerers, alchemists, and necromancers and were the famous Black Books of the Middle Ages, although the first genuine edition dates only from 1705.

Of course, the Mysterious Unknown, discussed in these books, was only a series of empirical ramblings. The learned and worthy Dominican monk, Albertus Magnus (13th century), would have nothing to do with them. Charles Daremberg has this to say on the subject. "What a curious destiny! A genuine scholar has become godfather to the necromancers associated with the Middle Ages and the Renaissance." And Querard agrees that it was "Idiotic rubbish to attribute so many errors to a famous Dominican."

Albert the Great's Black Book abounds with spells, each more amazing than the one before. It tells how to make the terrible Greek fire, how to become invisible by wearing a ring, and has recipes to ensure against being cuckolded, to bring back lost virginity, to tie ornamental shoulder knots, or to make a girl dance in just her nightdress.

From time to time, a grain of commonsense is found among the billy-goat grease, wolves' eyes, and plants picked by the light of the full moon, as in the recipe, for example, "against getting drunk on wine." Before sitting at table, it suggests, drink two spoonfuls of betony water and a spoonful of good olive oil, and you will quite safely be able to drink wine.

In order to cure a man of drunkenness "wrap his genitals in a cloth which has been soaked in vinegar," and for a woman, "put a similar cloth on her breasts." We don't guarantee success!

Magic communication across great distances

Albert the Great also reveals secrets of a parascientific Mysterious Unknown, but unfortunately they are unfounded! The title is long, but inviting:

A marvelous secret for making a magnetic sundial or compass, by which one can write to an absent friend and let him know one's thoughts, at the moment of, or the moment after writing

In short, it was communication by radio-electric methods which, in the 15th century, must have seemed very clever but needed simply a compass needle cut in two lengthwise! These are the instructions.

> Have made two fine steel boxes (like the ordinary boxes for mariners' compasses) which should be of the same weight, size, and shape, with a wide enough edge to hold all the letters of the alphabet. Each must have a pivot at the bottom on which a needle can be balanced, as on an ordinary sundial. Then, from several fine magnetic stones, choose one which, on the side pointing toward midday, has white veins and cut the one which you find to be the longest and straightest into two parts, as equally as you can, for your two boxes. They must have the same thickness and weight, with a little hole so that you can balance them on the pivot. That being ready, give one of the boxes to the friend with whom you wish to communicate and arrange with him a set time on a certain day of the week. It can be the same time each day, if you want.

When you want to speak to each other from your respective studies, quarter, half, or even an hour before the appointed time, you must, as quickly as possible, place your needle on the pivot in the box, keeping your eye on it all the time. You must have with you a cross, or some symbol of the beginning of the alphabet, so that when the needle reaches the marker you can see that it is time to speak to one another, for the needle must spin toward the marker of its own accord, after your absent friend has positioned his correctly.

Thus the friend, to make his meaning known to the other, will move his needle to a letter and, simultaneously by magnetic attraction, the other needle will move to the same letter. When you reply, you must do the same thing and, when you have finished, put the needle back to its old marker. Remember that you must be careful to shut the box firmly after speaking, and put the needle away separately in the cotton wool, in a wooden box, and above all keep it free from rust.

To change lead into fine gold

Nowadays, newspapers sometimes give information which appears to relate to the supranormal, or publish communications from the World Beyond, an activity which seems highly suspect!

This happened with a winning ticket in the French National Lottery, the number of which had been divulged to some fortunate woman during a dream, either by her dead husband or someone particularly dear to her. Yet, if one wanted to buy a ticket numbered, for example, 28753 from the next series, how could one foresee the town or village where this number was going to turn up for sale?

Alchemy belongs to the most intriguing part of the Mysterious Unknown because there is no way of proving whether, in the course of time, some particularly gifted experimenter did succeed in making gold or in creating the philosopher's stone which had the power to confer all kinds of benefits, such as luck, health, and knowledge.

Albert the Great's Black Book gives precise directions for changing lead into gold, as instructed by the learned chemist Fallopius and approved by those renowned alchemists, Basil Valentin and Odomar.* Here is the secret.

> You must steep a pound of Chypre copperas [leather ash or sulphate of leather] in a pound of tempering water, which you have strained well to make it clear. This infusion ought to continue for twenty-four hours, so that the copperas is completely liquified and mixed with the water. Then distill it by straining it through pieces of clean felt and keep this distillation in a strong glass phial, well corked. Then put one ounce of good-quality quicksilver, which has been purified, into a crucible which you must cover to prevent evaporation. When you see that it has begun to boil, add an ounce of high quality gold-dust and take the crucible off the heat as quickly as possible. Having done this, take a pound of highly refined lead, as directed below, which you must melt and mix with the composition of gold

*Basil Valentin is one of the most famous alchemists of the Middle Ages, but in fact it is not certain that he existed! It is possible that some hermetists may have used the name Basil Valentin (in Greek = powerful king) to protect their anonymity. In any case, real or hypothetical, Basil Valentin helped to advance the chemical knowledge of his time considerably.

Odomar, a 14th century French monk of almost the same epoch, was an alchemist and a chemist with a great deal of scientific knowledge.

and quicksilver you have just prepared and, as soon as the concoction has cooled, you will find that it has turned into fine gold.

Is there any connection between the secret of Fallopius and, the recent, curious rumors about a certain elegant, learned gentleman living in the Place des Vosges in Paris? A publication devoted to secret sciences and bearing the name of the Dominican alchemist already mentioned, claims in its fourth issue to have proof of it.

The hero of the affair, claiming to be the true Count of Saint-Germain,* made his appearance this century on January 28 at 9:30 in the French ORTF television series, *The Third Eye.*

The Count of Saint-Germain

After asking whether the ''new'' Count of Saint-Germain was genuine or an imposter, the publication asserted that he was without a shadow of doubt an Initiate. He could speak seven languages fluently, including Sanskrit and Chinese, and he could write equally well with both hands! Finally, the editor-in-chief affirmed that the new Saint-Germain could achieve transmutations. ''He has managed to change lead into gold on five occasions, and the last time did so in front of a team of experts from ORTF. This transmutation was filmed while it was in progress, so it seemed that it could not possibly be a trick, a sleight of hand.''

*The Count of Saint-Germain was an adverturer, possibly a Jew of Portuguese origin, who died in Eckenfoerde, Schleswig, in 1784. He astounded Louis XV's court by his grand ways and the confidence with which he claimed to have lived in the 16th century. He was banished from France. Cagliostro boasted of being his disciple.

Nevertheless, the author of this astonishing testimony was prudently noncommital, and declared himself equally torn between belief and disbelief. The program was given enormous publicity, because it was remarkably well presented, authoritatively enacted, and from beginning to end was fascinating to watch. The young, handsome, and charming "Count of Saint-Germain," always escorted by pretty girls, would have proved in front of ten million French people that he possessed the powder of projection, had the experiment been genuine!

The screening took place in the offices of the publication's managing director, on Wednesday, January 5, 1972 at 9:30, the day and hour chosen by the alchemist himself. As convention demanded, he did not touch anything. The materials consisted ot a camp stove and some lead supplied by the ORTF and examined by the witnesses.

In order to adjust the heater, Saint-Germain plunged his hands into the flame and made the necessary alteration without suffering any ill effect. (To prevent burning when exposing one's hands to fire, Albert the Great gives the recipe for an ointment made of marshmallow juice, the white of a fresh egg, the seed of fleabane, some powdered limestone, and horseradish juice.) The alchemist had brought a crucible and the journalist presenting the program put in it the three centimeters of smelting lead that he had dusted with the powder of projection which the magician kept in an amulet around his neck. The crucible was covered and put on the stove for five minutes and then immersed in cold water.

Finally, the crucible was opened to reveal a little darkish residue of some black substance, (the lead?) and a small piece of gold.

No miracle on television

Miss Jacqueline Baudrier, the charming director of the TV color channel has, at my request, given her opinion of this mystery.

Dear Sir,

It does not seem to me that an explanation regarding the young man who calls himself the Count of Saint-Germain presents any problems.

He claims to be able to change lead into gold on a camping stove and, to all intents and purposes, his conjuring trick has worked perfectly.

To be fair, he might have shaken some of one's convictions had he not also claimed to be 17,000 years old, regularly visit the planet Mars, and to have hatched out a Coleoptera beetle weighing 17 kg, and heaven knows what else besides. It is just too much . . ."

The Count of Saint-Germain tells a variety of astounding tales. For example, he says that he has known Louis XV, Frederick the Great, actually lived with Ninon de Lenclos, and also that he is one of the twelve genuine Rosicrucians who secretly control the world. (Of course the Rosicrucians do not in any way corroborate this assertion.)

The Count of Saint-Germain's real name is Richard Chanfray, and even if he does not actually possess the power to change lead into gold, one can nevertheless credit him with a very extensive knowledge of the esoteric.

The fact which he successfully pulled off in front of the ORTF cameras in the middle of the 20th century poses the question of whether one should believe that transformations were effected by alchemists in the Middle Ages.

Professor Rameau considers that the miracle-worker "is not the real Garoczy-Saint-Germain, but undoubtedly, as his knowledge shows, an extraterrestrial being!" The professor adds, "If he claims to be a traveler in time then he must prove it by making himself luminous in public. This must be done without the help of luminous salts or trickery, simply by ionization of his clothes; this would be evidence of his power over time."

Thus the enigma of the Count of Saint-Germain takes a new direction, which will delight devotees of the supernatural.

The Red Man of the Tuileries

In the early 19th century, a strange personage known as the Little Red Man of the Tuileries hit the headlines in Saint-Germain fashion. A writer by the name of Christian Pitois told the story in 1863.

After miraculously escaping the holocaust of the Rue Saint-Nicaise on December 24, 1800, Bonaparte went to thank the old Benedictine, Dom Guyon, who had warned him of the danger. The old man gave him a sealed envelope containing his horoscope, which included a reference to his astonishing rise to fame, but also prediction of his downfall. This upset Napoleon so much that from then on he ceased to consult his friend the astrologer.

On the night of March 20, 1804, a grenadier on sentry duty in the Tuileries Gardens caught sight of a human form, illuminated by a red glow, which seemed to be floating along the walks. After challenging him three times, the soldier fired; the light which had illuminated the phantom went out, and the alarmed sentry went to investigate, but he could only find a recently extinguished lantern and a large red cloak.

A little later they discovered the name of the apparition: It was Dom Guyon. He was disappointed because the First Consul was no longer visiting him and, having become somewhat unbalanced, had adopted the habit of walking at night in the Tuileries, draped in a large red flag. In his unhinged mind, this gave him the appearance of a hierophant. The shot had frightened the poor devil and he had fled, abandoning his lantern and his cape. When he reached his garret he had a seizure and died.

"Poor devil," Bonaparte is supposed to have said, on learning of this tragic end. "He hadn't foreseen that in his black books!" He gave orders for Dom Guyon to be buried secretly, forbidding the affair to be made public.

Such was the history of the Little Red Man of the Tuileries, who had been Bonaparte's astrologer. After the coup, the soldiers of Egypt looked upon him as a kind of genie of the Pyramids, invulnerable to bullets and incorporeal like a ghost.

Chapter Eight

The Magic Portraits In Belmez De La Moraldeda

When the Mysterious Unknown manifests itself in our tangible universe, either by chance or for reasons which we don't understand, scientists are generally unable to explain the phenomenon and prefer to ignore it or to put it down to trickery.

However, there is one exceptional case which seems to have shaken the convictions of many a rationalist. It concerns Belmez de la Moraleda, a small town which basks in the Andalusian sun on the slopes of the Sierra Magina. The actual geographical situation is forty kilometers as the crow flies (sixty-two kilometers by road) east of Jaen.

There, like all the peasants in the area, Juan Pereira farms about ten acres of barley and olives, and rears a herd of goats. He is the second husband of Doña Maria Pilar Gomez Camara, by whom he has two sons, Diego and Miguel, the elder of whom wants to join the *Guardia Civil.* Juan and Maria cannot read or write, but they are highly respected in the neighborhood for being hard workers who guarantee good service.

The enchanted house

One day in August, 1971, Marie was preparing a meal. When she was brushing aside the ashes in the fireplace, she saw what looked like a drawing on the hearthstone, which intrigued her. Sweeping it more thoroughly, she saw something resembling a face emerging, and nearly fainted with shock.

Coming to her senses again, and being superstitious like all God-fearing Spaniards, she suspected some trick of the Devil, and arming herself with a cloth set to work to efface the suspicious picture. But in vain! The more Maria washed and rubbed the hearthstone, the more clearly and richly colored the face came up. It was undoubtedly female, with large, almond-shaped eyes, straight eyebrows, a nose with narrow, pinched nostrils and a half-open mouth with thin lips. The hair seemed to be braided and at the base of the neck one could make out the top of a dark bodice.

One curious detail was that two dark lines ran from the nostrils, two streams of blood perhaps, coursing down the cheeks and even spoiling the perfect oval of the face. The picture was nearly life-size and was painted in gray sepia with reddish highlights.

Maria was frightened and called her husband and then their neighbors, who all hung over the fireplace, examining the ghostly apparation.

"Who could have done this drawing?" asked Jean Pereira. But his question was purely rhetorical because it was perfectly obvious that neither he nor his family could have created the fresco.* It was all so bizarre and inexplicable that soon the

*In his book *Les Faints Maudits,* George Langelaan tells a story which bears a certain resemblance to that of Mrs. Pereira. Mrs. Euna Lowe from Nassau, the Bahamas, saw images of Christ, Buddha, and an unidentified third person on a blank well of the church of the

curious from Spain, Portugal, Germany, Italy, and France poured in to look.

A tomb under the hearth

A month later, tired of being plagued by crowds which were becoming larger and more unmanageable, Juan Pereira asked a mason to come and cover the hearthstone with a layer of cement at least three centimeters thick. The furor died down for awhile, but as the cement dried, the phantom head reemerged through the limestone and was eventually just as clear and highly colored as ever. Then, a magnificent drawing of an old man's head took shape among the ashes.

This was too much for the Pereiras' nerves, and they decided to put an end to the business once and for all. In October the flagstone was taken up and when the mason dug under the fireplace he found a deep tomb 2.60 meters deep, out of which he pulled some human remains mingled with the earth.

They then remembered that the house, which had been built in the last century, stood on the site of an ancient cemetery dating back to Philip IV's time (1650). That explained the human remains but little else. The hole was filled in, the hearth entirely rebuilt with fresh cement, and at last the apparition seemed to have been defeated, for nothing happened for a month.

Meanwhile, Maria had made them put the excavated flagstone in a corner of the kitchen, and she religiously left flowers there as if it were a conventional tombstone.

Tabernacle of Glad Tidings. The same evening, the vision became reality and the faces appeared as frescoes which the rest of the world could see.

The spirits speak

On November 15, a new and larger face appeared on the fresh cement. It was fainter, but the same features were clearly recognizable. It took eight days to emerge completely, during which time miniature faces seemed to be hatching out in its hair, making a garland, or as some have described it, "The form of a planetary system where the centerpiece was the sun." The central face seems to surge from a spiral in a centripetal movement, while the faces of the cherubims suggest a centrifugal movement, as if they were separate from the main image.

Every one of these pictures is very expressive; it is almost as though the mouths wish to speak and reveal a secret. Grief and horror are portrayed in the eyes and the features, giving a very unpleasant effect, and all the faces have two lines on either side of the nose.

By this time, it was inevitable that the miracles of the *casa encantada* should have excited intense curiosity, and Belmez de la Moraleda was deluged not only with amateur connoisseurs of art, but also with journalists and specialists in the occult sciences.

The priest in this small town, Don Antonio Molina, was reluctant to believe in the supernatural aspect of the apparitions, while by contrast, Rafael Lafuente, a futurologist and radio-electric expert from Malaga, declared his conviction that this was a manisfestation of the World Beyond which had materialized through the intercession of a medium. He did not wish to name the medium, but it was clear to everyone that he thought the dark and unsociable Maria must be unconsciously involved in the affair.

The newspaper, *Pueblo,* appointed itself the spokesman for an inquiry and the house was invaded by reporters, an archaeologist, and a chemist. There was even a parapsychologist, Don German de Argumosa, who came equipped with a recorder which could register noises imperceptible to the human ear. It was all very disturbing!

At midnight, as they had been expecting, Don German's wonderful apparatus recorded information which, if genuine, is most interesting. The recordings were supposedly of "lamentations," "love trances," "heavy breathing," "a piercing cry which seemed to come from a woman," the words "*no habe . . . mujeres . . . no quiero . . . pobre quinco*" (do not . . . have . . . wife . . . from . . . I do not want . . . poor quinco).

Also recorded were : "*Borracho! Aqui no accepto borrachos!*" (Drunkard! We do not accept drunkards here!), "The cries of a dying child," "*Va con todos los hombres*" (She goes with any man), and "*Entra, mujer, entra*" (Come in, woman, come in).

Pueblo states that toward the end, one could hear "noises and sounds associated with lovemaking, brutality, and drinking, and one could distinguish brothel brawls, quarrels, and above it all, the horrible wailing of babies. Perhaps they were being massacred!" The witnesses who attended the recording, Juan and Maria Pereira and the mayor of Belmez, could hear no noise, or word. One must therefore deduce that the magnetic band was either more sensitive than the human ear, which is not generally the case, or else that the "beings from the world beyond" registered directly on the ferrites. On the other hand, unless it was a fantastic coincidence (but why not?), Don German was extremely lucky to chance on an emission at his first attempt, assuming that the beings do not speak all the time.

Some witnesses, on reflection, thought they might have heard "a hymn to the glory of God Almighty."

The house is haunted

These pseudo-messages sent by the spirits invited the following comments and speculation.

"We now know that house number 3, adjoining the Pereiras', had been the site of a parapsychological phenomena.

"A certain Lopez Sanchez, a cousin of the Pereiras, sold it because he was continually disturbed by peculiar noises, ghostly visitations, and the removal of objects. For example, he arrived home on one occasion to find the sheets had been violently torn from the bed." The house frequently changed hands, yet all the owners kept quiet about the strange incidents so that they would not prejudice the sale. They only divulged the facts when the portraits appeared on the stone.

It was also said that two men fought to the death in the room where the faces appeared. Soon it was alleged in the little town (2,500 inhabitants) that the pictures could even speak!

Another face appears

Friends of mine, Jean and Denise Larroque, went from Malaga to Belmez de la Moraleda to investigate for themselves.

"The face which emerged first," wrote Denise Larroque, "had been removed with the hearthstone, and this fresco had been placed near the wall under a protective pane of glass. Another slab had been removed in the same way from the chimney wall (at the back of the fireplace), but one could only guess at rather than see the picture on it, and it seemed to get fainter every day. It depicts an old man with a long beard, and is so astonishingly drawn that it could be by Leonardo da Vinci.

"I questioned fifty-three-year-old Mrs. Pereira, who seemed sincere, and maintained that the pseudo-scientific explanations given by the *Pueblo* journalists had no foundation. 'I was frying some eggs,' she said, 'when the first face appeared in front of the fire on the floor itself. I was very frightened and called my neighbors and children. We tried to clean the cement, but the image still remained and resisted all detergents.' "

The entire village believes in these apparitions and opposes the journalists, who must often have been jeered away by the inhabitants.

Don German's recordings, however, were not taken seriously by the Pereiras or their neighbors, who maintain that they have never heard an unusual sound in the house.

Maria Pereira is a strange woman, and has been greatly affected by the phenomenon, but the police and inhabitants of Belmez, as well as the local authorities, consider that she would be incapable of partaking in a fraud of this nature.

Belmez de la Moraleda, an attractive town set in pleasant surroundings, has an excellent hotel with a park, which encourages the skeptics to say that the whole thing could have been fabricated in order to create a new Fatima or Lourdes. Don Antonio Molina, the priest, insists to anyone who cares to listen that the phenomenon is absolutely divorced from religion.

Ultraviolet rays

How can these strange pictorial apparitions be explained? One can only put forward theories, nearly all of which relate to communications between the world of the living and that of the dead, providing, of course, that one discounts trickery.

The recordings on the magnetic band can certainly be dismissed as erroneous or fraudulent, but it is difficult to question the authenticity of the frescoes, bearing in mind that no member of the Pereira family can draw well enough to be the artist.

Pueblo believes that it is a matter of science. Mr. Angel Vinas, the chemist representing the newspaper, thinks that the apparitions could be the result of a chemical combination of silver chloride, Ag Cl and silver nitrate Ag NO^3. The reaction 2 Ag Cl + 2 Ag + Cl would be induced by an ultraviolet light and the silver could turn brown if combined with sulphuric hydrogen H^2S which is present in the air.

We do not know, however, what miracle enabled the chemical process to draw human faces or how simple, illiterate people like the Pereiras carried out the operation. Mr. Vinas omits explaining the mystery!

The supernatural

The possibility of its being a supernatural manifestation is not absolutely convincing, but it nevertheless comes nearer to satisfying the logical mind.

Mr. Joaquim Grau, a parapsychologist known in Spain as Uttama Sitkari, is of the opinion that there may be a medium in the Pereira family: undoubtedly Maria. Unconsciously, "By focusing her thoughts on the departed," she may be able to make pictures appear.

We can go further into the realms of speculation. Thought waves, transmitted in the past under particularly dramatic circumstances, have accumulated under the influence of an outside source of energy, forming a kind of knot of time (a singular universe), instead of diffusing throughout time and space. Our universe would be (in the same sense) one great thought enclosed in a circle from which it cannot escape. Intense sources of energy all around ensure that the circle remains closed.

Thus, in the present, favorable circumstances, disembodied chemical elements or the catalyzing power of a medium may have set up a process comparable with the force by which iron filings collect around a magnet. One might also compare it figuratively with the grouping of electric elements, arranged by the intervention and unconscious will of a medium serving as a conductor.

Another possibility is that the Pereiras' house is a favorable place for materializations and for the particular influence of electric currents which could act as the motivator and creative will in reviving scenes and situations of the past.

The simplest solution to the problem, however, is that a natural or supernatural creative force is acting in such a way as to reveal a secret or liberate a consciousness, in order to bring about a dialogue between this world and the world beyond.

Telluric currents and materialization

Viewing the subject from this angle, one sees that there would in the past have been magnetic and photographic recordings, by supposedly inert matter, of scenes or events of great intensity which were enacted on this earth. Perhaps it only needed an exceptional electromagnetic and chemical coincidence to reproduce a recording, one such as interference in the duration of time waves, possibly. Nature expresses herself and is involved in the lives and anxieties of man. The man-made object, even cement, can manifest nature's will when it is in harmony and agreement with its surroundings. Thus in certain places, the communion is so perfect and so harmonious that everything blossoms, heals, succeeds. Then the inert matter vibrates and unites, through a conductor (such as galena or a medium), with the person whose nature is fundamentally identical to its own. Their destinies, which are practically parallel and complementary, then join together and a dialogue takes place.

The opposite is equally true. When telluric currents do not circulate, a "predestination of place" occurs; thus it is that vice congregates around Subure, Montmartre, or in Las Vegas. Money in Paris collects around the Bourse, commerce in Le Sentier, and speculation occurs on the Left Bank.

Occultists believe that telluric currents are particularly favorable to this type of phenomenon, but that if these currents are absent when the materialization is to occur, other forces are capable of replacing them.

The creation of a world

One can imagine a thought being enclosed in some kind of "organic ferrites"; as these decompose and are transformed, the thought is released and can create supernatural phenomena.* Or else the thought, imprisoned in a closed circle, absorbs immense creative energy (to the point of becoming a kind of god) which sets in motion the appearance of *intelligent material elements* endowed with a chromosomic memory linking them to a previous life. *It is like actually creating a world, and perhaps this is the way the universe came into existence.* Creative energy, or thought liberated in this manner, is capable of reproducing the image of a past world.

There occurs an analogous process of physiological-pathological action, or hysteria, with the natural creation of stigmata, in very neurotic or credulous people. Thérèse Neuman, for example, was meditating on the stigmata of Christ when the intelligence embodied in her cellular system *(i.e.,* outside her conscious mind) reproduced the image in the appropriate places. In the same way, if a hysterical woman is

*Scientists, and in particular Doctor Jean Charon, admit that thought waves or intelligence can curve to form a circle that imprisons itself near an energy field. When by chance or necessity, the circle is opened, the intelligence or thought is released. An explanation of this thesis can be read in Chapter 14.

infatuated by a film star, and she dreams of or hopes for some form of identification with him, she can actually induce a picture of her idol to appear on her body. Could she make this image appear somewhere else? On a slab of cement, for example? It may not be impossible, but biophysicists have scarcely begun to study the question. It is a matter of transference then, and one might also say of mutation.

One could apply the mystery of Belmez de la Moraleda to a phenomenon like the transmutation of thought, and the projection of desire.

Chapter Nine

Agpaoa: Telekinetic Surgeon

Since 1971, a color film has been circulating around private projection rooms, intriguing scientists and specialists in the supernatural. If the pictures that make up the film are authentic, this is the most extraordinary documentary ever to have been screened. Should it be a fraud, it is an expensive one, with no obvious profit motive.

It provides evidence of a science associated with the Mysterious Unknown which far surpasses the Count of Saint-Germain's magic.

His hands plunge into flesh as though it were water

Tony Agpaoa is a Philippine from Baguio, a small town north of Manila, who has recently completed a tour of Europe and Mexico promoting mystical propaganda.

He is an extraordinary kind of envoy, representing a sect of deeply pious faith healers. They believe that god is omnipresent and diffuses himself through fields of energy in such a way that there is no longer such a thing as the impossible. By drawing on this divine potential they receive supernatural powers which enable them to cure most illnesses.

"In our sect," says Agpaoa, "we need an unshakable faith, and know that with the aid of spiritual strength anything is possible."

With the help of these principles—irrational and completely contrary to the laws of our universe as they are—the Philippino practices incredible surgical feats, which were filmed in Manila by the cinema enthusiast, Juan Blanche, in front of Dr. Naegeli, from Zurich, and several other witnesses.

Even these witnessses, who saw the operations take place, now doubt the evidence of their own eyes and the authenticity of the pictures recorded, because they are so fantastic as to be suggestive of a miracle!

Briefly, the film shows a healer plunging his bare hands into the bodies of invalids, without making an incision in the flesh, and removing tumors or diseased organs. When he withdraws his hands, the flesh closes up again as mysteriously as it opened, and no trace of a scar is left, yet the invalid is cured! Strange to relate, the vehicle of this miraculous power does not even realize what he has done. "There are mysterious forces who know," he says, "and it is they who control my fingers!"

One gathers that even with the film as proof, the witnesses wonder if they were the victims of an optical illusion.

In a simple movement wounds open and close again of their own accord

This is how reports describe a tumor operation filmed in 1971.*

*In actual fact, there were several operations: Two were abdominal, one was on the head, and another on the pancreas of a diabetic patient.

In a kind of open-air amphitheater, a staircase at each point of the compass descends towards a small, very simple hut with a table, thus making four large entrances, and providing an almost perfect view, if one disregards the four supports.

The healer comes down by the northern staircase, the invalid by the southern one, while the relations, surgical assistants, photographers, and the witnesses use the other staircases.

The photographers withdraw in order to film the procedure in comfort, using spotlights to illuminate the scene. Thus, nothing escapes their cameras, and the witnesses have every opportunity to direct the operation.

The healer is usually dressed in a loose white shirt with short sleeves and buttons down the front. He wears no mask, and sometimes wears rings on his otherwise bare hands. He meditates to collect his thoughts, alternately touching his head and his solar plexus before carrying out the operation.*

The patient lying on the table in the hut is perfectly conscious. He pulls his clothes up to his chest while the assistants arrange a white linen cloth and towels around the operating area. The healer does not appear to look for the injured part, but his hands begin to knead the flesh like a masseur or a housewife making pastry. Suddenly, he digs his fingers into the stomach with his eyes closed in concentration.

He pulls out a bloody mass, which can be clearly seen in

*Doctor Edward Mathey, from Berne, thinks (if the operations are genuine) that the phenomenon could be explained as a kind of entelechic (from *enelekheia* = completion or perfection) which makes use of the "vital forces" of the Aristotelian philosophers or vitalists.

his stained fingertips, and gives it to one of the helpers. A second assistant gives him a wad of cotton wool with which he carefully cleans his hands. Everyone believes they can see the opening made in the flesh, which is bleeding slightly, and which is cleaned with a second cotton-wool pad.

Then, when the healer has finished, he begins to tremble all over, particularly his hands, which he gradually withdraws from the open wound, which is emitting a little, very fluid, pink blood followed by a transparent liquid. He pulls his fingers out a little farther, passes the flat of his hand over the incision, and then rises to his feet. No further trace of the operation can be seen.

Three operations with the bare hand

This is the account given by Antonio Pitasi, the editor of a Genoese newspaper, of various surgical operations which were performed in Italy.

"We have seen Agpaoa extract from a patient's stomach a pad of infected cotton wool which had been forgotten during a previous operation by a 'scientific' surgeon. He did this without leaving any scar.

"One of the participants in our inquiry was cured of two hemorrhoidal swellings by the healer. Each was about five centimeters long and removed by simple penetration of the anus.

"Then, *by the same process of directly penetrating the stomach with his bare hand,* the healer extracted a growth which had been causing an intestinal blockage.

"He thus carried out three successive operations, without washing his hands, and yet caused no infection."

Kirlian emanations

On March 27, 1971, Dr. Hans Naegeli-Osjord, an eminent psychiatrist from Zurich, presented his film on faith healers at the Third International Congress of Parapsychology at Campione in Italy, rendering the audience speechless with amazement. Never before had a specialist in the unknown and the supernatural been involved in a manifestation of the most farfetched fantasies of Edgar Poe and Bosch.

"The pictures which you have seen bear no trace of duplicity," said Dr. Naegeli. "I can guarantee their authenticity." The film was shown several times in Lausanne and Zurich. Dr. Naegeli-Osjord is President of the *Schweitzer Parapsychologische Gesellschaft*, a doctor of international repute, and his evidence is above suspicion. We must accept it unquestioningly, even though we are conditioned to reject any phenomenon which is unacceptable to pure logic. We are naturally reluctant to believe in miracles, but will in fact do so when the sacrosanct scientific institutions fail to give us an explanation. We do, however, calmly accept anything to do with science proper, such as protons, electrons, and mesons, without even seeing them.

This is how Dr. Naegeli describes and interprets the surgical operations.

> In order to make an aperture in the flesh, the faith healer uses his finger (or someone else's finger if he transfers to that other person a kind of *mana*.* I have taken part many times in these operations, which were conducted in the

**Mana* is a mysterious power attributed to the statues on Easter Island. It resembles the *kundalini* of the Hindus and the "fluid" possessed by some miracle workers.

presence of two other people. There was no question of trickery.

The phenomenon is identical to that of psychic injections, where the symbolic image of a hypodermic syringe punctures the skin, either with or without producing any blood. Agpaoa and thirty other healers from the Philippines actually plunge their hands into the bodies of sick people.

I believe in the authenticity of a phenomenon which cannot yet be fully explained by natural science. Kirlian emanations probably play a part, but do not explain everything.

These Kirlian emanations may be high-frequency waves radiated by the human psyche. They are not accepted in scientific circles in the West, but the Russians take some interest in them as regards attempts to remove organs in the fashion of the Philippine healers.

Psychic surgery

Healers practicing psychic surgery have been famous in the Philippines for about thirty years, and in 1960 their methods were examined by Dr. Hiroshi Motoyama, from Tokyo, by the Englishman Sherman, by Russian doctors, and by Dr. Naegeli.

All experts on the matter state categorically that the miracle is genuine. The only black spot in the affair is the behavior of Agpaoa, who exploited his power for commercial gain. According to information from Mexico, the healer would not accept any honors or distinctions, but did take gifts of between $50 and $500 per operation. Furthermore, he is said to have organized an extensive charter service for his clients, bound for Manila.

There is a psychic healer in Brazil, called Ze Arigo, who

operates in an almost identical way, but he does so in a state of trance and uses a very sharp knife as a scalpel.

Ze Arigo claims to be telepathically directed by the spirit of a German, Dr. Fritz, who died in Rio de Janeiro in 1944. Fritz is a surname which, to say the least, seems strange, banal, and even comic! The operations performed by the Brazilian were supervised by the American professor A. Puharich, but to tell the truth, little is know about them.

For his own part, Dr. Naegeli believes in the miracle of the Philippine healers, and insists that the operations are performed on fully conscious invalids, without aseptic treatment, without anesthetic, and without the help of a scalpel. The hand alone carries out the removal of diseased organs and the therapeutic process of instant healing. He says that the hand plunges straight into the body as though it were a liquid, and extracts the diseased tissues and tumors; when the hand is pulled out, the flesh closes up again, leaving neither scar nor hemorrhage.

A legacy from extraterrestrial beings?

This process, although completely outside the norms of academic learning, may possibly be a form of extraterrestrial science bequeathed to us thousands of years ago by Initiators from outer space.

In fact, the Philippine healers work from secrets handed down by tradition to the Igorots, sorcerers of the isles of the North, who were allegedly visited 15,000 moons ago by the Kabunian gods who descended from the heaven in flying saucers. From that moment onward, they were able to walk unscathed through fire, and practice their miraculous surgery simply using the biomagnetic forces of their hands. According to Dr. Naegeli, they rarely go into a trance, but, as when walking on fire, prepare themselves by chanting songs all night and by praying all day. Their operations never take longer than two or three minutes.

"Sometimes," says the Swiss practitioner, "they remove animal hairs, string, human hair, and other objects from the bewitched body! I myself have seen a healer extract three cloves of garlic from the rectum of a patient. I kept one as a souvenir.

"It is possible that a few of these operations are tricks, but in my opinion this is extremely rare, and has never happened in the chapel of spiritual invocations where the operations are definitely all legal and above board. Besides, it is always possible to verify and to examine as the healers are not opposed to this kind of supervision, in fact quite the contrary."

A corner of the veil is raised

Dr. Naegeli may have raised one corner of the veil by presenting the details in a rather curious light, which must reflect the truth, if only in the description of the healing.

To sum up, these may be purely psychic operations, employing paranormal science and certain dimensions (if not a universe) which doctors do not understand, but which is occasionally glimpsed by mathematicians and biologists.

"There are several kinds of operation," specifies Dr. Naegeli. "Some healers make no incision in the flesh, neither by Kirlian manifestations nor with a scalpel. Everything happens as though it were on another plane."

These psychic surgeons transform the diseased part, a tumor for example, into waves or highly penetrative subatomic particles of the neutron type, which pass through flesh and skin to reappear in our universe in the form of a liquid discharge. This discharge then accumulates in a cavity which generally appears spontaneously on the abdominal wall.

Witnesses have only two or three times seen the healers remove tissues corresponding to Lipoma or to the histology of orthodox medicine.

Taken as a whole, these phenomena, which are only admissible in metaphysics, consist of disembodiment, transmutation, telekinesis, and rematerialization. The same process occurs in metaphysical experiences which involve mediums, and the healer is indeed a medium.

In order to explain this miracle, Dr. Naegeli suggests that a bio-electric current is emitted by the practitioner, particularly from his fingers. This current, which has been only briefly studied in scientific circles, would be the complementary element necessary to produce a supernatural effect. Among the Indians, this mysterious power is called *kundalini*, and is developed in the *chacras*, or psychic centers in the spinal marrow.

Dr. Naegeli says: "In the interests of contemporary science itself, it would be desirable for this psychic surgery, practiced by people with undeveloped intellects, to be studied and corroborated by biologists, as it would undoubtedly extend the still narrow limits of our rational knowledge."

Illusionism and magic

Among the Amazon tribes, and doubtless those of Africa and Polynesia, sorcerers can apparently root out disease in the same way.

They ostentatiously throw away a piece of bloody flesh which they have supposedly extracted from the body of the patient and, because witnesses of these magic performances are generally credulous and primitive people, they are prepared to swear that the operation works. Other, more skeptical witnesses, have divulged that it was merely achieved by sleight of hand.

Professor Granoni, an Italian neurologist, has analyzed the "blood" which flows after the healers have made the psychic incision and found that it did not have the properties of blood!

In Japan, by contrast, some analyses have been positive; others have shown it to be pig's blood!

Some healers were at one time imitating Agpaoa in France, and are possibly still practicing their craft, which one must accept as genuine. Mrs. R, from L'Isle-Jourdaine, has told me that when her husband was young, he once had a large inflammation rather like a boil on his neck near the jugular vein. He went to see a healer, who has since died, in the village of Ages. He said he could remove the pain very quickly, and pulled from his pocket a knife which had obviously been sharpened with care. The young man was rather alarmed at the idea of an incision being made, but the man said to him: "Do not be afraid, I am neither going to cut nor prick you. You can even, if you wish, put your hand over the inflammation." About ten centimeters away from the flesh, the healer pretended to make an incision, or possibly made a magic gesture. Then he said: "You can go away again. When you reach home the infected area will drain and you will be cured."

On reaching home, scarcely an hour later, Mr. R felt something hot running down his neck. He put his hand up to it and found it covered in blood. The abscess, or to be more precise, the inflammation, suppurated, the swelling disappeared, and in a short time the neck regained its normal appearance.

The rationalists reply

This is a frank exposure of the facts and interpretations advanced by people who have attended the surgical operations performed by Philippine healers.

The film recordings of Julian Blanche and Mr. Fuchs have inspired contrary reactions.

The rationalists denounce them as trickery and do not accept that the unbending laws of science could ever be contradicted. They may, of course, be right. Experience, and our scientific knowledge, tell us that it is impossible for a hand to enter a body as it if were a liquid or soft paste. One might as well suggest that one can walk through walls, or believe in the permeability of all solid matter, which is unacceptable to a physicist. Can the healers put their arms through walls, or through the armored plating of a tank? If they can, let them prove it; of course they don't comply! In a film by Fuchs, however, Tony Agpaoa has been seen to cut an adhesive band, seven centimeters wide and four layers thick, either with the tip of his finger or the end of his tongue, without actually touching it. If this story is true, how does one reconcile the theories put forward, such as the Kirlian emanations and electric currents, or the fact that the phenomenon appears to be quite different at the dematerialization and rematerialization stages? Such is the reasoning of those who contest the evidence of the miracle!

Even if one is prepared to believe, however, it is difficult to visualize a Mysterious Unknown, or a power possessed by the "psychic surgeons," but capable of being transferred, as it was to Dr. Naegeli. One might ask who donates this power, God or the ancient Kabunians? And why doesn't this god give similar power to the Pope, Jesus, or to other religious personages?

The problem is a real Chinese puzzle, with no satisfactory explanation. The rationalists deny the facts, *even if they have witnessed them*, while the believers insist on the accuracy of what they have seen with their own eyes and perhaps taken part in, but no one is consistent in his opinion.

It is all a sham

Let me repeat that I do not doubt the sincerity of the scholarly Dr. Naegeli, but there are, nevertheless, certain details which are somewhat suspicious.

There is no consistency among descriptions; sometimes the flesh is cut, sometimes the operation is a mere pretense carried out by supernatural intervention. The removal of an organ, such as the resection of an intestine, never occurs.* It is quite illogical to imagine that diseased cells or tissues could ever condense into infected matter inside a bag which has appeared out of the blue. Everything ought to come out and remain in an incorporeal state so that it can disappear all the better!

The removal of animal hair, string, human hair, and other objects from the body of a patient ought to have made the Zurich doctor smell a rat; and the extraction of three cloves of garlic, inexplicably stuck in the rectum, undoubtedly smacks of legerdemain and the most deliberate, clumsy quackery. All the same, these "psychic surgeries" in Manila are disturbing.

Witnesses of these conjuring tricks must have been deceived, and this fact casts an ineradicable slur on the phenomenon as a whole.

It is true that Dr. Naegeli does sometimes abandon his noncommittal position as, for example, when he says that the occasional operation is faked, and when he demands the supervision of biologists.

Lastly, there is Agpaoa's peculiar behavior. It is strange that a man claiming to be deeply spiritual; the prophet and undoubtedly the champion of his sect, does not hesitate to compromise

*There may have been a removal in some cases. Certain German newspapers have alleged that Agpaoa operated on false plastic flesh arranged over the body of patients, sometimes with their consent, sometimes without their knowledge.

himself by involvement in the most coarsely commercial and worldly situations.

Moreover, if one were to check the stories from Mexico, a number of the healer's clients confirm that he is a charlatan who only pretends to operate, and in fact effects the transfer by skillful manipulation of animal entrails.

This information was collected by the Geneva *Tribune*, September 18, 1972. On the other hand four people who underwent operations in Manila have testified to their effectiveness, however they may have been carried out.

Miss Sangemann, a German medical assistant, takes parties of invalids to the Philippines and has been present at more than 3,000 operations, 72 percent of which have been successful.

Certainly, a clever illusionist, such as the famous Kassagi in France, could easily substitute himself for Agpaoa, but not effect the cures, if they exist.

It is equally certain that we do not understand the Mysterious Unknown, which is very different from science conditioned by official disciplines; we treat it with absurd hostility.

We might hope that Agpaoa will emerge victorious, that a miracle will at last be confirmed, and that the time will come when man might return to what was, perhaps, his original path, and discover how to pass through walls like a neutron and see the mysteries of hidden universes.

The mummy in the sealed crypt

While considering this question of the penetrability of matter, it is interesting to take into account another phenomenon peripheral to it: the little American mummy of Pedro Mountain.

The most subtle detective-story plot is based on the mystery of the locked room; perhaps a room is bolted from the inside, yet the victim is within its walls, stabbed through the heart and killed with a single blow! Where has the assassin gone? How could he have committed the crime? Well, the Mysterious Unknown sometimes produces enigmas of this kind.

In October, 1938, some workmen digging in the quarry of Pedro Mountain in Wyoming stumbled on a mine. It was in a monolithic granite cliff which seemed to have neither fault nor fissure, and they had to use a pickax to bore a hole for the dynamite charge. Some of the blocks fell onto the road, revealing a cavern, five meters long, in a vertical wall. Two men went in and, to their intense astonishment, found sitting on the ground a little mummy twenty-two centimeters high, with a bronzed skin, a low forehead, and a flattened nose.

The curator of the Boston Museum, to whom it was taken for an expert opinion, declared that it was of the same type found in Egypt, except that it was not bound with thongs. Professor Henry Fairfield named this mummy *Hesperopithicus*, (a species of monkey from the Hesperides) and classified it as a hominid from the Pliocene period of the tertiary epoch, which lasted from ten to one million years B.C. His theory was not accepted by classical prehistorians, and the little creature was left neglected in the window of a museum in America.

One can certainly query the tremendous age attributed to the mummy, but not necessarily explain how it came to be in a cavern situated in the middle of a solid granite mountain block or how it could have been in a cavity which was hermetically sealed. Thus one comes back to the miracle of Agpaoa and the Mysterious Unknown which pervades our ordered universe: the incredible idea that some people are able to penetrate solid matter and to walk through walls.

Chapter Ten

The Hidden Mysteries of Fire

If one doubts that Agpaoa could really thrust his hand into a patient's body, what is one to make of those extraordinary beings who are able to lie on live coals without getting burned? There is reliable evidence of this further manifestation of the impossible, but before going on to examine the subject, let us consider a certain ancient tradition and some mysterious cases of combustion which are relevant to this subject.

Strange conflagrations

Legend has it that 2,550 years ago King Nebuchadnezzer II set up a great golden idol before which the Babylonians were commanded to fall down and worship. When the three young Jews, Shadrach, Meshach, and Abednego, who were in captivity in Babylon, refused to obey this order, they were thrown into a fire. It was of such intense heat that it consumed the idolatrous soldiers who were in charge of stoking it, but when the flames died down the three Jews stepped from the fire unscathed, singing hymns of thanksgiving to Jehovah. The Lord had preserved them.

Nebuchadnezzar was so struck by the miracle that he showered gifts upon the three who had been spared and proclaimed the power of the one *true* God.

Unfortunately this miracle was not repeated for those who were thrown into the gas ovens at Auschwitz, or for the victims of napalm bombs in the Sinai desert. Nor were the lives spared on October 8 to 9, 1871, when fires broke out all over Chicago as if they had been started by malefactors or by destructive angels. A veritable "tempest of fire" followed, giving off a terrifyingly supernatural red and green glow.

"No one could ever discover the cause or give even the shadow of an explanation," write J. W. Sheahan and G. P. Upson. "Something in the air seemed to feed this fire, which was quite unlike any other."*

On July 2, 1951, seventy-eight-year-old Mrs. Reeser of St. Petersburg, Florida, was burned to death in her apartment, in extremely bizarre circumstances. Near the open window the remains of her large armchair were found with the springs still hot. An electric plug, and some candles on the mantlepiece, had melted. The glass in a mirror had shattered and the uppermost parts of the walls were covered in soot and showed traces of exposure to intense heat. All that remained of Mrs. Reeser were eleven or twelve pounds of ashes, her left foot, a few vertebrae, and her shriveled skull.

There was another strange phenomenon. Apart from a small burned patch, the carpet on which these still smoking remains were lying was intact. Professor Wilton Forgman, the forensic

**History of the Great Conflagration*, J. W. Sheahan and G. P. Upson. 17,500 houses were burned in the Chicago fire.

expert, stated that never in his life had he come across so incomprehensible a case. A normal fire would have needed to reach a temperature of 1,500° C to produce such results. It is most odd that the carpet and the things which were less than a meter above floor level, were not burnt.

Mysterious fires

According to the French Press Agency, numerous cases of spontaneous combustion of the human body have been observed and documented.

In 1930, Peter Vesey, an American researching this phenomenon, was found completely burned in his study. Nothing else in the room had been touched by fire.

A similar thing happened on board the English vessel *Ulrich* when she was off the coast of Ireland. The body of the pilot was discovered to be completely burned, but his shoes were untouched and the navigational instruments, which were within reach, showed no trace of a fire.

On the same day, by coincidence or otherwise, a driver was burned to death in his truck, which had overturned in a ditch, although in the cab where his body was found there was no sign of fire.

Numerous cases of similar fires could be quoted, all equally mysterious, and producing unaccountable effects, but none would throw the faintest light on the mystery.

In *Bleak House*, published in 1852, Dickens affirmed that he had studied thirty cases of combustion of this kind.

For a human body to be incinerated it needs to be left for several hours in a heat of at least 1,000° C. In India, Nepal, and Ceylon they use enormous pyres, often soaked in fuel, to incinerate dead bodies, and even then most of the bones remain.

God's judgment or the devil's?

In bygone days, the salamander was believed to be impervious to fire, and indeed gave its name to a type of asbestos, a silicate of calcium and magnesium which really does have this property.

As well as fire-walking, which is certainly a custom among some of the peoples of Bulgaria, the Philippines, the South Sea Islands, and Africa, it seems that even in the West there are people who can stay for a very long time in the midst of flames without apparently coming to any harm. It is just as incredible as the case of the witch doctor Agapoa, and just as difficult to doubt the validity of official documentation of the subject.

As far back as the Middle Ages the practice of *Judicium Dei*, or trial by ordeal, was used to reveal the divine or accursed powers of those who were put to the test. The most usual form of ordeal was to make the accused hold an iron bar weighing about three pounds, which had been blessed and then heated, according to the gravity of the fault and the social status of the accused, sometimes until it was redhot. It was ritually placed in the church, where the accused fasted for three days, heard mass, and received communion. Having solemnly sworn that he was innocent, he was made to carry the redhot bar for as long as it took him to walk a certain distance. If after three days he bore no signs of being burned, he was declared innocent.

Sometimes the test involved walking through fire. There is the case of Peter Igneus, or Peter of the Fire, who was a member of a religious order in Vallumbrosa in Italy. In 1603, wearing his priestly robes, he walked unscathed over redhot coals between two lighted pyres and then went back again to find the maniple (a strip of cloth which a priest wears over his left arm) which he had dropped.

Strabo, in Book Twelve, tells how the priestesses of Diana walked over burning coals to prove their purity, and St. Epiphanus related how priests in Egypt would rub their faces with certain drugs and then plunge them into caldrons of boiling water without seeming to feel the least pain.

There is a story of an 18th century "charlatan," one Gaspard Touravant, who traveled round the country washing his hands in molten lead as if it had been water. Does it seem feasible that a "charlatan" washed his hands in molten lead at 327° C? Judge for yourself!

The English medium, Home, made a coal glow by blowing on it and then carried it on a handkerchief which showed no signs of burning. He performed the feat in the presence of a Miss Douglas' guests. It might have been a mere conjuring trick but that still needs to be proved.

Deacon Paris

We no longer live in an atmosphere of faith. No believer, not even the Pope, would have the exemplary courage to walk on hot coals. What happens at Lourdes is ridiculous and derisory, the only miracle being that of arriving there without a road or train accident. As recently as the 18th century, though, there were still men and women of unshakable faith, called the Jansenists.

It goes without saying that they were harried by the Church. Clement IX fulminated against them and issued the bull *Unigenitus* which aimed to establish the naked truth—Roman, apostolic, and obligatory. This gave rise to heated disputes and religious persecution and, as always happens in that kind of situation, miracles soon began to take place. M. H. Martin wrote, "When one expects wonders they always occur."

They came about through the intercession of Deacon Paris, a

devout, visionary ascetic who was a Jansenist and therefore vehemently opposed to the Papal bull. The deacon was charity incarnate: He gave everything he had to the poor and, whether it was his turn to do so or not, he gave his morsel of daily bread to those who were hungrier than he. Admittedly he was self-motivated because he wanted to reach paradise. Nevertheless, judge him for yourself!

When Paris died in his garret in the Faubourg Saint-Marceau on May 1, 1727, while the persecution was at its height, the fanaticism of the Jansenists turned from fevor to delirium, then to folly, and finally to a depraved kind of madness. This was the period of the famous Convulsionaries. The sick would drag themselves to the deacon's grave, then stretch out and eat the ''holy'' soil to which they ascribed extraordinary divine healing powers.

Miracles of hysteria

So-called miraculous cures took place which attracted the faithful to come along in crowds along with the blind, lepers, and paralytics. Electric tremors ran through these crowds, which were quickened with the same fevor. These were *vrils*, which will be familiar to those interested in the occult.

Some of the women would stand up with transfigured faces, others would burst into tears or start shrieking. Then, among the crowds, keyed up to an extraordinary pitch, there would be outbursts of nervous hysteria, convulsive spasms and people going into ecstatic trances. Finally, when fever pitch was reached, the infirm, the paralytic, and the crippled would rise up and walk; the blind would see and the dumb would speak! It was even said that illnesses which were not of nervous origin, such as cankers and sores, disappeared in an instant.

These facts and miracles are to be found in the writings of

Cardinal de Noailles, Archbishop of Paris, "a man of charity, faith, and compassion."

In the end these exhibitions by the Convulsionaries became cruel and indecent. H. Martin claimed that the women played the principal role in these scenes which combined hysteria and the phenomenon of analgesia which normally goes with it.

Pop concerts of the discos of Saint-Germain-des-Prés, produce the same sort of hysteria and analgesia, even to the point of total insensitivity. In the cemetery of Saint-Medard the women barked, mewed, or leaped about, allowing their bodies to be trampled on and beaten violently. They underwent ordeals by fire, the spit, and all sorts of other forms of torture, claiming to receive divine consolation by so doing.

Naked women crucified

People armed with daggers or iron skewers pierced their limbs, without of course taking any antiseptic measures, and there were no fatalities or infections as a result. Others rolled naked on hot coals and came away foaming at the mouth, their eyes starting out of their sockets, delirious, but without any burns.

"Four or five young men were seen placing all their weight on a girl who was lying stretched out on the ground, and afterward they beat her with sticks but she felt no pain."

Several beautiful women, who became still more beautiful when they were transfigured, wanted at all costs to be crucified naked, in the manner of "Our Lord." They allowed nails to be driven into their open palms, and their feet to be nailed, one over the other, to the cross. They showed no sign of pain, but their Messiah, perhaps of lesser faith than they, endured a terrible martyrdom.

Women in a state of exaltation asked to be crucified several times in succession, "To atone by their penitence for the depraved conduct of Louis XV and his court of debauched nobles who were without scruple or conscience, but who were nevertheless great believers in the bull *Unigenitus*."

Voltaire gave a terse judgment on these scenes, which defied his understanding. "Do you know," he wrote, "what a Convulsionary is? It is one of these demonaics from the dregs of society, who, in order to prove the error of a certain Papal bull, go from garret to garret performing miracles, roasting little girls without hurting them, beating them with whips and sticks for the love of God, and crying out against the Pope."

It is curious to note that every year at the traditional time and on thousands of other occasions, men amuse or condemn themselves by being crucified as Christ is supposed to have been. They do not seem to suffer from this rather useless and stupid ordeal.

How God shall not perform miracles

Were these Convulsionaries hysterial or possessed; were they being martyred or inspired? The hysterics in their convulsions needed remedies, "medicines" or "assistance" as they were called, and in these particular circumstances, they were given two kinds, major and minor.

Major relief consisted of being beaten with sticks, stones, hammers, fire-irons, and swords, on and in different parts of the body.

Minor relief was less effective and comparable, one might say, to homeopathy nowadays (everything is relative!). It was limited to people being beaten with canes, kicked, punched, trampled on, slapped, and battered.

In search of solace, one woman condemned herself to 100 strokes on the head, the stomach, or the buttocks. "Others had their covered breasts twisted with pincers until the metal was almost on the point of bending."

In this nightmare of madness and hysteria it seems that some true miracles did take place, and these were discussed in Parliament. In turn the theologians and doctors of the Sorbonne examined the nature, causes, and results of the phenomenon. They did not want to ascribe them to God, so they asserted that the Devil had a certain power over nature, and in some measure the power to work wonders. In the end the Jesuits banned these nightmarish scenes in the cemetery of Saint-Médard, but it was the Jansenist wits who had the last word with the well-known epigram.

> By royal decree God shall not
> Perform any miracle in this spot.

How Marie Sonnet slept on fire

If the astonishing Agpaoa case gave rise to some legitimate doubt, the incident involving Marie Sonnet, "the Salamander," was even more extraordinary. One cannot help wondering whether, in this instance, the miracle was genuine. The story was told by Councillor Carré de Montergon, who lived at the time of the Convulsionaries, and more recently by Oliver Leroy.

In about 1730 Marie Sonnet, a girl of humble origin who had been won over to the Jansenist heresy, far outstripped in prowess the fantastic happenings at the Saint-Médard cemetery. Dressed only in a white sheet, she lay down on a bed of fire and slept unscathed "for the time it takes to roast a piece of mutton or veal." The whole of Paris was able to witness this miracle, and an account was duly drawn up by those whose testimony may be believed. The following is the text of the report, dated May 12 1731.

> We the undersigned, Francois Desvernays, priest, doctor of theology at the Sorbonne; Pierre Jourdan, licentiate of the Sorbonne, Canon of Bayeux; Lord Edward of Rumond Perth; Louis-Basile Carré de Montgeron, Councillor at Parliament; Armand Arouet, Treasurer of the Exchequer; Alexandre-Robert Boidin, esquire; Monsieur de Boibessin; Pierre Pigeon, burgher of Paris; Denis Villat, burgher of Paris; J. B. Cornet, burgher of Paris; Louis-Antoine Archambault and Amable Francois-Pierre Archambault, his brother, esquires, hereby certify that we have this day, between the hours of eight and ten in the evening, seen the girl named Marie Sonnet, being convulsed, her head on one stool, her feet on another, the said stools being placed entirely on either side of a large fireplace, and under the mantel of the same, in such a way that her body was in the air above the fire which was of an extreme heat. She stayed in this position for thirty-six minutes, on four different occasions, without the sheet in which she was wrapped, she being without clothing, being burnt, although the flames sometimes rose above it, which seemed to us altogether unnatural. In witness whereof we have signed this day 12th May 1731.
>
> Signed: (Here follows the list of names as aforesaid).
>
> Futhermore, we certify that while we were signing the present certificate, the aforementioned Sonnet placed herself again on the fire in the manner described above and stayed there for nine minutes, seeming to sleep above the fire, which was extremely hot, fifteen logs and a bundle of faggots having been burnt during the said two hours and a quarter."

Where the physical and psychic meet

Olivier Leroy, who has made a thorough study of this phenomenon, draws a parallel between Bernadette Soubirou and Marie Sonnet.

When Bernadette was in a state of ecstasy, she could put her hand in the flame of a candle for a quarter of an hour, as timed by Doctor Dozous, and her fingers would show no sign of burns. In her normal state, Bernadette said that the flame burned her if the candle was held near for only two seconds.

"It is certain," says Olivier Leroy, "that in the relationship between man and fire there is something quite extraordinary. There is no reason why the world of physical laws should not have its duck-billed platypus and flying fish. So why not admit, as experience suggests, that these strange phenomena are normal where the physical and the psychichal meet?"

According to M. E. Mangoli, director of *Metapsichica*, "With the methods of three-dimensional science it is not possible to verify the veracity of phenomena which occur in a four-dimensional world." That is why he thinks that the penetrability of opaque matter by Agpaoa and the incombustibility of Marie Sonnet may be attributed to ultraphysics. The recent discovery of fire without heat suggests the existence of this particular science.

One should nevertheless make a distinction between Agpaoa, a real healer-conjurer who misled his audience insofar as the details of the surgical operations were concerned, but who nevertheless healed the patients, and Marie Sonnet, who quite genuinely seems to have slept on a burning fire. For some obscure reason, either the fire was giving out no heat, or Marie Sonnet's body had temporarily become noncombustible, due, perhaps, to some effect of exaltation or faith which counteracted even the best-established laws of physics.

How natural man is not bound by physical laws

There might be two different types of men: those who are protected by the Lord, or the Devil, and others who are not.

We know that different religious sects have always tried to use miracles to prove that theirs is the true God and that the miracle which they most often resort to is the incombustibility of the human body, as exemplified in the divine judgment of the ordeal by fire. These days, however, the mysteries of fire and invulnerability are associated only with "savages," or pagans.

Certainly, in Bulgaria and Greece there are a few "*anasterarias*" or fire-walkers who ascribe their powers to Saint Helena or Saint Constantine, but it is well known that these fanatics are not at all Christian. On the contrary, they are really celebrating the ancient cult of Dionysus, which is 3,000 years old and thus predates Jesus by a long way.

Twentieth-century biologists, mathematicians, bishops, Hindu religious leaders, or great Islamic theologians may all fully understand the laws of physics, because in a sense they invented them, but they are still incapable of walking on burning coals or sleeping on a fire or walking through a wall. On the other hand, ignorant men and people who do not *believe* in the religion of science, can, to some extent, make child's play of the theorems and premises of chemistry and physics.

"Natural" man can have concepts and powers which seem supernormal because his thoughts have not been reduced to a systematized plan, or affected by the laws, framework, and tenets of our scientific inventions and conventions. Consequently his nature, physiology, and psychology are different from ours. "Natural" man can move about in his universe in the same way as birds, foxes, and bees can move about in theirs, obeying their own physical laws and using faculties, such as their mysterious senses of direction and divination, which to us often seem miraculous. In other words, miracles, when they are genuine, emanate from an unknown, mysterious universe which is parallel to ours.

Chapter Eleven

The Sibyline Books and Joan of Arc

Nature speaks a Sibyline tongue which men interpret in their own ways, which are often incorrect.

In 1971 some gardeners in the Lot-et-Garonne region of France noticed their beans were growing upside down inside their pods. It was thought to signify calamity, but the year went by without any particular mishaps so, fortunately for them, their interpretation was wrong.

The Sibyline Books and the fall of Rome

Should one believe in predictions? In his book *Messages du Sanctum Celeste*, the Grand Master of the French Rosicrucians, Raymond Bernard, gives the opinion that no predictions are ineluctable.

"Every Rosicrucian knows that the law of the triangle is fundamental and is applicable in all spheres, from the most subtle to the most obvious, in the visible and invisible universes of creation," he writes. This law therefore applies just as much to prophecies and predictions as to any other questions which baffle the human mind. In short, a prediction must tally with the conditions which have been established in order for it to be fulfilled, and this is not always the case.

In ancient times, the Sibyls enjoyed great renown, and it is claimed that one Athenais attested to Alexander's divine origins, which one is inclined to doubt. For in fact these prophetesses were just the docile instruments of governments, and often their predictions were not made public until after the event which it was their purpose to foretell. This was even true of Nostradamus.

The Sibyls made their prophecies orally, in sealed envelopes, or on palm leaves. The Sibyline Books, or Oracles, which were prized by the Greeks, Romans, and neoplatonists, consisted of three volumes, only one of which has survived, even that having been tampered with.

Tradition has it that in 615 B.C. the book, by an unknown prophetess, came into the hands of Tarquin I (Tarquin the Proud), fifth King of Rome. The woman presented the king with nine books which, she said, contained the destiny of the Romans, with directions which had to be followed so that the events would take their predicted course. In payment she demanded 300 philippi of gold, which at that time was a considerable sum. The king refused the offer and the Sibyl burned three of the books and then asked the same price for the six books which remained. When Tarquin again declined, the old woman burned three more of the books, but still demanded the same price for the three books which were left. The king was much impressed and gave her the 300 gold philippi, being by now convinced that his purchase was of immense value.

In the 671st year after the foundation of Rome, under the

dictatorship of Sulla, a fire destroyed the Capitol and the precious manuscripts could not be saved.

In the year 76 B.C. the Senate put three Senators to the task of reconstructing the substance of the ancient books of the oracles. These were later rearranged by Augustus before he had some 2,000 of the oracles burned. He preserved only the so-called Sibyline Books, and these, when they had been copied and correctly arranged, were placed under the base of the statue of the Palatine Apollo. It is thought that they were destroyed by General Flavius Stilicho, who was of Vandal origin, "in order to cause the ruin of the Empire by getting rid of its guarantee of eternal life."

Basing their claims on the lost prophecies of the Sibyl of Cumae and of Nostradamus, occultists predict that in the year 2088 Rome will be destroyed by a terrible fire and that nothing will remain of the Eternal City but a pile of smoking rubble.

End of the world; destruction of New York and San Francisco

In a remarkably well documented book, Josane Charpentier enumerates prophecies from all over the world since a very early date. On the subject of the end of the world, the author recalls a text by Berosus, based on annals kept in the temples of Baal:

"These natural disturbances will happen according to the movements of the heavenly bodies, and one can foretell when the fire will take place, and the deluge which will follow it, for the whole earth will burn when the stars all come into conjunction under the sign of Cancer."

Germany's fate was proclaimed by the prophecy of Hroswitha, the 10th century Abbess of the Convent of Gandershein in Saxony. Having described the wars of 1914-18 and 1940-45, Hroswitha said, "There will be no more Holy

Roman Empire, and from its ruined there will rise up the Empire of Christ and of the Antichrist. There will be war between the two parts of Germany, and the enemies will reunite. This will continue until the time of the Red War, foretold in the Book of Wrath, and the time of the Great Empire in the East, which will be the last emperor of the Earth."

The Antichrist had already been foretold in the prophecy of the Tiburtine Sibyl. "A prince of iniquity will then come forth from the tribe of Dan, and he will be called the Antichrist. A child of perdition, full of mad pride and malice, he will perform on earth a host of wonders to support the lies he will preach; through his magic sacrifices he will astonish true believers who will see fire come down from heaven at his command. Then there will be great persecution such as there has never been and such as there will never be again."

Some wanted to regard Jesus as this Antichrist, but He was not of the tribe of Dan and it would be unjust to attribute to Him the wonders and evil intentions imagined by the Sibyl.

More appropriate in these times is the 15th century inscription on a tombstone in the cemetery in Kirby:

> When pictures look alive with movements free,
> When ships, like fishes, swim beneath the sea,
> When men, outstripping birds shall scan the sky,
> Then, half the world deep drenched in blood shall lie.

The famous American clairvoyant, Edgar Cayce, who died in 1945, foretold that New York would be destroyed in 1970, just before the end of Los Angeles and San Francisco. In 1944 he said that New York would disappear during the next generation. This would mean 1944 + 25 = 1969. So Cayce made a mistake. No natural or fortuitous catastrophes actually occurred, although in 1969 and 1971 there were earthquakes of considerable intensity in Los Angeles. (Sixty people died in the 1969 quake).

Seismologists know that the San Andreas fault, the cause of the terrible earthquake which destroyed San Francisco in 1906, is composed of two masses of rock under California, which move in opposite directions (southeast and northwest) at the rate of a few centimeters a year. The seismologist Don Anderson has stated that the crushing of the two magmas in the rock could occur during a Sun-Moon-Earth conjunction.

Oracle stones; the end of Marseilles

Near Rennes-le-Château, in the Aude, there is an irregular mass of rocks. Legend has it that they were thrown down from the skies by a giant who prophesied, "When the rocks fuse, the end of the world will come."

An old man from the area recalled that when he was small the children from the nearby village played hide-and-seek among the stones. Today children of the same size would have difficulty in getting between them.

Are the rocks moving according to the giant's prediction or merely because of landslides? Is the end of the world just round the corner? The people in the village obviously believe the prophecy, as they have put iron bars between the blocks to stop them coming together.

On the Naurouze Pass, northwest of Castelnaudary, at an altitude of 215 meters, an obelisk has been erected on three blocks called Nauroze stones, in memory of an engineer named Riquet. These stones are bare and fissured and there is a local legend which says that when these fissures close up there will be a period of general debauchery, followed by the end of the world.

De Novate, a clairvoyant living at the beginning of this century, wrote in 1905 that Marseilles would be swamped by a tidal wave just before momentous events which would change the face of the Earth.

The sign of the end of the world

During 1971 and 1972 about fifty signs representing an *M*, the last downward stroke being longer than the others and crossed by a bar, were mysteriously drawn on road signs and other surfaces along the roads between Sisteron and Pûget-Théniers. Enquiries made by the police drew a blank, and the sign did not appear to belong to any occult sect or any known ancient alphabets.

It does, however, bear a certain resemblance to the Thai *ru*, the Javanese *go*, the Japanese *na*, and a letter which is found on the Moabite stone of Mesha.

Believers in UFO's were certain that the signs were drawn by extraterrestrial beings, and it is a fact that the *M*, with the last stroke crossed by a bar, figures in the supposed Venusian alphabet which is known as *"varkulets."* There is no room for further speculations along these lines. The sign is painted very evenly in black on a white background, very probably using a stencil.

The riddle would have remained unsolved if we had not come across the same design in a book called *Geheime Wissenschaften* (secret sciences), *Magische Werke* (works of magic) handed down to us by Petrus von Apono.

Formerly the sign was part of a secret language known only to priests who had been admitted to the mysteries, and was only for use in sanctuaries or for divine purposes. Also, by a somewhat disturbing coincidence, the *M* with the barred stroke relates to the planet Venus and signifies the end of the world, or a great terrestrial catastrophe. Its origins probably go back 5,000 years to the appearance of the comet which devastated the surface of the Earth.

One might be tempted to see this sign as a bad omen for Provence, but a characteristic of predictions, thank God, is that they seldom come true.

Black's telepathy

While we are wary as far as visions of the future are concerned, we are intrigued by the mysterious senses of certain animals and by another mysterious phenomenon called telepathy.

M. Valembois, a machinist who worked for a firm in the Pas-de-Calais, left Bethune early in 1971 to take a new job. He left his faithful Flemish sheep-dog, Black, with his cousins. Both man and dog were very attached to each other, but because his master was constantly on the move, Black unfortunately could not go with him.

On June 17, six months after their separation, Mr. Valembois, (who at the time was in Châteaurenard in the Bouches-du-Rhone) heard that a black dog had been seen wandering in the streets of the village. It was Black, who was overjoyed at finding his master. The dog had crossed France and walked more than 1,000 kilometers in order to find his beloved master.

What was even more extraordinary was that by going to Châteaurenard, Black had walked to a place that he had never been to before. His sense of direction, therefore, would have been no help, so the journey must have been accomplished by some mysterious system of remote control or mind-to-mind telepathy, since Valembois certainly thought about his faithful friend very often. In all probability Black was guided across

France by Valembois' thoughts, in the way that control-tower beams guide planes coming in to land.

Thought waves

We shall never know whether Jesus really performed miracles, but we do know that Chairman Mao, the Messiah of China, has made the blind see and the lame walk. Of course one must beware of political propaganda, but it is known that in the space of two years a team of Chinese doctors have used the phenomenon of "Mao's invisible thoughts," along with acupuncture, to cure more than a thousand people who were blind, dumb, deaf, or paralyzed.

According to the *New China News Agency*, the cured people danced on the stage of a Peking theater in 1969 and expressed their heartfelt admiration for the "great Chairman."

Following the Russian example, Americans are beginning to put their trust in telepathy and are exploring the possibility of making contact with astronauts by this means in the event of a failure in electronic communication.

This means that a proven electronic system would be replaced by a system which is as yet unproven. The Russian scientist, Professor Kogan, has put forward the theory that thoughts can be transmitted by using electromagnetic fields on waves of extremely variable length, ranging between 25 and 965 kilometers. Successful experiments have been carried out between England and the University of Los Angeles involving a distance of 8,000 kilometers.

Furthermore, NASA has confirmed that the medium Olof Jonsonn "guessed" which four playing cards the astronaut Edgar Mitchell had taken out of a pack of twenty-five cards while he was in an Apollo spacecraft more than 150,000 kilometers from Earth. Mitchell, who had agreed to take part in this experiment, had concentrated for a considerable length of time on the cards, which he had picked out at random.

An Italian psychologist, Signor Inardi, caused a great commotion by answering all the questions put to him during a TV contest called *Dare Devil*. He won 35 million lire, and viewers accused him of using telepathy to read the thoughts of the chairman, who of course knew the answers. The rules of the contest were changed, and the answers were opened only when the participants had given their replies. From then on, Signor Inardi was no longer infallible!

Joan of Arc's third eye

Was it clairvoyance, premonition, or chance that made Jules Verne send off his moon "rocket" 100 kilometers from Cape Kennedy?

In Canada a clairvoyant by the name of Henry the Great frequently surprises the public by making predictions which often come true. In 1972, for example, he announced that Prime Minister Trudeau would not finish his term of office and would withdraw from the political arena.

Although the Mysterious Unknown has been condemned and denied by sectarian rationalists, it has nevertheless played a leading role in the politics of all nations, particularly in French history.

One might wonder whether Joan of Arc did have a third eye or what magic powers enabled her to recognize the king who was mingling in a group of his favorites.

The story of Sainte Catherine de Fierbois's sword was not a totally convincing experiment, but in the eyes of the chroniclers it belongs to the realm of the inexplicable.

Historical fact borders on legend at the beginning of the tale, which was written by Canon Bas and Abbé Charles Pichon, a former priest of the parish. After the Battle of Poitiers, according to ancient tradition, Charles Martel placed the sword which had routed the Saracens in the sanctuary of Sainte Catherine at Fierbois. Seven centuries after these doughty deeds, France was once again in peril, threatened by the invasion of Henry VI's English troops. France's sovereign, Charles VII, was in a very bad situation when the miraculous Joan of Arc, the Maid of Orleans, appeared, reviving the national spirit and liberating the land.

Everything seemed lost that afternoon of March 5, 1429, when the inhabitants of Fierbois saw a little group of horsemen approaching on the Loches road. It went toward the chapel and the young woman in men's clothes who was leading the party prayed for a long time at the altar dedicated to Sainte Catherine.

One of her companions, Jean de Metz, recounted how Joan of Arc, the daughter of country people from Domremy in the Barrois, had just been made Commander by Charles VII, who had given her "troops to command so that she could fulfill her promises." The armorers in Tours had fitted her with a suit of armor, the embroiderers had made her standard, and her warhorse was a gift from the Duke of Alençon, but the Maid would accept no offer of a sword.

"My sword," she said, "has been prepared for me by my celestial friend, Sainte Catherine, and it is in the chapel at Fierbois."

The magic sword

This was an extraordinary utterance and needed to be proved. There were many votive offerings in the chapel—a statue, flower vases, *prie-dieux* for the faithful, but there was no trace of a sword.

"Yes, there is one," affirmed Joan. "The one which will drive the English out of France."

From the record of the trial, we know that was not the Maid herself who went to Fierbois, as the good priests relate. This is her testimony which was given in Rouen.

> "While I was at Tours, or Chinon, I asked for a sword to be brought from behind the altar in the Church of Sainte Catherine de Fierbois. One was found immediately and it was all rusty."
>
> "How did you know that the sword was there?"
>
> "The sword was in the ground, rusty; there were five crosses on it; my voices told me where it was. I had never seen the man who went to fetch it. I wrote to the priests asking if I might have the sword and they sent it to me. It was buried, not very deeply, in the ground behind the altar. In fact I am not quite sure whether it was in front of the altar or behind it, but I think that, at the time I wrote, it was behind it. As soon as it was found, the priests rubbed it, and the rust came off immediately with no trouble. It was an arms dealer from Tours who went to fetch it. The priests of Fierbois made me a gift of a scabbard, and those of Tours gave me another. One was of vermilion velvet; the other of gold cloth. I had a third one made of very stout leather. When I was captured I did not have this sword with me. I had always worn this sword, from the time that I had it until my departure from Saint-Denis after the attack on Paris."
>
> "What blessing was given to the sword you are talking about?"
>
> "I did not give, or have given, any blessing; indeed I would not have known how to do so. I was very fond of the

sword because it was found in the Church of Sainte Catherine, who is very dear to me."

Joan had said that the magic weapon bore five crosses on the escutcheon, which in her eyes was of the greatest significance and she felt she must have this sword, and this one alone. Canon Bas and Abbé Pichon say that the provenance of the sword was most uncertain. Legends attribute it to Charles Martel, Guillaume de Pressigny (said to have been given it by the dying Saint Louis), to Godefroi de Bouillon, or to King René of Anjou.

Joan did not have it with her when she was taken prisoner. She may have left it at Saint-Denis, or hidden it at Compiègne when she thought that she was lost.

"We possess no relic of Joan," wrote Canon Bas and Abbé Pinchon. "The English burned her body and threw her ashes into the Seine, which became hallowed from Rouen to the sea. Her arms have disappeared and this angelic being has ascended to heaven leaving no traces other than her good deeds."

The mystery of Joan of Arc

In the cause of truth we have to say that the story of the Maid of Orleans is suspect in many points.

There is no doubt that Joan was a heroine who contributed very considerably to the liberation of France, and we believe that she was burned at the stake at Rouen. But despite this statement of faith we try to present the other side of the case, too.

Her voices, as she calls them, deceived her if she was burned at Rouen, and most of her predictions were false, except that she told the King at Chinon that she would be wounded "above the breasts," which did in fact happen during the siege of Orleans.

Joan said this herself during her interrogation, and we have irrefutable evidence on the subject.

She received the wound on May 7, 1429. About a month previously, on April 12, a Flemish ambassador at the court of Charles VII wrote a letter to his government in which the following sentence appears. "The maid will be wounded by an arrow before Orleans, but she will not die." This part of the letter has been preserved in the records of the Exchequer in Brussels.

On the other hand, when Joan said that "before seven years have passed the English will run a greater risk than they did at Orleans and will lose everything they have in France," her prediction was only partially justified. In fact, by 1438, only Paris had been liberated.

These points are very minor, though, compared with the strangest claim that the whole affair of Joan of Arc was nothing but a vast hoax plotted by a powerful political faction. This extremely well documented case is presented by Pierre de Sermoise, who maintains that *Jehanne* was the illegitimate daughter of Queen Isabeau, and Louis, Duke of Orleans.

"Both subject to and protected by the machiavellian skill of Bishop Cauchon, she escaped the stake. After a marriage to Robert des Armoises which was never consummated," she continued her mission.

Opinion among historians is divided, but all recognize that the affair is very hazy.

Was Joan the Queen's daughter?

The *Comptes de l'Hôtel Saint-Pol* show that on June 12, 1407, five years before the presumed date of the Maid's birth, a village girl called Jeanne Darc came to offer chaplets of flowers to Charles VI.

Queen Isabeau had given birth to twins. The boy, Philippe, had died, and the girl, Jehanne, had been placed with a wet nurse in the Darc family in Domremy. Joan would have recognized her brother at Chinon for the simple reason that he was her brother, and she could have received all the information she needed in order to identify him during the two days she spent in the Queen's apartments, before she had an audience with Charles VII.

The Lords of Poulengy and Novelompont would have made of her the brilliant rider that she was, for a peasant girl would not have known how to ride. She was a virgin because physically she was gynandrous (a hermaphrodite).

The armor, which cost 100 Tournois pounds, was given her by the king's mother-in-law and it was a "royal" suit of armor. Her sword had belonged to Du Guesolin, who had left it to Louis of Orleans, Joan's supposed father. It had in fact been placed in the church of Sainte Catherine de Fierbois, so Joan would have recovered *her father's sword.*

Who was burned at the stake?

The *Chronique du Doyen de Saint-Thibaud-de-Metz* affirms that Joan, "in the city of Rouen in Normandy, was burned at the stake, or so it was said, but since then this has been disproved."

The Maid was led to the stake with her head covered and the victim's face was hooded to the last. Her name does not appear on the list of witches burned in Rouen between 1430 and 1432, but there are three other Jeannes on it: Jeanne-la-Turquenne, Jeanne Vannerit and Jeanne-la-Guillorée.

A manuscript in the British Museum says, in these very words, "Finally she, or another woman like her, was burnt publicly at the stake. Many people have been, and still are, of differing opinions over this."

We also know that in 1436, in Orleans, a certain *"dame des Armoises"* claimed that she was the Maid, which was verified by her brother, Pierre du Lis, by her own mother, and by the treasurer, Jean Bouchet, who had previously received her in his house.

The King of France's cause was in such need of a heroine of Joan's stature that Charles VII's councillors conjured up a visionary; for a shepherd from the Gevaudan also performed miracles.

A Spanish history book, *La chronique de don Alvaro de Luna,* includes a chapter entitled *How the Maid of Orleans being without the walls of La Rochelle, sent word to the King, and what the Constable did with her help.* Alvaro de Luna was a contemporary of Joan, living from about 1400 to 1453.

These often contradictory testimonies and documents are disconcerting and lead us to believe that Joan's mission was perhaps not as spontaneous or clear as we are normally given to believe.

It was a magical affair

History, like prehistory, archaeology, and sometimes science, can sometimes be illuminated by the logic of facts, even if these smack of the esoteric—indeed, *especially* if they smack of the esoteric.

The story of Joan of Arc is, without question, steeped in magic. It is the product of an age completely given over to witchcraft, incantations, spells, sabbaths, and demonic practices. As in the time of the Caesars, it was the astrologer and soothsayer in the wings who held the power and made decisions.

The principal actors in the occult history of Joan were: Joan of Arc; Charles VII's mistress, Agnes Sorel; Isabeau, the king's mother; Charles VII; the Duke of Orleans; Gilles de Retz; and

Bishop Cauchon. It so happens that they all died tragically, one might even say cruelly, the victims of their own actions:

Joan was burned at the stake as a witch.

Agnes Sorel was poisoned, no doubt by the Dauphin, Louis XI.

Isabeau died forsaken, miserable, and spurned.

Charles VII starved himself to death.

The Duke of Orleans was killed by assassins in the pay of John the Fearless.

Gilles de Retz was justly accused of witchcraft and satanic alchemy as well as of celebrating black masses and sacrificing children. He was strangled and burned at the stake.

Pierre Cauchon, the infamous Bishop of Beauvais, was "struck dead of a sudden by the hand of God" (wrote Eliphas Levi) and was excommunicated posthumously by Pope Calixtus IV. His mortal remains, torn up from hallowed ground, were thrown on the roadside by the people.

Even a skeptic most surely concede that the convergence of these occult, if not diabolic, happenings cannot be the result of mere chance.

Many other things lend further weight to these extraordinary coincidences. For example, Joan's gifts of milk to the Bourlemont oak, the magic voices she heard, her defenses against the devil, the mysterious sword, the Bellator, the Fragment of the True Cross, which served as a talisman, and so on. Joan's visions and prophecies belong to a realm of inexplicable mystery. It is probably better not to probe too deeply if one wishes the shining image of the heroine to remain.

PART III

The Fantastic

CHAPTER TWELVE

THE WORLD-MOTHER, LILITH, AND MAN'S PRIMACY

So God created Man in his own image, in the image of God created he him; male and female created he them. (Genesis 1, Verse 27)

A close look at the Bible might make one think that the first human being was created a hermaphrodite, that is to say both male and female, although Verse 7 of the second chapter of Genesis states that man was made of "the dust of the ground," and woman (Verse 22) of Adam's rib.

It was no doubt as a result of inaccurate transcriptions of older myths, Celtic, Egyptian, Phoenician, Indian, and so on, that the authors of the Christian Bible wrote this sort of nonsense.

The hermaphrodite World-Mother

Long before the Hebrews, very ancient peoples revered the figure of the World-Mother in whom they saw the mother of humanity, and often she was depicted as being bisexual, or hermaphrodite.

The Goddess *Mut* was both supreme Father and supreme Mother for the Egyptians; *Neith the Old* was Father of Fathers and Mother of Mothers and was depicted in the form of the male scarab and the female vulture.

The Assyro-Babylonian Ishtar, goddess of the morning and evening (Venu Lucifer and Venus Vesper) was depicted at Niniveh as having a beard, and at Carthage the Phoenician Astarte was also depicted with one. Most of the ancient gods are *syzygies* (inseparable divine couples).

The oldest book in the world, *l'Histoire phenicienne* by Sanchoniatho, states that the *Zophasemin* or Heavenly Observers which had issued from primeval matter, were originally androgynous.

The sexes became separate when light was separated from darkness. (*Preparation for the Gospel*, Eusebius, Chapter 1, Verse 10).

The Adam of our falsified and badly translated Bible is in actual fact the generic term for the recently created human species.

The *Midrash Schemot Rabba*, Chapter 20 a—Parasha XIV, Chapter XII, says: "When God created Adam, he created him man-woman."

According to Jeremiah ben Eleasar, God created man an androgyne.

Moses Maimonides says: "Adam and Eve were created together, joined together back-to-back. When this double being had been divided in two, God took the half which was Eve and gave her to the other."

Manasseh ben Israel wrote that Adam's form was dual: "Male in front and female behind."

Cybele, the mother of the gods, was an androgyne like the

Greek Aphrodite, who had the attributes of the male above the hips, and those of the female below. In Cyprus and Berlin there are statues which show Aphrodite with a beard.

Thus there is plenty of evidence to show that ancient peoples thought of the original human being as androgynous, and that the World-Mother, whom they worshiped above all gods, had both a phallus and a vulva.

The World-Mother and parthenogenesis

This thesis has been adopted by a number of biologists, as well as the thesis that the World-Mother reproduced by parthenogenesis. (Up to the present, parthenogenesis has been observed only in the lower unicellular organisms and in sea-urchins. It has never been observed or reproduced experimentally in vertebrates.)

Man has two breasts and we know that the two symmetrical halves of the human body develop "up to a certain point independently.* This would explain why the sexual organs situated on one side may be unlike those on the other. However, it does not explain how on the same side there are often sexual organs which belong to different sexes."

This fundamental duality, particularly in man, and the persistence of the disappearance of ducts whose purpose it is to feed and develop the reproductive organs, lead one to believe that woman appeared even earlier than man.

The Mullerian ducts

This is how Professor B of the University of Poitiers taught the life-history of the human fetus in 1917:

*According to the biologist E. R. A. Serres, surgeon and member of the Académie des Sciences (1821).

While there is as yet no differentiation between the sexes, in the peritoneal region there are two double symmetrical ducts of slightly different origin: the Mullerian duct and the Wolffien duct.

In the course of the development of the female type, the Mullerian duct develops into the Fallopian tubes, the uterus, and the vagina.

In the male, this duct atrophies and produces the Morgagnic growth in the prostatic vesicle.

The Wolffian duct is the origin of the urethra in the female and of the deferent duct in the male.

In the female then the two ducts are separate, whereas in the male there is only one, as a result of a later mutation or adaptation.*

Thus, in men there is more specificity, more complexity, which according to accepted biological laws, proves that the female is anterior to the male.†

This conclusion drawn by the Professor from Poitiers has been reiterated several times by biologists, particularly at the Sorbonne.

Another indication that the female is anterior to the male might be that the female chromosomes are all XX, while those of the male are X to which a Y must be added. This denotes a differentiation in which it is quite reasonable to see a mutation.

*Today it is claimed that this physiological peculiarity in man is not the result of a slow evolutionary change in the organism, but of a natural differentiation, not the result of evolution.

†Matter and organisms always become more complex in the process of evolution. The more complex the organism, the nearer it is to the present; the more rudimentary or simple it is, the nearer it is to the origin of its species. To put it another way, the transistor radio is nearer to the present than the crystal set.

Twenty-two pairs of chromosomes + 2 sexual chromosomes: XX in woman, XY in man.

Today it is held that there are no pure types, whether in the human species or the animal and vegetable kingdoms, and this seems to go counter to the idea of the development of two completely distinct human types, male and female, each having dominant characteristics, as well as related and opposing characteristics.

Women live longer than men

Other observations seem to support the theory that Eve was anterior to Adam: feminine sexual characteristics show in the fetus before masculine characteristics, girls are less fragile than boys during their childhood; are better able to stand pain and to survive the hazards of living. The female embryo develops more rapidly than that of the male. One is also led to believe that the brains of men and women show quite significant differences. The hormone testosterone would seem to produce a sort of masculinization of the brain, or at least to give it certain characteristics.

Only men are subject to a certain number of hereditary diseases: hemophilia, myopathy, and twenty or so others. The average length of life for a man is shorter than that of a woman (by about seven years).

Here are some World Health Organization statistics relating to the average lifespan of the population in several different countries. These figures are quoted in *France-Soir*, August 10, 1972. (The first figure relates to men, the second to women).

Lilith

There are certain traditions, admittedly no more consistent than the Bible story, which claim that Eve was not the first

Norway	72	77
Sweden	72	76
Holland	71.5	76.8
Switzerland	70.5	75.8
France	68.2	75.7
Britain	68.5	74.8
Italy	68.7	74.2
Belgium	67.8	74
Luxembourg	67.1	73.4
Germany	67.5	73.3
America (USA)	66.3	74.4
Japan	63.5	66.8

woman to be created. The story of Adam and Even and their fall from earthly paradise reappears in these traditions along with the barely discernible symbol of the serpent, recognizable nevertheless from its role as Initiator.

This serpent was in fact the Devil who brought knowledge to mankind through the gift of the apple to Eve—unless it was to a concubine, since there is no real certainty as to who the first wife of the first man was.

The *Encyclopédie* has it that according to an old Talmudic and highly unorthodox legend, Adam had two wives: Eve and Lilith.

When Adam was expelled from the Garden of Eden, he abandoned the woman who had listened to the temptations of the serpent and who had tempted him to eat of the apple. This woman was Eve, and she, having sinned with the Devil, gave birth to Cain and Abel.

According to Bayle's *Dictionnaire* Eve lost her virginity straight after she had been created, and the serpent took advantage of this to tempt her while Adam was asleep, resting from his conjugal efforts. Other interpreters suggest that Adam, after the fall, was excommunicated for 150 years and these he spent with a woman, who like himself was fashioned from clay. Her name was Lilia or Lilith.

According to the Talmud the principle female demon was Lilith, who was depicted with a mass of long hair. She was very beautiful and aroused not only men, but also women to voluptuous games.

It is she who is addressed by the adept of ceremonial magic in the "Incantation of the Seven": *Torment us not, Lilith, and get thee hence, Nehemiah!*

According to Sepher-A-Zohar, it was actually she who seduced Adam, and it was the beautiful archangel Samael who seduced Eve.

The magic passion between Lilith and Adam was born of the Egregores or Watchers mentioned in the Dead Sea Scrolls, identifying them, or so we believe, with the "angels" or Initiators come from another planet.

A demonic grandmother

Whatever the case, according to the commentators, at the root of our genealogical tree we seem to have had an ancestor who was the Devil, or a grandmother who was a demon.

We did suspect something of the sort.

Another tradition has it that Lilith was the first human being, coming before Adam, to whom she gave birth, or whose birth she witnessed and whose first wife she was. This suggests the myth of the World-Mother giving birth by parthogenesis.

Both were fashioned from the red clay of the newly created earth, Lilith being formed particularly perfectly.

Adam nevertheless abandoned her for Eve, who was made of his flesh and blood. In fact, he "preferred" himself.

This tradition was embodied in poetic form in 1855 by the Marquis de Belloy, with one or two variants, since he makes both Lilith and Eve spring from Adam's rib. The Kabbalists gave the name Lilith to a small, dark star which was observed several times by astronomers; Riccioli, Cassini, Alischer, etc., among others. This star was thought to be a second satellite of our planet and to bear the name Lilith, the Black Moon.

A tradition attributed to the Pythagoreans has Lilith as an anti-Earth orbiting the Sun on a path exactly opposite to the Earth, so that it cannot be seen. This is of course a legend!

In the *Symposium* Plato mentions another very old legend: that of man created androgynous.

The riddle of the first woman of creation and a hermaphrodite Adam "preferring" himself in choosing a Heva born of his own flesh and blood, puts forward an interesting thesis about the antecedents of the creation of man.

This is in fact the real problem of the World-Mother.

The greater intelligence of man

All these traditions, legends, and superstitions relating to Lilith, the first earthly creature and rival of Eve, demon, Black Moon or dark star, prove that from the dawn of time our ancestors believed that the first human being may have been a woman: the World-Mother.

This hypothesis, which is in line with that held by certain biologists at the beginning of this century, would mean that woman's creation preceded that of man.

From this would follow the curious conclusion, which is nevertheless borne out by physiological evolution, that *theoretically man is more intelligent than woman since his bodily development is more complex.*

The atrophying of the Mullerian duct, which in an earlier

human type had an essential function, leads one to conclude in man's favor.

Further evidence of this is that the first human type to have both the Mullerian duct and the Wolffien duct (fallopian tubes, uterus, vagina, and urinary canal) was a woman.

Whatever the case, this human creature Number One was the World-Mother, mother and father of our most distant ancestors, "Mother of Mothers" as the Egyptians had it, and this would explain the universal cult devoted to her. This would give a deep significance to ancient beliefs, to the androgynous divinities of Greece and Babylon, and to the wonderful and perverse Lilith, who handed down to us her intelligence, her cunning, and her demonic curiosity.

Man may be divided into two main categories: the good and the bad, the poor and the rich, the ignorant and the wise. Mastery of the world is always in the hands of those who are evil, intelligent, and rich.

Chapter Thirteen

Chromosomatic Writing and Sin

The symbols water, Earth-Mother, serpent, grotto, etc., were drawn by men before they had knowledge of their profound nature, and they were probably handed down from before the development of writing. Likewise, knowledge of the external world preceded knowledge of psychology, both being simply faltering steps toward the understanding of reality which, if it is to have any value, must strike a universal chord.

Everything in the universe, from the stars to a grain of sand, shares in intention and interaction with the life of man. The Earth was able to form itself and distribute land in right proportions, the sea was able to carve out the continents, and the mountains spread themselves over the land. Even created objects, when they are fearless of men who can perceive their true nature, show their goodwill. There is no notion of precedence, of humility, or of sacrifice in nature, but collaboration and communion; for all things partake of one essence and one understanding in working toward parallel but complementary ends.

The psycho-sphere

According to Jean-André Richard, the Earth was born of an original plasma which then evolved slowly into polymorphous structures, which became more complex stage by stage and finally produced the different kingdoms, from the mineral to the higher animals.

The plasma was a field of electrical forces of which a variant, the psychic force, made up earth's psychosphere.

It is from the psychosphere, which is eternally present, that life (everything which is alive, particularly organic matter) draws its spiritual and mental energy: the visionary his visions, the sage his meditations, the miscreant his instinct for evil, the Initiate his knowledge, and chance its law of averages.

Water acts as a catalyst and solvent for this psychical force, which is partially carried by hydro-telluric currents which feed springs, wells, lakes, and rivers.

Water witchers and numerous observers have noted a constant connection between these currents on the one hand, and on the other, points where lightning strikes, cursed houses and other places, and also, so they say, "black spots" on the roads.

Others put in a different but related category electro-telluric currents, which are, in fact, the same thing.

Telluric currents

M. G. Theiux, of the Compagnie Générale de Géophysique, says that telluric currents are caused by the displacement of ions, that is to say, electric particles formed by an atom (or group of atoms) which have gained or lost a certain number of electrons.

According to this thesis, streams are electronic baths with secondary reactions carrying ions (cations and anions) from one electrode to another with the function of losing certain elements and electric charges.

The exchanging and recharging take place between a natural electrode such as a menhir, tree, rock, ground, etc., and a second electrode with a different potential which man himself constitutes.

Ions have quite specialized properties, notably that of losing their charges, and they can, depending on factors of equilibrium and potential, enrich or impoverish man's physical and psychical organism.

Malign places are those where the ions cause a cellular (or at least electrical) disequilibrium, or cause a loss of potential. *Benign* places are those where the charge carried compensates for a lack of potential, recharges the human accumulator, or, through *syntonization* (accord, harmony, resonance) reestablishes the electrical balance which has been disturbed.

What one needs to do therefore is discover the electrode which is complementary to one's own, and which will emit not harmful but revitalizing impulses. Such electrodes are often trees, stones, or a particular type of ground.

In former times the Druids made this discovery empirically. They chose the oak from all other trees as their life-giving father, and the menhir as their health giver.

According to Thieux, telluric currents are formed under the influence of the sun, and they have a periodicity of twenty-seven days. They interact with the Earth's magnetic field and gravity. If one fed properly programmed punched cards into a computer, it would be able to give each individual an indication of the places where telluric currents were favorable for him. This would be prohibitively costly.

Fortunately, man has his own natural computer which is much more effectively able to detect the benign white spots and the malign black ones. And its use is free!

The great ancestral fear

In former times human migratory patterns were governed by forces which were then obscure but which we now understand.

Archaeological sites and tourist attractions are frequently situated at particular magnetic foci.

Prehistoric man had to sharpen all his senses of perception in order to escape from the real or imaginary perils which threatened to complete the destruction caused by the Flood, when he ventured to reconstruct civilization. Man had only to make one mistake and he would have disappeared from the earthly stage. In his personal and collective unconscious man experienced with extreme intensity the drama and gravity of each of his acts.

The Earth-Mother had submerged him; unleashed the oceans, and caused the mountains to erupt: Her wrath had been terrible, and it was sound politics from that time on to secure a lasting peace with her. But there were areas here and there which remained in a state of insurrection: swamps, valleys subject to repeated flooding, massifs which were periodically split open by telluric earthquakes, and mountains from which the Earth's living fire burst forth.

Asylums of peace

So the men of olden times would move about from place to place, guided perhaps by a woman, or by the most sensitive person among them: the leader or priest before his time. And the leader would say: "I will not stop, for I am afraid. I cannot stop, I must not stop." And then one day he would drive his leader's staff into the ground and say: "Here in this place we may build our dwelling." As a thank-offering to the Earth-Mother for providing a safe shelter, men would pile up stones to form a cairn, or build an altar.

Wherever the leader thrust his staff into the earth, our ancestors would build a monument, thus leaving a sign of thanks, in which other men knew that they could put their trust. In this spot man would establish a modus vivendi, an equilibrium between man's biological, economic, and social needs.

Here man could live secure and sleep undisturbed. Here he found water, stone, wood, fruit, game, clay for making pots, and iron for making tools. If a mine were exhausted, or if game and fruit became scarce, then the men of ancient times took it that the pact was broken for a time, and they would move on in search of somewhere new. But the altar remained as a token of thanks.

It is very probable that the magnetism of ferruginous soils influences biological structures and magnetism in man. It is thought that the dry-stone enclosures of the Gauls, traces of which can be seen in the woodlands and heaths of France, derive from an atavistic memory of an area which was secure and taboo and which in prehistoric times was circumscribed by a stone circle or a ditch. Within the circle certain taboos operated: hunting, stealing, and violence were forbidden. This was an early form of the protective magic circle, the inviolable sanctuary of the church. Woe betide the man who broke the taboo; only death was fitting punishment for such sacrilege.

It is another product of inherited belief that churches and necropolises were built within the magic circle of the taboo, and that cities were built within a circle of safety, which was called the ramparts.

The taboo in churches and cemeteries, within a circumference of thirty paces, was instituted at the Council of Charroux in 986. This was followed by the Councils of Narbonne in 990, Limoges in 994, Poitiers in 1000. This was the time of the Peace of God which was later to become the Truce of God, which forbade warfare for between 230 and 260 days in the year.

If the magic circle were defiled it lost its privileges and powers. For these to be restored there had to be a special ritual service.

The cities of old were in all probability built around the spot where an inspired leader had driven his staff into the earth. Those which were not, such as New York, Tokyo, Bombay, etc., and which were built in these places for commercial reasons only, will never enjoy the privileges resulting from telluric currents.

The Mayas, a pre-Celtic people, settled for a long time in Canada and then in the USA. One day their leaders had a premonition that they must immediately leave these regions, however hospitable, and establish themselves farther south. (It is possible that the northern regions were destroyed in an atomic disaster. The Mayas fled "like blind men lost in fog." There were several months of total darkness and nearly all perished. This is related by the Popol Vuh.)

All the Mayas set out in search of the Promised Land, led by their priests. They would recognize the place in which their city was to be founded, by a tree in which there would be an eagle devouring a serpent. It was in this way that they came to settle in Mexico.

The Hebrews, being more materialistic, chose Canaan because it was rich. Moses never drove his staff into the earth there, and as a result Palestine was never protected by a taboo.

The serpent and the spermatozoa

The swimming serpent is the symbol of the rite of initiation transmitted by the telluric currents. It is the greatest symbol of Initiation, for it represents life, the penetrating spermatozoa, lightning, and energy. In all countries and all traditions, the serpent is the guardian of treasure, the one who knows all the secrets.

It has wings, and may change into a man or woman, (Quetzalcoatl, Melusine) and indicates that the Initiator belongs to another planet, which is nearly always Venus.

Everywhere in the ancient world it also represented the flying machine and the flyer, the spacecraft and the cosmonaut. That was why it was rigged out with the head of a ram, the leader of the flock, guide and progenitor, or the head of a bull or dragon. This is how one should interpret the falsely named sun "ship" of the Egyptians which in their oldest temple at Abydos is represented in the form of a serpent with a ram's head.

Nature herself seems to have chosen to introduce the shape of the serpent into the primordial elements of life: the spermatozoa and chromosomes.

Nature's alphabet

One might think that the chromosomes, those little flexible rods which transmit hereditary characteristics, constitute nature's alphabet and that they are components in the text of our biological "programming," the future story of our lives.

Due to the way in which our unconscious knowledge works, the earliest form of writing must have derived from this biological script of which very striking examples are found on the Mesha stone in Palestine, in the alphabets of the South Sea Islands, in China, Japan, and so on. They are particularly noticeable in Sanskrit: the letters *a, p, m, s,* in Pali; and in the Phoenician: *y, x, c, u, v, l*; and in the writing at Glozel, *y, u, c, i, l.*

In the filaments of the nucleus of the cell there are forty-six chromosomes. When the spermatozoa and the ovule meet they produce twenty-three groups which in turn form the forty-six divisions of the cell which makes up the future being. If one accepts these twenty-three groups as a basis for an alphabet of twenty-three letters, one may take it that the true proper name of each individual is already programmed, inscribed in alphabetical characters during the process of the evolution of the organism.

This is man's *chromosomatic name*, his name which is unknown, unknowable, and unpronounceable like that of God. Thus it is a *divine name*. His other name is merely his human, officially registered name which may be changed or modified by administrative decree. The chromosomatic name is the *hereditary* name, which corresponds to the characteristics handed down by the father but not by the mother, although hers are usually more important.

In actual fact, a child should hereditarily bear its mother's name, and more logically still, it should have its own, individual name which would describe it and distinguish it from the rest of the family. This is now the function of the forename.

The invention of the name

Originally, individuals names were certainly common nouns—Carpenter, Fisher, Field, Stone, Wells—and thus they denote a trade, an object, a place, etc.

The Law of Manu in India recommended that women should be given a gentle-sounding name and men a name of a positive kind, *i.e.*, having some moral or physical overtone. Many Indians chose to add to this the name of some divinity whose qualities they particularly admired.

Among the ancient Hebrews the name of the patriarchs had a mystical meaning usually related to God and the sentiments attributed to Him.* After that names would refer to elements of nature: Thamar, palm tree; Sarah, princess; Rachel, ewe; Deborah, bee; then to names of prophets, and lastly, as the race and its moral qualities degenerated, so the names became typically materialistic: Gold stone, Silver stone, Gold mountain, Silver mountain = Goldstein, Silverstein, Goldberg, Silverberg, etc.

The law of July 20, 1803, concerning foreign Jews residing in France, forced them to adopt names which would distinguish them from each other, and recommended the names of French and foreign towns. The Lisbons, Ratisbons, Carcassonnes, Cremieux, Cremonas, and Freibourgs date from this period.

Among Moslem communities, patronymics are of recent creation; it is still the practice in many states for the name to disappear at the death of the individual. Nordic and barbaric peoples set great store by a distinctive, essentially personal name which could not be handed down, except in the form: "son of."

The nickname or chromosomatic name

The ancient Greeks had only one name and it was not handed down from generation to generation; the Romans usually had both a name and an agnomen. The Celts—Gauls, the Welsh, Dacians, etc.—had a name as well as an individual, descriptive

*Eli, Joel: two names for God; Nathaniel, Elviathan, Jonathan, Nathania: Gift of God; Joshua, Jesus, secret, prophetic names.

name, an agnomen, like the Indians in both India and America.

The *nickname*, which is as old as the hills, is in fact the most significant personal name, describing a quality or physical deformity. It is very evident, however, that the true name of the man of the future will be coded by a computer in terms of equivalents of gene-letters, or chromosome-letters, which will express his profound, and unalterable identity. Man will thus be the image of his name, until biologists are in possession of the terrible power of tampering with genes, that is, of modifying an individual's identity and changing his sacred "self." This will be the *sin* which will inescapably bring about the loss of the earthly paradise in which we live. And this will again be the fault of a king or serpent!

Woman denounced

As we know, according to the Bible, original sin was perpetrated by Eve and Adam, who stole the fruit of the tree of knowledge and who, when they saw their nakedness, allowed themselves to be carried away by the lusts of the flesh.

With the exception of puritans, people are no longer offended by either the greed or the "turpitude" of our ancestors; on the contrary, marital instruction and consummation are, in all latitudes of the globe, virtues which are praised and encouraged by religions and governments. So the infamous sin must originally have been some crime the nature of which has been obscured by the mists of time.

The third of the five Chinese canonical books, the Chi-King, which predates the Bible, holds women responsible for the original sin: "We had pleasant pastures; woman has taken them from us. We were masters of everything; woman has thrown us into slavery. What she hates is innocence, and what she loves is crime. The good husband raises up the enclosing walls, but the woman, who wants to know all there is to know, throws them down.

"Oh, how enlightened she is! She is a bird with a fateful cry; she has been given too much latitude. She is the ladder down which so many of our ills have come. She has brought perdition on the human race; first through error, then through crime."

A Chinese proverb says that one should not pay heed to a woman's words, for she was the origin and root of evil.

It was an excessive desire for knowledge, says the sage Hoi-nan-Ise, which caused the downfall of the human race; but he does not say who was responsible for it.

The ancient Persian Zend-Avesta, when speaking of the first human couple, gives this account of original sin: "In the beginning Mesquia and Mesquiane were pure and pleasing to Ormuzd.* Ahriman, who was jealous of their happiness, came upon them in the form of a grass snake, offered them fruits, and persuaded them that he was the true creator of the universe.

"Mesquia and Mesquiane believed him and became his slaves; from that time on their nature was corrupt and this corruption affected their descendents."

The Scythians called their common mother the Serpent-Wife; Chautcoatl was the same thing for the Mexicans.

The strange sect of the Cainites

Thus, in the Zend-Avesta and the Bible, original sin was disobedience of God's law; but theologians have never been able to give a clear explanation of what divine law was.

*Ormuzd or Ormazd is the supreme divinity in Mazdan mythology, the good and light giving creator of the universe; Ahriman is the god and principle of evil who is the opposite of Ormuzd.

The Bible has borrowed the symbol of paradise and the fall of man from Zend-Avesta.

In about 159 A.D., the Cainites preached a strange philosophy concerning the problem of good and evil. They were members of a Gnostic sect who claimed to have transcendental and total knowledge of God's nature and attributes. They venerated Cain, Abel's murderer, and the Sodomites, with their questionable morals, and they honored Esau, Korah, and Judas Iscariot. On the other hand they abominated all the Old Testament patriarchs: Abel, Enoch, Noah, Abraham, Isaac, etc.

In their system of philosophy, so the *Encyclopédie* tells us, the Benign Intelligence and Malign Intelligence which were responsible for creation, produced Adam and Eve. Then the spirits imprisoned in the Intelligences, having taken on bodily form, had intercourse with Eve. From this union came children, each of which had the character of the power which created it.

Abel was subject to the creator of the Earth and was thought to have issued from a God who was called Hister. Cain, on the other hand, was begotten by wisdom and the higher principle, and thus he was to be venerated as the first of the sages.

According to the Cainites, only Judas, of all the Apostles, knew the mystery of creation, and that is why he delivered Christ, who wanted to reconcile man with God, to His enemies.

In their opinion, Jesus would have been the Messiah if He had preached discord, as He had proclaimed He would, and not love, which is fundamentally loathsome. For Jesus said (Matthew 10, Verses 34-35): "Think not that I am come to send peace on earth: I came not to send peace, but a sword.

"For I am come to set a man at variance against his father, and the daughter against her mother," etc.

Perfection, these Gnostics asserted, consisted of perpetrating the greatest possible number of outrages.

Their gospel was that of Judas, and a bizarre book called *The Ascension of St. Paul.*

These extraordinary doctrines were very popular, and some people might see certain youth cults of our own day as a revival of the Cainites.

Double standards

All things considered, these ideas of good, evil, and sin are not very different from the ideas held by certain churchmen in the Middle Ages and even by some nearer our own day. Theologians and Popes have often gone too far in their interpretation of deadly sin.

In the Middle Ages complete remission of all their sins was given to Christians who fought the enemies of the Church: Moslems, heretics, and even other Christians subject to kings misguided enough to fall foul of the Holy See. Julius II (reigned 1503-1513) for example, pardoned all the sins of anyone killing any member of the excommunicated family of the Bentivoglio! When Clement V (reigned 1305-1314) had excommunicated Venice, he gave absolution and dispensation from all penance to anyone killing a Venetian.

In 1797 Pius VI gave a similar free pardon to anyone who slew a French Revolutionary. The substance of what he said is as follows: "Any man who kills a Frenchman will be making a sacrifice which is pleasing to God, and their names will be inscribed among those who are the Lord's elect." God was not a Revolutionary at that particular time!

In contrast to this benelovent attitude, the Church was intractable when confronted with the odious crimes which were the really deadly sins. Such as drinking a spoonful of broth on a Friday!

Innocent XI excommunicated women who "did not cover their chests from the bosom right up to the neck." This order was renewed by Pius VII and Leo XII, who, moreover, extended its scope to include all dressmakers, milliners, and tailors who made up such indecent garments.

Benedict XIII sentenced to excommunication "everyone of whatever nationality who gambled on the lottery, and all those who organized such activities." Clement XII (reigned 1730-1741) fell in with this virtuous edict, but having himself set up a state lottery, he anathematized only those "who lost their money elsewhere."

In praise of racism

These anecdotes are useful for anyone who wants to have a relatively clear idea of the concept of sin as it was understood in those obscurantist times, and for anyone who wants to study its real nature in the light of present knowledge.

In fact, there is one cardinal virtue: racism, and one deadly sin: contravening the law of racism.* The aim of life, in its broadest sense, is for man to guarantee the progressive evolution of the species, and to use all his intellectual and physical condition. Those who work towards these ends lead a good life, but those who on the contrary destroy their true and original nature through drugs, alcohol, vice, evil thoughts, and criminal actions, are going against the universal law.

There was a time when men indulged in heinous intimate relations with species other than their own. One finds reference to these aberrations in myths and most sacred writings; they

*It may be that here the word "racism" does not correspond exactly to what is generally understood by it. In the absence of any other more appropriate term we would define racism as being the desire to preserve, and allow no deterioration in the hereditary and genetic patrimony of the whole human race, without making any distinction among individuals, peoples, or ethnic groups. We emphasize this problematic definition in order to minimize any possible misunderstanding or malicious interpretation.

resulted in monstrous offspring which caused a deterioration in the genetic inheritance and endangered the existence of humanity.

We must draw attention to the Lord's commandments to His people in the Bible.

Leviticus, 18:

22. Thou shalt not lie with mankind, as with womankind; it is abomination.

23. Neither shalt thou lie with any beast to defile thyself therewith: neither shall any woman stand before a beast to lie down thereto: it is confusion.

24. Defile not ye yourselves in any of these things: for in all these the nations are defiled which I cast out before you.

This much is quite clear: In former times couplings between humans and lower animals did take place. The result was the degeneration of the human race, which perhaps only just escaped sinking into a monstrous form of animality. This would not have been the end of the world, but it would have been the end of man. Man's gradual and wonderful ascent, achieved over thousands of years, would have been reduced to nothing.

This is why we think that the deadly sin par excellence is that which is perpetrated against the human race.

The whole of nature is "racist"

Sin against the laws of racism (or the species) has universal validity.

Even though the intelligence of animals is not as highly developed as that of man, they do not attempt to procreate with any race other than their own. The cuckoo lays its eggs in a warbler's or robin's nest, but there are no sexual relations between these birds.

Plants are even more racist. The wind carries pollen and

disperses it on to the pistils of thousands of different types of flowers; bees carry the pollen of the iris to wallflowers, acacias, boxtrees, and lilies, but no fertilization ever takes place. Even from orchid to orchid, if the species is not identical, antibodies immediately appear to neutralize the alien pollen.

And there is no diminution in the strength of this law. In all sections of its vast organization, nature sees to it that its species are protected, and great pains are taken to see that no dangerous hybrids are allowed to appear, especially in the higher echelons, that is, those whose evolution is most advanced.

It is possible on the other hand for Norwegians to have children by Balubian or Papuan women, and the Chinese by Mexican women: They all belong to the human race. Nevertheless, it would certainly be a mistake for an intellectual, cultured, erudite man to marry a woman of an abnormally low intellectual or psychical capacity. Man must try to increase his capacity for consciousness and action and not diminish it.*

The ancient Hebrews established laws to avoid this crime, which went against good sense. The Talmud advises women to marry, whenever possible, a member of the Sanhedrin, or failing that, a schoolmaster, or failing that an intelligent man who is familiar with Holy Writ. Ignorant or stupid men "were a disgrace to God" and were to be stoned or even eliminated (euthanasia). Mosaic law orders the death penalty for anyone marrying a close relative.

Taking the notion of sin and racism too far, the Israelites were advised, wherever possible, to choose their wives from among

*"Cancer is the despair of living matter at the highest levels. God says to those with cancer: 'How have you used the energy I gave you. . . . What disorder have you sewn in my scheme?" From *Hygiène et Médecine naturelle*, No. 849.

their own tribe in order to reduce complications in questions of inheritance.

Marriage between Hebrews and Canaanite women was strictly forbidden. (Exodus 34, Verse 16, and Deuteronomy, 7 Verse 3, etc.)

Deadly sin

If one plants an acorn, an oak tree and not an acacia or beech will grow of it. Oak trees know that their job as trees is to make certain that the species survives. If by some freak or miracle one of them produced a poplar, the world would end in unimaginably fantastic and nightmarish chaos.

For the peasant would sow corn and reap grass; dogs would produce mice, fish produce birds, and once the scheme of the universe had been upset and disturbed, monstrous forms of life would replace organized existence. The great certainty that makes life not only tolerable but admirable is the confidence we have in universal order. Each thing in the universe obeys a rhythm and order which has been preordained by an Intelligence which is infinitely more subtle than man's.

Everything in creative evolution is part of an infallible plan in which everything is accounted for, even chance, and the punch cards of the cosmic computer tolerate no mistakes.

No computer devised by man will ever be able to guarantee a mathematical, physical, and spiritual scheme which is as complex and sublimely intelligent as the scheme of reactions, links, messages, and increasing complexities which since and before the DNA all work toward developing and producing a rose, a swallow, or a man; a cloud or a galaxy.

In one way man is such a miraculous product that it would be sacrilege to interfere with him. It would be as stupid as wanting to break a sculptor's masterpiece, to smash it to pieces and use it to make a road. No one has the right to commit such sacrilege, and worst of all, as far as we are concerned, is to interfere with our genetic code. The law of racism is universal and unbreakable. Whoever contravenes it commits the great *sin*.

One could imagine a tyrant capable of annihilating three million men and sparing merely a thousand or a hundred people. This would be a great crime, but it would not be the great *sin*, for life could start all over again; and nothing is lost so long as all is not lost.

On the other hand, we will almost have reached this situation when biologists start to interfere with genes and chromosomes;* they will then commit the unforgivable sin and the human race will be cast into nothingness.

Nothing will be able to save it; our earthly paradise will be lost; this will be the *fall of man*. This is how we understand the story of original sin. This seems to be the real and terrible truth of the symbol of the fruit of the tree of knowledge of good and evil; that is to say: science. It is a terrible possibility which hangs over man's destiny.

*Biologists have already begun to interfere with genes and cells. They are studying ways of being able to modify at will certain hereditary characteristics. At cellular level, they have, in the University of Oxford, been able to marry plant with animal.

Chapter Fourteen

The Creation of the World

In attempting to come to grips with the mystery of the creation of the universe, physicists start by trying to explain the exact nature of Life. Some believe that matter is inert and that the step or borderline separating it from life is somehow connected with a revolutionary concept of space-time; a concept which involves *a fundamental difference between matter* and life, or in other words, between death and life.

This barely tenable viewpoint is not shared by true scientists, who, on the contrary, tend more and more toward a concept of a living universe-entity, or to quote Robert Linssen: like an "immense mind."

Life in all things

"The work of the English scientist D. Lawden," writes Linssen, "as well as that of the mathematician and philosopher Stefane Lupasco, of the mathematician and chemist Tournaire, of the physicist P.A.M. Dirac, of Dr. Roger Godel, Robert

Oppenheimer, Jean Charon, Teilhard de Chardin, Chauchard, etc., all points clearly to the existence of some form of memory, of intelligence, not only in organized matter, but also in unorganized matter."

In brief, *life exists everywhere, with its physical and psychic qualities, ranging from the purely mineral to man himself, for their essence is identical.*

It therefore seems probable that matter and energy are also identical, merely being seen from different viewpoints.

The theory of the Unknown Master

The theory held by one Unknown Master points to the position of clay at the center of the electronegative scale, equidistant between fluorine and caesium.

Clay lies halfway between:

Fluorine: acidity, cold, low-density, negativity, space and spirit.

Caesium: basicity, warmth, high-density, positivity, mass and psychism.

Flourine (- 223)   Al-Si   Caesium (28)

Aluminum is a metal (male), silicon is a metalloid (female): combine them by mixing in water and you have clay (silicate of hydrated alumina).

What is interesting in this theory are the qualities: the acid function of space-spirit, and the basicity function of mass-psychism, which have a natural connection with the problem of the creation and origin of man when seen in relation to Mendelejeff's table of 143 elements.

There are, traditionally, four simple elements: fire, water, air, and earth, but this Unknown Master restricts the number of *matter-elements* to two only: time and space.

A more widely accepted theory reduces the number of element-matters to one: the space-time continuum.

In Einstein's Theory of Relativity space-time is a continuum (the opposite of discontinuity), that is to say, according to André Gueret and Pièrre Oudinot: "A certain curve of continuity without interruption, evoluting in space. It is therefore impossible to go from one point to another without passing through all the intermediate points."

To put it another way, time and space cannot be separated, they exist simultaneously, the one through the other, reciprocally: The space-time continuum is curved and is therefore identical to the universe, which is likewise curved.

Proteus, the time traveler

The basicity function implies a curious connection between mass and psychism, a connection which conforms remarkably well with Einstein's matter equals energy.

There is a curious echo of this in the myth of the sea god Proteus, son of Neptune, who like DNA and the chromosomes, had the gift of possessing the future: He could travel in time and knew all things.

Proteus, whose name comes from the Greek *protos*, meaning first, would only impart his knowledge to those who could force it from him. (The Initiate teaches only those who are worthy; the dragon must be killed if one would have its treasures; one must await the death of the master to inherit his knowledge.)

Another connection with the Initiates: Proteus had the power to change into a rock (matter), into a tree (vegetable kingdom) or into an animal, which leads naturally to the thought that the protonic function, first and positive, has the power to decide the direction of the evolutionary processes.

Looking for other connections between the Intiates and science, we notice that in Proteus, the primeval water of the first oceans is intimately bound up with action, in the same way as the biologists regard this primeval water as necessarily involved in the formation of amino acids, the first link in the chain leading to so-called biological life.

In conclusion, the god's powers of metamorphosis and prophesy imply the existence of a universe other than ours, similar to that predicated by Jean Charon, in which is enclosed the electromagnetic waves which he calls "mnemonics," probably because he sees them as close relatives of the chromosome-memories and the "akashic archives of the universe."

These speculations and arguments definitely suggest the existence of a universe of four or five dimensions, a concept which simplifies enormously further speculation on the mystery of the Creation.

Plus time, minus time, and zero time

When traditional wisdom and classical physics agree, one can usually be confident of moving toward truth.

The Initiates' theory of the birth of the universe is very close to that of Jean Charon on the birth of life: *The cell program may well be enclosed in a ci*r*cle curved by energy and enclosing the electromagnetic waves containing its information, for example in the form of the spiral chain of the DNA molecule.*

The borderline between matter and life may be closely interwoven with an aspect of the space-time continuum. This approach to the mystery of the Creation does away with the dilemma of the ancient cosmologists: Did the world have a beginning or is it eternal?

It would certainly be humiliating to have to hold to the Biblical explanation of the Christians and Jews, for whom the world was created by the God of Abraham!

Strangely enough it is legend, mythology, even fairy stories, which come closest to the truth.

The Mayas of the Popol Vuh had a conception of history and time of a purely miraculous nature, having no connection with the duration and space of our three-dimensional universe.

Metamorphosis, "proteusism" ubiquity, time travel, have always been the basis of sorcery and religion, of magic and the fabulous exploits and romances of the Round Table. They come very close to the truth, to the disgust of conventional religion.

But truth does come close to the miraculous, the unbelievable, which is why Teilhard de Chardin claimed that only the fantastic has some chance of being the truth.

Occultists suspected as much and introduced into their speculations, and often into their teachings, an extrascientific element in relation to nature, time, and space, having to do with the metamorphosis of matter: an element never accepted by rationalists.

It is in the light of this heretical element that certain Initiates teach cosmogony. According to this hypothesis Nothingness existed, exists still, conjointly with the Creation if one reduces space-time to its simplest expression: zero.

According to Frederic Joliot-Curie and Chadwick, primeval matter would not have had an electric charge. One has to imagine it as a neutron. This neutron would therefore be *protomatter*.

This primordial universe, in which plus and minus were absent, is identified with zero, *i.e.*, Nothingness, but a Nothingness full of potential plus and minus, just as zero implies continuation: 1,2,3, etc.

In this way we are led to envisage a beginning which is no beginning, a "full-void," neutral, containing both positive and negative.

Graphically, the universe is represented by a symbol consisting of a horizontal stroke, followed by a circle, followed by a horizontal stroke crossed by a vertical stroke: -0+.

Let us envisage the universe

When man tries to envisage the universe he comes up against two obstables:

Is it limited or infinite?

Did it have a beginning or is it eternal?

The Wise Man knows the answer: I am ignorant, I know nothing of these mysteries. Nevertheless, man, wise or not, is curious and wants to build hypotheses, so with regard to dimensions he says: "The universe is infinitely large." As for its creation, he opts sometimes for eternity, sometimes for other explanations: energy as the starting point; the will of some Power or of an Entity called God or Universal Intelligence according to circumstances.

In Einstein's Theory of General Relativity matter and energy are essentially the same, which permits of a hypothesis that the beginning of creation was in energy-matter.

These attempts at a solution, these explanations, are pure fantasy, completely erroneous, and physicists know it.

The ignorant, of course, have certainty: a faith, a belief.

In fact man comes up against an almost insurmountable obstacle in that human reasoning relies generally on a logical base, of which reality and the laws of physics are an integral and unavoidable part. But these laws and realities are only valid in the imperfect universe which is the one we perceive.

The paradox of Zeno

Zeno of Elaea (490 B.C.) philosopher, dialectician, claimed that there is no such thing as movement, time, or space and believed in absolute motionlessness. Indeed he denied that these properties are capable of logical proof by the use of absolute principles. According to him only singleness and its relative plurality exist as the properties of bodies.

He established the impossibility of motion by the paradox of the arrow, which can never reach its target if it follows a line consisting of an infinite number of points in space.

Classical science, with its atom, its curved universe, relativity, and advanced mathematics, make constant use of paradox and dialectic in building valid hypotheses. According to Zeno's system all space is divided into an infinite number of points, so that between 0 and 1 and between 1 and 2, or, to help us visualize more easily, between the first meter and the second meter there is, certainly, one meter, but there is also 10, 100, billions of points.

According to this system a train which leaves Paris, kilometer 0, never arrives at Bordeaux, kilometer 585, even if it runs at 100 kilometers an hour, or even 100,000 kilometers an hour. This is a well-known mathematical curiosity, but one to which no particular significance is given. If the train has to pass an infinite number of points between Paris and Bordeaux, there will always remain an infinite distance still to go, no matter how high the speed. The train will never reach its destination.

And yet an apparent fact: The 12.15 from Paris always arrives at Bordeaux at 5.45 or thereabouts. When it comes to mathematics reality appears to beat fantasy. But is this really so? In absolute reality the train never does reach Bordeaux: It only reaches certain parts of the city, but certainly not the Place des Quinconces, the Porte de l'Hôtel de Ville, the Palais Gallien, the Saint-André Cathedral, etc.

Now, Bordeaux is not simply the station, but *all* the city, from its outer limits, which one can trace on the surface, down to its microscopic infinity, which can never be reached, by any means whatsoever. This little digression serves to prepare our minds for a quite another form of thought.

Neutron Man

Let us pursue further our investigation into the absurdity in our reality.

For a being living on the neutron of an atom, the infinite would be at the other side of the proton, out toward the unreachable depths where the electrons circle, by the billion, some twinkling like our stars, others so distant that their light is lost in the impenetrable depths.*

Beyond this unmeasurable electronic corona, more crowded than our own night skies, flashing, crisscrossed with falling stars. comets and UFO's caused by constantly changing orbits, a being living on a neutron would be unable to visualize other types of space.

In the same way, a sentient being, living on a mumps virus, would probably have some sort of perception of the ear and the brain, but the rest of the head would simply be beyond its powers of apprehension and investigation, and the idea that it was dependent upon an even larger organic system would never even occur to it.

Man, living on his planet, envisaging "his" universe as billions of light years in extent, as shown by his radio tele-

*In the atom, between the corona of electrons and the nucleus there is proportionally as much space as between the sun and the earth. A stream of particles discharged in order to detach a neutron from its nucleus has to be numbered in billions if it is to have any chance of one hitting the target.

It should be noted however that the hypothetical structure of the atom is now questioned, following the discovery by the physicists Danos and Gillet that the nucleus is organized in quartettes.

scopes, is in the same position as the proton of an atom or a mumps virus.

The concepts "large" and "small" therefore have no consistency, since the infinitely near is no closer than the infinitely distant, and vice versa. Both correspond to this theoretical central zero which is our *physical* self, as the future corresponds with the past and that theoretical central zero which is our *present* self. Our perceived reality is, in this sense, unimaginable, out of reach, illusory.

Here we are, at last, nearing a relatively positive conception of our universe, of its space and time, for if we can bring ourselves to admit and to imagine *that space and time do not really exist*, we shall attain a perception of sorts of the mystery of the Creation and of life.

One dead and one living

A similar process allows us to envisage outside time a particular way of viewing the *existent*, or primordial, element, from which everything flows in a *"complexification"* which is truly beyond explanation.

But a "complexification" presupposes an adding of something. It is at this stage that one brings into play the space-time continuum and the idea of uni-matter, as well as spirit or energy existing in a past-future continuum which, with an effort of imagination, can explain how 1 contains +1 and −1.

This 1 is at the same time finite and infinite, creation and creator, a sort of entity containing the universe. 1 alone is uncreated, dead, since it contains no continuation, no duration, no distance. It is living if it contains a potential for "complexification," *i.e.*, space-time, energy-matter, and intelligence. If it contains this trinity, everything becomes possible.

For the conventional believer this trinity is God and his hypostasis. It represents an esoteric concept of real validity. For the man without preconceptions it is the indispensable "possibility" needed for further progress.

The system, in both cases, consists of adding to the dead 1 something *which is not living, which does not exist,* but which is going to make life: space and time. Then 1 becomes dynamic, living, and creator of the possible, even of ubiquity.

The experiments of Bernard d'Espagnat, professor at the Collège de France, have demonstrated this phenomenon of ubiquity possessed by certain waves. Fiction comes to join science.

The Father, the Son, and the Holy Ghost

We are thus able to conceive of a phenomenon of creation one and multiple, without beginning in time, since made of Nothingness, of the past, of the future, and this process leads us to invent further indispensable fantasies: the infinite-finite, intelligent energy-matter, and nonexistent and all-powerful God, "creature of the heaven and earth, consubstantial with the Holy Spirit and with the Son who is flesh and life manifest."

To be sure, all this is little more than energetic self-deception, but nourishing to man's avid curiosity.

Buddha, the great Initiate, analyzed this concept more than 2,600 years ago and defined it in the wonderful word *maya.*

Other seekers after knowledge, the theologians, half a milennium later, also came to understand that it was necessary to provide God with a son, so that the Holy Trinity might become esoterically the symbol of the Creation. These seekers were Initiates.

The illusion of time: the instantaneous universe

Are we now sufficiently free of the illusion of reality to try a new hypothesis?

The past, the present, the future are one.

The measurable, the infinitely big, and the infinitely small are one.

These terms correspond to no absolute reality; they are merely the expression of our conventional universe. They exist and do not exist, have substance and are insubstantial, are equal and superior to zero in a sense that we cannot grasp with our imperfect senses, and all is illusion.

This is the opinion of real scientists: "Only nonsense stands some chance of being the truth," said Niels Bohr; Teilhard de Chardin was of the same opinion.

Now, using this data, we can venture an explanation of the creation of the universe: It is not eternal, yet has no beginning and no end: It is in a constant state of creation and dissolution.

The universe was created an infinite billion of light-years ago; it will be created in an infinite billion of years in the future, its creation is beginning now, at this instant, *all this simultaneously*, with an exact coincidence of time and space, void and fullness, positive, negative, and neutral.

This fantastic concept, which is already guessed at by some advanced physicists, has more chance of being right than the Creation described in the catechism: God created all things. Or the cosmogony of the lay school: The universe has always existed.

If the idea of God, Father of Jesus Christ, arbiter of good and evil, of heaven and hell, teacher of Moses in the Sinai, military advisor to Joshua, observer from on high of our sins, is totally ridiculous, that of a Superior Intelligence is considerably less so. As far as the concept of an eternal universe is concerned, it is not fundamentally misleading, but it is impossible to explain it and impossible to grasp.

It was already in the Rig Veda

The introduction of space-time is not a new element in this attempt to define a cosmogony.

The Initiates for millennia past have been ahead of the physicists with this argument; *In the nonexistent and the Nothingness of the primeval void, everything was created with the existent of the ultrafuture universe.*

This is what the esoterics had already found in the Rig Veda: "There was neither being or not-being, neither ether, nor the canopy of the heavens, neither containing or contained . . . but *That One, He*, breathed alone with *Her* of whom he held the life in his bosom. Other than He nothing existed which has since existed. Desire, given substance by the intelligence of Him became the original seed (desire equals energy); this seed became progressively Providence, sentient souls, matter or elements. *She*, who was supported by *Him* in his bosom, was the inferior part; and *He* who sees, was the superior part. Who in this world knows and can exactly affirm how this creation took place? The gods came *after* this creation of the world.

Whichever hypothesis is considered, we invariably come back to a non-understanding, a paradox. Even in the Rig Veda: "Nothing exists except some thing."

God was created by the intelligentsia

The idea of Creation is completely foreign to the theologians of India. For them God did not *create* the universe: he *vomited* it.

To create implies to give birth in conjunction with some outside matter. To vomit implies a creation which partakes of the creator, which is part of him.

They describe creation as: "The birth of elements, of elementary molecules, of sentience and intelligence, a birth produced by Rahma, by means of an unequal mixture of qualities; the secondary emissions coming from Purusha (the constructive element)."

In reality nothing happens in this way, for all is maya (illusion).

If the different concepts of Creation are taken more or less seriously by ordinary people, for the intelligentsia they are simply amusing conundrums.

In the Bhagavat Purana, Bhagavat (God) is the first of beings who, in the form of Purusha, is at one and the same time, agent, container of all things; cause and effect; he creates and uncreates himself in each *kalpa* (cycle) than continues and discontinues himself by turn. God is the sum of beings emitted by him. *That One* alone is at the same time all things and God.

Here we are very far indeed from the dogmas and illusory gods of the Christians, Jews, and Moslems, all as equally nonexistent and invented as the dogmas and gods of Egypt, Peru, and Mexico.

More deeply Initiative than the Bhagavad Purana, the Bhagavad-Gita or Evangel, or Gospels (Good News) which Matthew, Luke, and Mark used for tracing their Christian Gospels, gives us some very interesting revelations on God and the higher spheres of Initiation.

According to the deeply versed Orientalist Edward Dumeril,

"The Brahmans, wishing to lead a contemplative existence in turbulent surroundings which were making their work impossible, wanted, by the use of reason, to give legitimacy to the superiority of their caste: They invented, from sheer necessity, a Supreme Being.

In introducing a god into a philosophical system which could not accommodate one without denying its own validity, the Indian intelligentsia performed a veritable *tour de force.*

By careful stage management the author of the Bhagavad-Gita still succeeds in keeping for his teaching the sanctity of those Truths of which the origins are lost in the mists of time, and the authority of a "revelation" above ordinary humanity.

This "revealer" whom the founders of the religions, in order to impress the ignorant faithful, called "God" or the "Supreme Being," is in fact a *maya*, an intelligence unknowable and impenetrable.

It follows that the Grand Initiates of India, and probably of the entire world, have invented a demiurge understandable to the ordinary people, which then instituted the cult of secondary gods, who were merely heroes, statesmen, and superior human beings.

Manou knew. . . .

The Code of Manou, it is worth remembering, states that "Veda is the principle and true sense of the universe, existing by himself; inaccesible to human reason, which is not able to grasp its significance."

Manou, the first man, the first Initiate, and the first inheritor of transcendental knowledge in our cycle (or *manwatara*), gave a symbolic representation of the creation of the world, rich in significance for those who know how to read it.

Brahma *neutral,* the unknowable, he who the mind cannot perceive, created the different creatures from his own substance.

First he created water, in which he deposited a seed which became a glistening egg, in which the *Supreme Being himself was born* (yet another interpenetration and use of a strange space-time) in the form of *male* Brahma, the ancestor of all beings. Brahma lived in the egg for a "year" (equivalent to 3,110,400 million human years), and by the sole use of thought divided it into two parts: the heavens and the earth.

It follows from this that the first creation was not clay, or even gas (H and O), but water (H_2O), from which all else came.

This is not accepted by physicists, who put the creation of water after that of the elementary gases: hydrogen, oxygen, nitrogen, carbon, which themselves came from energy-matter.

Nevertheless, tradition has it categorically—the first movement was in the waters, and Nara the Divine Spirit was called *Narayana,* he who walks on waters (taken over by the Gospels), because everything participates in the nature of water and the Divine Spirit.

The Vedic mythology therefore joins the mythology of Greece in associating water with the Creation: *Narayana* is a close relative of Porteus and the two symbolize the alchemic preparation of the real Grand Design: the Creation.

To be found in the arcanum of mythology is not only the knowledge of the Initiates, but also scientific secrets which physicists and biologists are probably wrong to ignore.

The cosmogony of the Initiates

The cosmogony of the Initiates may be expressed as follows: *In the non-existence and Nothingness of the great primeval past void, everything was created from the existing and the created of the future universe.*

Given the existence of the Living, the potential for evolution (the future) is more likely than the existence of the past. (A grain of wheat can result in a stalk of wheat; this is a near-certainty which can be proved. But we cannot prove beyond doubt that the grain came from another grain.)

Creation is present at all times, and must be seen as present in the future not yet arrived, as well as in the evolutionized past and in the ungraspable present.

The universe therefore has a beginning and a nonbeginning (nonexistence). It begins with the future, on condition of bringing it into the past, which is Nothingness and nonbeginning. In this sense we can almost say that the future preexists the past, but at the same time is contemporary with it.

Everything was created, not with hydrogen or carbon, as the chemists think, nor with fire, water, air, and earth, as the spiritualists would have it, but with original and indivisible matter: *space-time*.

The first second of creation was child of the next second, and its mother at the same time: The future gives birth to the past and is indistinguishable from it.

In our known universe, the concepts which we are expressing—following in the steps of the ancient Initiates—are made concrete in the present time, which does not exist.

The grilled meat that we eat contains at one and the same time not only the meat, but also the products of digestion, and it is only in appearance (illusion, the *maya* of Buddha) that the three times are disassociated in a triple space which satisfies our lazy minds.

In fact, it is impossible that the action of eating can be

confined to the simple expression: I eat. The past cannot exist without the simultaneous. The first breath of a child is a beginning which was present in the sperm of its father, of its grandfather, etc. It is the past made manifest.

But this first breath also implies and contains the children which will be born of this child, or the restitution of the constituent elements of the physical body, and contains a universe of past and future chains of events, from the beginning to the end of the world, for all eternity, indefinitely, without possibility of stopping, of end, of beginning, of finality.

The same phenomenon is present when a grain of sand is eroded from a rock; the whole universe is involved.

This is what Hermes Trismegistus meant by his axiom: Everything is contained in everything: That which is on high is as that which is below.

Those with open minds can begin to see at this stage in the argument that these contradictions have nothing to do with the irrational!

It is not impossible to imagine the "first" present time having a past; and easy to accept that it had a future; it was present in its genetic code, and one can therefore conceive of it as the nonexistent past of the present time. The near-certitude of the future is one of the keys to the understanding of our cosmogony.

The past belongs to a three-dimensional universe and presents no insoluble problem for our physical perceptions or for our intellects. The future belongs to a four-dimensional universe; it includes the dimensions of our normal world, and in addition that of the probable but unknown world toward which we are moving.

Belief—religious or otherwise—also exists in a four-dimensional universe, since it involves conjecture about the unknown.

The creation of the world, impossible to conceive of in our three-dimensional universe, can be approached, if not completely understood, if we can imagine it in a four- or five-dimensional universe.

Chapter Fifteen

Life and Intelligence

Life consists of an incredible will to engender, to become space-time. The purpose of life is unknown; perhaps it is quite simply to demonstrate existence, but it is probable that the search for a purpose and the desire to demonstrate existence is a human concern which has no absolute significance.

Human life must harmonize with the universe. In ancient times the role of religion was to accomplish this harmony, *i.e.*, to establish a close liaison between the destiny of man and that of the cosmos.

Life is the superior essence *par excellence*, it is the created universe, the Essence, God, Supreme Intelligence, and the Grand Architect of the Masons. The life-essence preexists and exists in all things.

Primitive life in the cosmos

According to astronomists and physicists, living organic matter originates from animo acids to be found everywhere in interstellar space. It is now regarded as fairly certain that very complex organic compounds are created and develop in the quasi-void and absolute cold of the cosmos.

According to Sydney Fox, these interstellar organic compounds must be microspheres, prebiological cells, or, rather, blueprints as it were, of biological cells.

God and the space-time continuum

The greatest physicist of all times, who was also the first Great Initiate, Hermes Trismegistus, taught that life had neither beginning nor end, birth nor death, that it was eternal and existed in all things, as much in a grain of sand as in the brain of a priest. He summed up this doctrine in the famous proposition: "What is on high is as that which is below. All things are in all things."

He was, according to Manethon, the Initiator of the Egyptians. He is said to have written 36,525 books of sacred .eachings. The Initiate speaks at suitable moments and speeds up the evolution of man and his civilization. There are still in existence about twenty fragments of ancient Egyptian science attributed to Hermes Trismegistus. His work was a culmination and continuation of Egypt's oldest traditions, its monotheism, its philosophy, and was an influence on Pythagoras and Plato.

He also said: "Mind (energy) existed before humid nature (the oceans), which came out of the dark places; all was confused and obscure before the Word (organization, structure of matter, complexification) came and gave life to all things."

This is exactly how most physicists view the matter: If one is to dare and try to imagine the nature of the universe, it must be seen as a condensation of energy, transmuting into hydrogen and water.

To sum up, one could say: In the beginning there was the *mother sea*, the fecunding water.

This view is certainly erroneous in the absolute and infinity of space-time, but it can be used for convenience in the restrictions imposed by our known universe.

Who, according to this hypothesis, is God? What is the Supreme Intelligence?

Here again Hermes Trismegistus agrees with the best minds of our time:

"The Master of creation is all and one, the entire universe and the smallest imaginable part of it, a part which represents, contains, gives birth to the totality. The Only Master is preexistent and postexistent; he is the eternal traveler of the ages. . . ." (*i.e., the space-time continuum.*)

One is dumbfounded, meditating on these profound words, which the physicists and astronomers of the 20th century have come to accept, 4,000 years after the great Egyptian Initiate.

Tradition and science are therefore in agreement: There is as much likelihood of intelligence in a grain of sand as in a molecule of animal flesh.

Atoum, the atomic God

We give the word "atom" a Greek derivation: *â*: privative and *temnô*: I cut.

Its true etymology is lost in the mists of time, thousands of years before Democritus; nevertheless, Pythagoras, his teacher, learned of it during his stay in Egypt.

The Esoteric College at Heliopolis, the most ancient in Egypt according to M. Guéret, worshiped the Creator of the world under the name *Atoum*, the noble God whose name was not known to the other gods.

He is the primordial God who created gods and men and all

that is out of his own substance, who attracts, repulses, positive, negative. (God must sacrifice himself in order to create. It is the miracle of transmutation. The noblest attribute of the Initiate or saint is not sublimation but the offering of himself as a sacrifice.) He is the unknowable, outside our normal time and space.

In other words, Atoum is the primordial substance, protomatter (neutron) and, let it be said at once, *Atoum* is the original *atom* made of space, time, and desire.

This etymological connection would not be so convincing but for the fact that an Initiate king in the 14th century B.C., Akhenaton, gave the name of atom to the Only God in whom the Egyptians were to believe, the name being *Aton* (pronounced "atone").

The atomic gods

In fact, Aton was a resurrection of Atoum, the first and only God, who in the inescapable decay brought by the millenium had been replaced by Ra, Rê, Amon, and even by Horus and Osiris.

The identification of *Atoum* with *Atom*, the physicists' prime matter, and, in fact, father of all creation, results from the very etymology of the god's name, which comes from the root: *A*, meaning "nonbeing" and *Tou*: "to be complete."

The Initiate priests of Heliopolis taught that "in the *Noun* (chaos, primordial ocean, in which lay all creation and the seed of all things and all beings, but in a nonliving, nonmanifest form), lived an undefined spirit *carrying within itself the sun of all existence.*"

He was called *Atoum* and had created from his own substance all gods, Man, and all beings. From this neuter Atoum, identical to the neuter Brahma of the Vedas, came, without external influence, +and −, man and woman. Atoum, therefore, was the very source of life, from which flowed the universe.

Physicists and biologists are more and more inclining to the hypothesis that the life-essence is protomatter, without the electric charge, which they identify with an isotope of the neutron, which is in fact a primitive neuter atom. One should note the extraordinary fact—something which proves the existence of authentic Superior Ancestors—that in the Hindu cosmogony the life-essence is Brahma neuter; in that of the Egyptians the essence is Atoum, positive and negative at the same time, which results in neuter, and *Aton*, the etymology of which derives from: neuter!

This Initiate knowledge of the Egyptians was shared by the priests of the majority of the religions of antiquity.

The Great Soul of the Brahmans was a unique god, *Atma*; the sacred word of the Tibetans was *Aum*; *Adonaï* was the Supreme Master of the Hebrews and *Adonis* that of the Greeks.

Attis, husband of Cybele, the Magna Mater, was the "Papas" (father) of the Phoenicians and one might well see the etymology of Atoum in *Athena* who emerged living from the brain of Zeus, as well as in Hathor or Nout, the Egyptian goddess of the sky.

Gueret and Oudinot write in relation to these strange etymological coincidences:

"We do not believe that all this is a result of chance. What we call *atom* the Ancients called Atoum, Aton, Atma, Aum, etc., but giving the concept a wider, more complete philosophical and religious significance."

This hypothesis receives further support from the mythology of ancient Persia, one of the oldest in the world, where *Atar*, the Fire of the Aryans, was the son of the supreme god, Ahura-Mazda.

"But the critic," writes P. Masson-Oursel and Louise Marin guesses that *the son is older than the father.* He is the life-essence and in this role regards the burning or cooking of dead flesh as an unpardonable crime.

Imprisoned

For the physicist Jean Charon, all the phenomena of the universe had a common origin, but no one has succeeded in laying bare the detailed structures and deep hidden meanings of life.

From chaos (but what was this chaos?) the mysterious Existent became elementary corpuscles, and then, under the influence of magnetic fields, which are assumed to have been preexistent, by a series of "complexifications" they took on an atomic structure.

The impulse had been given, the first step taken; the atom became molecule, then a simple chemical element, then a compound, etc. Life manifest, controllable life, had formed; Jean Charon calls it: The Living (*le Vivant*).

He reasons that structures and liaisons came about by means of "memory" profoundly knit to "the Living" by the "mnemonic field," a sort of memory of a specific past.

In General Relativity, space-time is bent in the neighborhood of a zone of high-density of energy. Jean Charon believes that the space in the interior of a DNA structure, assuming that it obeys this law, may curve in such a way as to form a circle which would imprison the electromagnetic waves and their "information." This phenomenon would apply equally to vegetable and animal cells, which for this purpose are identical.

The borderline between Matter and the Living would therefore be intertwined with the space-time continuum.

Charon believes that the liaisons between physical fields in different states are achieved through plane topology in the case of space-matter, and by cylindric topology in the case of the Living; with the help of energy, but in minute quantity.

Through cylindric topology, liaisons which are "impossible" for matter, could happen *suddenly* in this new sort of space, in which electromagnetic waves have the power to remain enclosed.

How intelligence originated

As early as the 5th century B.C., the heretical philosopher Diogenes of Apollonia had identified matter with energy: "*Ex nihilo nihil fit*" (Nothing can come out of nothing) . . . since intelligence obviously existed he concluded that air (ether, atom) and all creation was permeated with thought.

Our physicists through their experiments and speculations, have rediscovered Hermes Trismegistus and caught up with his theories.

They have come to believe that energy, eternal, infinite, psychic, and intelligent, preexists the universe.

It becomes matter spontaneously (condensation, transmutation of joules into corpuscles), *i.e.*, elementary corpuscles which by successive complexifications end by forming themselves into atoms of hydrogen, oxygen, carbon, etc. It is in this way that visible matter is created, from a grain of clay to a giant galaxy.

More and more complex and subtle processes produce intelligence and show signs of a type of consciousness in the matter, showing the ability to choose, and evidence of memory and initiative.

If intelligence, as is generally accepted, is characterized by an aptitude for coping with new situations, then that matter which is falsely called "inanimate" is infinitely more intelligent than organized matter!

"Every second," writes the German physicist Jordan, "something new and unexpected happens at the atomic level."

This is also the view of Robert Linssen when he writes that, "At every millionth of a millionth of a second intranuclear constituents respond to the demand . . . of lightning processes of change, the complexity and speed of which are simply beyond our ability to imagine.'

Many thinkers also agree that the most authentic forms of intelligence are to be found in the farthest reaches of the material world, where it is not only a question of intelligence, but even of a certain capacity for "love," although different from the personal, egotistic love of humans.

This sort of love, as seen by some physicists and philosophers, is present in energy and matter and would be, as stated by Robert Linssen, like a state of being, free from servitude, attachments, and pain.

This capacity for love, like that for intelligence, would exist in its most sublimated form in energy-matter, corresponding to that *loving-energy* spoken of by Teilhard de Chardin, who was one of the first in our time to put the accent on the spirituality of matter.

Charon proposes as the possible catalyzing agent which produces intelligence—perhaps the very nature of intelligence—the "chromosonic" memory of the universe or mnemonic field, which is part of all things.

Nature's memory-chromosomes

In this hypothesis one has to envisage matter at its earliest creation, still suffused with all imaginable energy, and subject to natural laws at a point in time when the space-time continuum is close to zero (close to eternity, immobility, prime matter). Such matter would be possessed of a "memory" of the future, which would function rather like the punched tape of a computer program.

The computer has an intelligence of sorts, derived from man. Chalk, for instance, also has intelligence, but derived from itself, or to be more accurate, from that universal, eternal intelligence contained in its chromosomes and from *the time when it will exist* in a more elaborate form: as water, plants, animal, man.

This universal memory is obviously the same as the *akhashic memory*, which was somehow already known to the spiritualist Initiates.

For physicists, on the other hand, this phenomenon is linked to space-time, which as we have seen is bent by powerful energy fields, just as the path of the photon is bent when it passes close to a sun.*

If the energy is very powerful, the curve thus produced will form a circle from which neither the photon or space can escape.

In Initiation, space-time, in the Invariable Mean (the center of centers) curves back on itself to form a snake biting its own tail.

In this way the waves of future-memory may imprison themselves with their infinite potential and their intelligence, in the labyrinths of nature's original thought-matter.

The magic circle without space-time

The imprinting at the level of the chromosome of the totality

*There is every reason to suppose that the real essence of life, present in everything, but principally in DNA and the mysterious depths of the cell, is a source of intense energy, although of infinitely small dimensions.

of data contained in the life-essence is probably achieved by electromagnetic waves, or, more accurately, by concentric magnetic axises, the original of which, self-contained, develops, according to Einstein, thirty billion light-years.

We believe that these memory waves carry the memory of all that is present, all that is past, and *all that will come to pass.* These waves, which are imprisoned in the "magic circle" (rather after the manner of magnetic tapes) of our chromosome-memories, belong to a more complex and complete universe than ours, and contain the *memory* of past, present, and future time.

In the magician's circle strange phenomena occur, demonstrating that the magic circle is indeed an *alien* zone—outside the earth and not subject to its laws, a veritable island in the universe.

According to the Initiates the chromosome-memories contain the soul of the world (or of God, if one prefers this hackneyed concept) and constitute the really essential element in the human body and brain—its energy center in fact.

The chromosome-memory theory has been known to physicists only since 1950. Initiates, on the other hand, have known of it for centuries, and have attributed to the universe the faculty of registering all events, past, present, and future. They have called this faculty the Askhashic memory of the universe.

To sum up: It is possible, indeed probable, that biologists will shortly discover that the secret nature of life and of the phenomena at the chromosome level are governed by laws operating at a higher level in which the space-time continuum is different from the one familiar to us, and in which the future and the past are absorbed into a time other than ours.

Intelligence (or psychism), an integral part of life, is present then in all matter, and we have come to believe that certain imperatives, certain degrees of energy decay, serve to free this intelligence from its imprisonment.

We should establish a distinction between intelligence and psychism, but this would involve endless discussion. Some philosophers even equate psychism with intelligence.

Chapter Sixteen

Nature Thinks

The intelligence of plants

Intelligence at its most elaborate, as defined at the human level, consists of the ability to choose and to understand, to synthesize, analyze, classify, orientate in time and space, memory, generalization from the particular, comparison, establishment of relationships and consequences of ideas, imagination, deduction, subjection of instinct to reason, and coping with unexpected situations.

Naturally intelligence does not imply the possession of all these abilities, but it may be fairly claimed that the presence of any one of them constitutes a proof of intelligence.

All human beings are endowed with intelligence, but to a greater or lesser degree. The intelligent person demonstrates this quality by his ability to generalise from the particular, and by avoiding self-centredness in his more banal activities: avoiding excessive attention to his self in idle conversation and mundane matters: his family, children, health, car, food, clothes, etc.

The man of poor intelligence, on the other hand, personalizes everything and confines himself to limited, uninspiring matters.

Intelligence and the soul

If one admits the existence of the soul, a connection between it and intelligence is already established. According to this hypothesis the soul (consciousness and thought) is the spiritual essence of man, the golden chain linking him to the wider universe.

Exterior objects and phenomena create impressions which by means of our senses are transmitted to the brain, where they become sensations, images, ideas. Between physical perception and its mental consequences there is a borderline where a certain mechanism comes into play; this mechanism being intelligence.

According to the 18th century thinkers, the soul, normally existing at the level of potential, becomes actual intelligence when it reaches the level of activity. One classic definition: Intelligence is the faculty of living in harmony with the laws of the universe.

Georges Cabanis, a disciple of Locke and Condillac, wrote:

"It is well known that the condition of our internal organs, particularly that of the viscera of the lower abdomen, affects our powers of feeling and thought. The resulting illnesses can change, disturb, and sometimes completely reverse our normal feelings and ideas."

The large intestine of men of action is always short, less than a meter in length. Mystics, on the other hand, tend to be prone to constipation, the large intestine measuring up to two meters. The toxins reabsorbed by the large intestine condition our state of mind!

This connection of the soul with one of our more gross organs, the large intestine, proves that intelligence and matter inter-react to an extent which makes them virtually identical. Yet the matter which makes up the human body has no obvious superiority to that of other species.

Animals and plants receive sensory impressions, observe, compare, judge, calculate; all of which can be taken as proof of their intelligence. To explain these phenomena man talks of instinct in the case of animals, and of exterior intelligence in the case of plants, but this is merely an avoidance of the problem.

The intelligence of flowers

It is possible to develop conditioned reflexes in mimosa.

Plants are just as capable of learning as are animals, says Dr. Arumus of the University of Toledo, Ohio; it is also true that insects and plants share a very close biochemical relationship shown by the sterols and terpenes (secretions of alcohol) which condition their physiology and behavior.

Maurice Maeterlinck writes: "Plants have a repertoire of tricks, traps, *machinery*, which from the point of view of mechanics, ballistics, aeronautics, take precedence over the discoveries of Man."

He describes the intelligence shown by a root, observed by Brandis (*Uber Leben und Polaritaet*) which, finding the sole of a boot in its way, divided itself into as many rootlets as there were holes in the leather, then, once past the obstacle, joined together again to make a single root.

The author of *Intelligence in Flowers*, having improved sage by hybridization, noticed that the less developed sages adopted without difficulty the more advanced characteristics of their kind, whereas the reverse situation was rare. This experiment shows that plants are capable of *choosing* those paths which are most advantageous for their evolution.

They can even, for the protection of their species and its genetic code, secrete poisons which destroy or sterilize alien pollens. Pure racism, in the best sense of the word, and part of the struggle against the real sin: deterioration of the species.

On August 19, 1972, the American government announced that biologists had succeeded in creating by hybridization (starting from the actual genetic cells of two different species) a new plant which was entirely edible, roots, leaves, and fruit. This plant is as yet unnamed. If its taste is well received it will be grown on a wide scale.

This is not the first time that geneticists have sinned by breaking universal laws. One day they may well create a gigantic (or microscopic) monster which will destroy humanity.

The inspired orchid

The Pentecostal rose, which grows in damp meadows in April and May, has a flower which looks like the fantastic, gaping mouth of a Chinese dragon. At the bottom of this mouth can be seen two stigmata joined together and surmounted by a third, which has at its extremity a sort of half-basin full of a sticky liquid.

Two ovules, each full of pollen grains, are steeped in this strange little pond. When an insect lands on the bottom lip, which is ideally designed for landing, it is irrisistably drawn to the bottom of the mouth by the scent of nectar.

It is now that the orchid demonstrates its amazing architectural skill: It has deliberately designed the passage leading to the nectar, narrowing it in such a way that the insect cannot avoid touching its head against the half-basin. As if worked by an electric signal, the basin tears, and the two ovules immediately come into contact with the visitor's head, and are stuck there by the sticky liquid which coats them.

The insect drinks the nectar, crawls out backward, having apparently grown two horns, formed by the ovules and their stalks. The insect then goes on to plunder a nearby orchid and crawls in the same way, horns first, which one might think must lead inevitably to it pollinating the second plant with the pollen of the first! But no: Pollen on pollen will not lead to fertilization!

The counting plant

"It is now," writes Maeterlinck, "that the genius, the experience, and forethought of the orchid come into play. It has exactly calculated the time required for the insect to drink the nectar and go on to the next flower; an average of thirty seconds.

"As we know, the packets of pollen are carried on two short stalks which have been steeped in the sticky liquid. At the point of insertion each stalk has a tiny membrane disk, the sole function of which is to shrink within thirty seconds, so that the stalks are made to form a curve of 90°. This is the result of a new calculation, not of time, but of space."

The pollen horns are now horizontal, pointing to the front, so that on the next visit they will, with minute accuracy, touch and fertilize the stigmatas above the basin. Not bad for a simple little flower completely lacking in intelligence!

But that is not all: "The stigma that is touched by the packet of pollen is smeared with a sticky substance. If this were as powerful as that inside the basin, the mass of pollen, their stalks broken, would adhere to the stigmata, their mission apparently accomplished. This cannot be allowed to happen; the chances of the pollen performing its task cannot be left to the hazard of a single attempt. This flower, which can count seconds and measure angles, is also a chemist, which can distil two types of gum: *One very adhesive, which dries immediately on contact with air, so as to stick the horns of pollen to the head of the insect, the other, very much diluted, for the stigmata's part in the operation.*''

In other words, this second gum is ideal for holding a few grains, but too weak to retain the main mass of pollen, so that the insect is able to fertilize a good number of flowers.

What brain, inside or outside the plant, has designed this remarkable mechanism, and has even thought up further safeguards? When the membrane of the basin has torn itself open to liberate the sticky ovules, the lower lip is instantly raised in order to retain the little pollen left behind by the insect. Why waste!

All plants are endowed with this diffuse intelligence, from their roots which search, avoid, choose, to their flowers, which see through the many ploys used by insects, and which secrete aphrodisiac perfumes, explicitly designed to attract and deceive them. Their intelligence is obvious, often as pronounced as that of animals, whose degree of biological complexity is nevertheless enormously more advanced.

Intelligence in animals

Termites, through their powers of organization, and particularly by their ability to estimate the limits of their possible activities in relation to their numbers, appear to show quite remarkable intelligence.

But according to the more extreme rationalists, it is not intelligence which governs such phenomena, but simply instinct.

''Nature has created a regulating mechanism'' writes Vitus B. Dröscher, ''which may justly be called *reasoned.*''

But how are we to differentiate between what is *reasoned* and what is merely instinctive? And who has the boldness to state categorically that intelligence is independent of instinct?

The ichneumon's radar

The ichneumon wasp has talents which are quite fantastic. The female lays her eggs *in* or *on* other animals, such as caterpillars, spiders, or royal ants, which then act as live food for the newly hatched larvae.

Naturally the caterpillars, spiders, and ants die as a result of this system, which makes the wasp particularly useful, but this is not what we mean by fantastic talents. The remarkable thing is that the female ichneumon lays its eggs on larvae which are deeply hidden in tree trunks.

"In great excitement," writes Dröscher, "she scurries over the tree trunk in all directions. Suddenly she comes to a dead stop, goes back a little, sets herself, and swiftly sinks her abdominal drill (7.4 centimeters long) deep into the tree trunk. Almost every time she strikes a hidden larva."

That a small wasp should carry such a powerful drill is extraordinary enough; that she can sink it 7.4 centimeters into living wood—the length of a finger—is amazing, but that the ichneumon can detect a larva hidden at such a depth verges on the miraculous!

It must be instinct, one thinks: The insect's antennae act like a water-diviner's wand. There is, however, the essential difference that the water-deviner is almost always wrong, whereas the ichneumon practically never makes a mistake.

Even more fantastic: the echneumon megarhyssa *selects* the species of larva buried in the tree, since its offspring can only survive on the larva of sirex.

It follows logically that although this ability to choose so carefully, to locate an object so accurately, and to know the exact species involved, may be a form of instinct, intelligence certainly plays a part.

Bees, as is well known, can plan ahead, dolphins have an intelligence (memory, phonic communication, understanding, planned courses of action, etc.) almost as sharp as that of man. Rats are wily and astute, and we are familiar with the intelligence of beavers and crows, and our friends, dogs, cats, and horses.

Instinct and intelligence

This ability to investigate the unknown, invent techniques, and even to make and use tools—does it come from intelligence or from instinct?

Entomologists and naturalists plump for the latter explanation, because according to them the echneumon, for example, shows no sign that it is endowed with thought. Thought and "projectivity"—the ability to make plans—are the main criteria of intelligence, and imply in addition the ability to analyse, synthesize, and choose, as well as self-knowledge.

"Instinct is the antipode of reason" writes Dröscher, with some daring.

As we see it, instinct is the unconscious understanding of unlearned, unknown phenomena, spontaneously divined—for example, by the desert animal which almost always moves towards water which it cannot know is there. But all this is intelligence in the true sense of the word, even if only intermittent.

The entomologist J. H. Fabre commented early in this century that instinct leads animals into absurd and useless activities. Insects nevertheless have some discernment which allows them to adapt to slight changes of environment, and this implies awareness. The variations due to this power of discernment are individual and not transmittable to offspring. Fabre admits that insects are aware and adaptable but refuses to accept this as proof of even rudimentary intelligence.

Again, this is the unknown reason which causes an animal or a man to move out of the way of an unforeseen danger, and which enabled Joan of Arc to divine at Chinon which man was the Dauphin.

It is difficult to believe that it is only by chance, without the intervention of reason, conscious or not, that the echneumon is able to detect a larva 100 times out of 100, and its sex too, through seven centimeters of wood!

Surely it is impossible to believe, with the entomologist, that the megapod constructs its incubator blindly, without conscious purpose, without foreseeing its use, without intelligence, *i.e.*, without understanding, calculation, reflection, and knowledge.

It is even more difficult to accept that termites, whose degree of organization is the highest in the insect world, build their city-fortresses blindly, produce, harvest, and use their food, without an exact knowledge of the number of soldier-termites required to defend a given size of community.

The animal's ability to build nests, burrows, lairs, to know the optimum behavior to follow in case of danger, attack, or complete passivity, is not instinctive, but is, rather, subconscious knowledge, or, more accurately chromosome-memory.

It is inherited; part of the genetic code; there is nothing to indicate that intelligence is excluded from this phenomenon. On the contrary, we see here the presence of a superior intelligence, diffuse, manifesting itself in ways that differ from conscious intelligence, but not in essentials.

In the same way, it is impossible to accept that the development of a cell according to the program laid down by its species, or the course of evolution that begins with the explosion of a nova are automatic processes, instinctive, mechanical, owing nothing to intelligence.

Nature, by which we mean the universe, is "an immense mind," an organism which is intelligent in its totality and in its tiniest manifestation. In fact, we believe it to be Intelligence itself, complete and absolute.

The animal kingdom, like clay, like rock, like mountain, river, meadow and plant, is a "thinking reed."

Life in matter

It is admittedly not always easy to distinguish thought in stone or an oak, because it is not immediately obvious. But it is perfectly logical to accept that a superior, transcendent intelligence is to be found in chalk, and in trees, as much as in the brain of a scientist.

The mysterious intelligence of a grain of sand is no doubt more subtle than that of a physicist, but on the other hand could Einstein calculate and control the behavior of cells in dog, bee, or tree?

Yet it is beyond doubt that there exists in these entities a hidden intelligence which feels, computes, calculates, reacts, with the precision of an electronic computer.

The intelligence which governs this phenomenon is essentially unknowable by man, who can only take note of its presence, in particular in RNA.

The Russian chemist V.A. Firsoff believes that matter is alive, intelligent, and claims that the elementary particles possess a mental interaction; one of them, the *mentino*, being identified with what one might call the "wave of intelligence."

"*Mentinos,*" writes Charles Noël Martin, "constitute a disincarnate intelligence, which obviously makes their detection a matter of extreme complexity."

Our ancestors of stone

Man, imitating the god-universe creating humanity, tends to people the Earth with stone statues. The need to create is the hallmark of life and manifests itself in all the kingdoms of creation.

For a long time our ancestors believed that it was sacrilege to copy the divinity's most elaborate creation, man. This is presumably why the Celts have left very little by way of human images, and in very ancient times left the granite of their menhirs and dolmens uncarved.

The Hebrews and Arabs inherited this superstition and have rarely departed from it since the days of Moses and Mohammed, perhaps because, more than most peoples, they have been prone to practice magic.

Various traditions assert—probably symbolically—that there was a time when statues came to life and fought against the men who had created them.

Legend, no doubt, but truth itself is so fantastic that there can be no shame in allowing the imagination to wander in a world of science fiction, in which nature, scoffed at by our civilization, unleashes a cataclysm and amuses itself by replacing man by creatures made of so-called inanimate matter, or indeed, by the vegetable kingdom.

The Mayan Popol Vuh tells of ancient times when men of the Second Age were made "like wooden puppets, in the image of men that speak."

Guided strictly by observed phenomena, it is possible to conceive that the mineral world, in its attempts to become more live and to sublimate itself, tries and sometimes succeeds in taking animal form. When the Earth is "in heat," all miracles are possible.

These times of heat—the "desire" of Aryan and Phoenician mythology—are perhaps cycles of history which coincide with the birth of a new humanity.

The traditions of many peoples do seem to assert the creation of man from rocks, stones, and pebbles.

Has the Earth an unconscious need to give birth? Does it obey its "chromosome-memories," or a consciousness that in certain zones of exceptional irradiation (and therefore of exceptional intelligence) tends to create life in animal form?

It is tempting to believe so.

The amorous zones

One of my regular correspondents writes:

> It has often seemed to me that there are certain delimited areas here and there in the world, where the rocks, stones, vegetation, elements, configuration of the land, and even the activities of man—conscious or not—combine to produce, or have already produced, lines, surfaces, and volumes in the image of the human and animal kingdoms, as we know them, or indeed can imagine them.
>
> It is as if in these areas electromagnetic phenomena on a world, a cosmic scale, have amused themselves by endowing certain types of matter with a divine spark, a sort of "prime soul," which then guides the molecular structure into developments which result in quasi-live forms, which more or less resemble us, although often in grotesque dimensions.
>
> It seems possible that there have been periods when the

conjunction of all these phenomena, physical, chemical, biological, and others, have produced viable beings, animals, permanent mutations, and metamorphoses in different space-times.

Here the writer's views join those of the ancients, who believed that there exist areas on the earth's surface where teluric currents emerge. At such places they built temples on platforms (in Mexico) at an altitude which they judged to be particularly propitious for fertilization, birth, and reconciliation.

Although unproved as yet, it is possible that these areas of emergence have certain electrical properties, not only in the sense that we know electricity, as source of attraction, repulsion, flashes, and disturbance, but also in another, more subtle, more essential sense.

However this may be, there do seem to exist on the Earth amorous zones favored by strange phenomena, at certain chosen places where the currents of Intelligence of the Heavens and the Earth come together, unite, and give birth.

Anything is possible, including the extremes of improbability, miracles even, in these places where the spirit of love abounds, where matter crystalizes under the compulsion of energy and the pressure of an immense will to create. As at the dawn of life.

Here, men who were eager to appease the Earth set up altars, megaliths, chapels, churches. Here were shaped the first taboos, the first refuges built, the first cities erected.

Zones of aggression

Duality is an easier concept to grasp than trinity. + opposes –, good opposes bad, smallness-largeness, light-darkness: the earth has many zones of aggression which probably exactly balance the amorous zones. There are certain places where men are subject to inimical forces, animals become ill, trees die without obvious cause.

This theory, sketchy and imperfect though it may be, could nevertheless explain the continued existence of damned regions, ghosts, hallucinations, crimes, and sicknesses, which no exorcism seems able to dispel.

Woe to the land of Israel, the Gobi and Colorado deserts, there where the land was once atomized, and will be again. Woe to Rome, Venice and Naples, Tokyo and Berne, Zurich, Las Vegas, and New York. Woe to those men who from insensitivity or by tragic destiny leave the amorous zones—or are ejected from them—and go and live where there is cataclysm.

The wise man, from empirical knowledge or acuteness of perception, seeks to identify such places as are beneficial and seeks to live there. By the same token he tries to avoid the zones of aggression, the cursed places, where a beneficial equilibrium can never be established.

The earth has its revenge

The Earth has long tolerated the frenzied animal brutality, the injustice of man, who, not content merely to torture it, does not hesitate to show his contempt by abandoning its worship and whoring after false gods.

Whatever the superficial appearances, it is logical to assume that lics, trickery, desire are universal, and must be present in the unknown universe of matter.

The river has its soul, its intellect, its thoughts; the mountain dreams, the meadow sees, speaks, listens.

The Earth in its entirety is an immense, complex organism, full of strongpoints at which intelligence-energy accumulates, points of which, until now, only the sensitive have been aware.

As with all organisms, it possesses a womb: the oceans; a stomach: the soil; a nervous system: the circuit of telluric currents. It undoubtedly has also zones corresponding to its head and heart: those places where civilizations and the better instincts of man arise.

The Earth hides her ancient cities; she hides her history and lost civilizations—with slow, deliberate cunning?

In our times she seems to be diverting the currents of her nervous system, exposing her volcanic depths, spitting out her green poison, heavy with menacing, diabolical potentiality: pitchblende, from which the scientist-sorcerer extracts the hellish power of the atomic bomb, uranium 235.

Chapter Seventeen

The Prehistoric Museums of the Petrimundo*

Nature speaks freely to the man who cares for her and feels a sense of communion with her. Mountains, meadows, forests are alive, have intelligence, language, memory, and are always willing to communicate with human beings.

Objects have their whims and preferences, their moments of somnolence, their moments of lucidity, during which they express themselves and take an active part in universal evolution, and even in man's activities.

There are places on the earth where the nature of the ground

*We have coined this neologism ''petrimundo'' (world of stone, or precreation of the living world) because the concept must become part of the vocabulary of scientific research into our civilization.

It appears that the precreation (first sketches of creation, before the appearence of so-called organized cells) took rock or clay form, which closely echoes mythology, but one must also accept the possibility of precreations in metal or other forms.

speaks, thinks, cures, and others where it is hostile, dumb, refusing its secrets and miserly with its beneficial radiations.

He who does not believe in the intelligence of nature and the "inanimate," who does not believe that stones, forests, water, have language, is himself a mere lump of matter, of limited understanding and meager sensitivity; he is irremediably confined to the duller, emptier things of life.

Nature's hysterical pregnancy

Twenty-five million years ago, nature became bored with its decor of prairies, mountains, and oceans. Everything was wild, grandiose, sublime, but sad, silent. Admittedly, from time to time there would be a clap of thunder, and no doubt terrible storms, like a three-dimensional cinemascope in full color. But these gave only a very restricted range of sound.

Nature began to think, and being a woman, to dream—and what does a woman dream about if not love? Dreaming led to motherhood. She gave birth to things of color and brilliance and all sorts of strange creatures which scampered about her earthy skin or flew in her perfumed sweat and in her breath.

In those days she had formidable magic creative powers. Her subconscious fantasies conjured up vague images which she consciously elaborated, stripping them from their blurred contures.

This male seed found its way into her heart, her flesh, into the still-fresh creative molds, and gradually the dreams gained strength and will, then body and density, and began to appear as tiny aborted fetuses looking like lichens or protozoa.

She had dreamed vaster and more subtle dreams, but perhaps not precisely enough to act as viable blueprints. In short, it seemed as if this embryonic creation lacked life because its development has been too rushed.

Nature gathered together all the intelligence scattered throughout her infinite structure and concentrated it at its most sensitive, most cerebral point.

Then, midst fantastic temperatures and the irradiation of the barely receded chaos, there took place an interpenetration of times, and the future burst into the light of the present.

This infinite intelligence brought forth from the uncreated shapes like elephants, dogs, monkeys, men. . . . And to shelter this near-life, continually seeking equilibrium, she dreamed up and created protective boxes and screens, fixed structures which became walls, houses, towers, castles, roads, paths, furniture, and objects of all kinds.

Soon nature was large with the fruit of her imaginative labor, with the materialization of her desire.

In a desperate convulsion of her enraptured body she ejected, erupted, the palaces, the human forms now found in Montpellier-le-Vieux, the incredible "zoo" in the forest of Fontainebleau, the idols of the Vence plateau.

In the beginning these objects probably had life, intelligence, desire, but millions of millennia turned it all to stone, and it has come down to us congealed and apparently without life.

Nevertheless, flesh, blood, intelligence are still present in this matter, consisting of sandstone, chalk, and granite, but they are concentrated, savage, and one would oneself have to be sandstone, chalk, or granite to be aware of their existence.

This is how the poet and the wise man explain these miraculous zoomorphic and anthropomorphic rocks, which are to be found in France, Peru, Brazil, and Rumania.

As strange as all this may seem, biologists, geologists, and physicists are coming near to accepting this explanation.

Fontainebleau's fantastic museum

Of the various "zoos," Fontainebleau undoubtedly has the most dazzling variety of "animals," monkeys, rhinoceroses, snakes, birds, dinosaurs, toads, the entire cat family, sheep, bears, hippopotamuses, turtles, whales, sea lions, owls, elephants, etc., even a sphinx, and some human heads beautifully carved, all as in the wild, but mineralized in some way.

Most of these zoomorphic specimens are to be found in the val d'Apremont, in the region of Roches de Franchard (the highest point in the forest), in the Massif des Trois-Pignons, and in the area of Bas Breau, etc.

Edith Gérin, who has been studying and photographing these sites for some years, writes: "Can it be simply chance that these strange rocks are grouped as if belonging to some ancient center of ritual, particularly in the Gorges and the Apremont Chaos?"

There are two possible explanations for the petrimundo at Fontainebleau: an accident of nature or the work of prehistoric man.

The latter can be rejected out of hand. The rock, consisting of extremely hard sandstone, still has its natural surface, formed at the point when it solidified, about 30 million years ago.

The first explanation is hardly more satisfying, for the laws of probability, which might be stretched to explain the accidental creation of simple shapes such as sea lions, snakes, and turtles, can hardly account for three elephants, with their trunks, eyes, tails, bodies, and legs.

We are therefore forced back on the theory of amorous zones, and the conscious will of nature to give birth; in other words to make trial models of her most elaborate future creations.

This is the most reasonable explanation, however fantastic at first sight. We believe that the Fontainebleau petrimundo is a manifestation of the intelligence of matter.

Montpellier-Le-Vieux: the devil's city

It has been said that France is the most beautiful country in the world, and certainly the the Tarn Gorges contain some of the most wonderful sights imaginable. Montpellier-le-Vieux, in Eveyron, ranks in beauty with Sainte-Chapelle, Chartres, and other works of the hand of man. It is a place in which the creative genius of nature is fully manifest, demonstrating the intrinsic beauty and intelligence of matter.

It is perhaps the most fantastic, dreamlike spot on our planet, a scene from another world, owing nothing to the tools and hands of man.

Situated in the Causse Noir, above the Tarn Gorges, Montpellier-le-Vieux is a prodigious pile of jumbled stone needles, cliffs, and natural rocks.

The local shepherds believe that giants of long ago built this kingdom bristling with battlements, towers, fortified towns, ramparts, vast ruined cities; peopled by dragons, dogs, bears, camels, tiny shepherdesses, shepherds as big as mountains, as well as beautiful ladies of olden times, in sumptuous crinolines, Moorish kings, princesses, and queens crowned with diadems.

A city of alleys, streets, squares, avenues, triumphal arches, huge doorways, mysterious houses, sumptuous hotels, dungeons, lighthouses, doors opening onto celestial seas, exotically colored.

And in this immense city, in this kingdom looking like a Gustave Doré reverie: silence, the deep silence of eternity, of ancient things, of faded colors, and indefinable perfumes. Even if the cry of the cricket or blackbird, or the scampering of a bolting rabbit occasionally pierces the strange silence.

And yet, in this silence, one hears the faint sound of invisible crowds, ungraspable, ghostly, the rustlings of a life which flows and ebbs, disappears, returns, evaporates at the touch of a ray of sunshine or the stumbling of an unfeeling intruder.

And not a single manmade object. Everything made of natural rock, eroded, raddled, sculptured by time, rain, wind, ice, and sun. Everything: the fantastic castles, the solitary towers, the animals, the people, the artifacts.

A veritable fairyland in stone and rubble, an unbelievable miracle, a wonder, a film of the middle ages and the Arthurian legends, in color, with magic spells, mysterious disappearances, substitutions, transformations, changing with the changing light, the changing hours, the changing moods.

This is why the shepherds of Causses saw in it a city built by giant magicians, and since it was so vast, royal, and little known, they believed it to be some ancient capital. Montpellier being the largest town in the area, they called the site Montpellier-le-Vieux, ("the Old") as if it were the forerunner of the present Montpellier.

It seems that the writer Monteils was the first, in 1802, to write about the "black Causse," "with its decor of enormous rocks, shaped like cubic or pyramidal figures, presenting to the startled traveler, at a distance, the sad spectacle of towers and ancient castles falling into ruin."

The stone is dolomite, a natural carbonate of lime, of a greyish color, sometimes bluish, sometimes tending toward red.

Torrential gulleys are the setting for a landscape of dales like rocky amphitheaters: la Millière, les Rouquettes, les Amats and le Lac.

"These are," says the Joanne dictionary, "the four grand amphitheaters which make up the four principal districts of this city of rock. An excellent overall view can be had by climbing up to the highest rock, the Douminal, at an altitude of 830 meters itself looking like some prehistoric Acropolis."

From here one looks down on the city itself (les Millière), an amphitheater (les Rouquettes), a parade ground (les Amats), and a coliseum (le Lac).

Such is the simple layout of the Devil's City: to this can be added an outer circuit road; the long, narrow amphitheater of la Citerne, which runs parallel with that of les Amats.

Paiolive

Paiolive is a similar site, but much less rich in picturesque rocks. It is situated on the chalk plateau, Gras des Vans, in the Ardèche region of Southern France.

> To this marvelous setting of white rocks, sculptured by water, Nature has delighted in bringing all the riches of southern flora: The wild cherry, the spindletree, the terebinth, fig, maple, honeysuckle, soften the rocky crevices.
>
> The outstanding constructions in Paiolive are: the Chapelle Saint-Eugène, a remarkably rocky platform, the Défilé d'Endieu, the grotto de la Gleizasse, la Rotande, a veritable ballroom, covered in fine grass and surrounded by an oval of rocks, the Château des Trois Seigneurs, where vaguely shaped ruins rise confusedly from the rocks, the Bois de Gagniet, an immense labyrinth of rocks, covered in vegetation and brambles, where even the

shepherds rarely venture. At the far end of this chaos one suddenly looks down on an area of subsidence from which emerge obelisks joined together by bridges.

Taking care to avoid the crevices, one goes through a doorway, from which a narrow lane leads to the Salon. Here, on lawns shaded by magnificent trees, there rise the great monoliths, the Daughter of Loth, the Nun, etc., and then, not far away, a tiny ribbon of fresh water, coming from a rock—the only spring in this stony desert.

This poetic description was no doubt still valid in 1900, but nowadays the site has changed considerably, and it must be admitted that we were unable to find there all these marvels. Still, the woods are very enjoyable and there are undoubtedly strange rocks waiting discovery.

The village of Idols

In the remote past the gods bombarded the Vence plateau; the gods, or perhaps visitors from outer space, fighting earthmen, or possibly fighting other extraterrestial visitors.

Or perhaps there was a shower of meteorites which crashed into this area, digging out huge craters which can be seen to this day.

These are the thoughts which spring inevitably to mind when one first sees the stony, sun-drenched hills of Saint-Barnabé, to the west of the Chiers mountain.

The Village of Idols is a Montpellier-le-Vieux in miniature, situated in the Vence pass, about thirty kilometers from Nice. It can be reached by taking the N7 road as far as Cagnes, then turning north on the D36 and D2. A kilometer the other side of the Vence past a stony track leads to the village of Saint-Barnabé.

To the south and west there extends a plateau strewn with strange shapes: the Village of Idols.

The titanic, fascinating landscape is covered with shallow, craterlike depressions, perfectly round, in which water collects in the rainy seasons. Meteorite craters? Water erosion? The latter seems most likely.

Walking casually and pleasantly along trails covered with a thin, sparse grass, one skirts around outcrops of rock, looking like dismantled citadels or ruined houses, and here and there the giant statue of a barbaric god or some prehistoric divinity stands out against the sky.

The Marcahuasi Plateau

The Marcahuasi Plateau is to be found ninety kilometers north of Lima, Peru, at an altitude of 4,000 meters. In 1953 the archaeologist Daniel Ruzo, in the course of an excursion, suddenly found himself in a strange place, covered with an enormous number of stone animals which seemed to be guarded by giants cut from the Andean rock.

A fabulous animal, in the Inca style, its mouth open, guarded the ancient road which led to this kingdom.

Ruzo immediately wrote to the Academie des Sciences:

"I am convinced that the scientific world will soon have to admit that all over the world, prehistoric men, at a later date than the cave painters, took to rock carving as a means of expressing their higher aspirations."

He gave this civilization the name "Masma Culture."

His theory ignores the possibility of an orographic creation, and it does seem that in the case of the Marcahuasi fauna, even if it is natural in origin, it was later retouched by man.

At Marcahuasi one can see lions, a horse, a group of elephants, a camel, sea lions, etc., but also an Inca head, an Assyrian profile, numerous human figures, and some graphlike drawings in which the hand of man is obvious.

But these anthropomorphic and zoomorphic figures lack the precision of outline shown by the Fontainebleau material.

Futuristic machines hewn from the solid rock

Mother Earth, then, at Fontainebleau, Montpellier-le-Vieux, at the Vence pass, at Cieux, and in a thousand other places all over the globe, seems to have given birth to civilizations, and to have encroached on the uncreated and future space-time in order to accomplish this work.

It would appear that she must have put into this petrified world giants, towns, animals, and all sorts of objects (pots, bows, bowling pins, etc.) and in addition, if our theory has any validity, cars, planes, space rockets, and even the antigravity machines, which toward the year 2,000 will supersede the clumsy, primitive Atlas and Apollo rockets, plus a good many other machines at which we can only guess.

Fontainebleau has its sea lions, its elephants, its turtles, owls, and bears; Montpellier-le-Vieux has medieval streets, towers, belfries, castles, and titanic cities. . . .

Everywhere one finds pots, bells, vases, pyramids, feet, clogs, cheeses, hats, books, binoculars, and even rockets. But where are the cars, IBM machines, trains? It is probable that the richest, most impressive "whims of nature," produced millions of years ago, have totally disappeared, swallowed in earthquakes, eroded by the winds, rains, and frosts, dynamited by men, leveled by agriculture.

May not this petrified world be one which is parallel to ours, able to interconnect with ours? Is it not possible that the legends of giants, fairies and Ali Baba's caves are based on improbable but possible truths?

The petrimundo and the prehistoric museums

Still, the Earth continues and will continue to give birth. However, the investigation of out-of-the-way things and places is still too recent, too badly organized for it to have resulted in findings connected with the world of industry and electronics.

And how are we to recognize the shape of machines and objects, miniaturized perhaps, for which our civilization has so far no need, and the use of which we cannot even begin to imagine?

The intelligent observer of the petrimundo must know how to guess at functional possibilities; strange geometrical shapes which are obviously not natural to the material of which it is made. He must be familiar with the shape of things so far produced by our civilizations, from the clay bison of the caves to the sophisticated toys of today, from the racing cars of le Mans, to the Concorde jet and Apollo 17.

It is worth considering whether it is due to the almost miraculous power of our chromosome-memories that we imagine or recreate the civilization of Atlantis with architecture in the shape of pyramids. It seems possible that the same applies to nature, and that the chromosome-memories suggested the form of future creation, from the first man to the last cities to be destroyed by the final cataclysms of the dying world.

We believe that one day soon, before erosion has completed its destructive (and sometimes creative) work, an enlightened government will create a section of primohistory in its Ministry of Education or Fine Arts, whose task it will be to classify and preserve as primohistoric monuments the zoomorphic and anthromorphic material on these sites, and other numerous sites which will rapidly be discovered now that the public is informed and is aware of the phenomena.

Chapter Eighteen

The Machine for Filming the Past

That Superior Ancestors once existed is not doubted by those who are willing to face those naked truths which come from the depths of time.

From time to time, the clearing out of an attic, the opening of a tomb, the study of some heretical book, brings to light traces of inventions which we thought were the discovery of this age, but which turn out to have been known to the peoples of antiquity.

Machines of the future

Four or five thousand years ago the Egyptians knew how to hatch chicks by using artificial means, without the intervention of hens.

In May, 1972, an archaeologist searching through an old chest in the cellars of the Cairo Museum came across a sort of bird, made of sycamore, with a wing span of 18 centimeters, but with a tailfin instead of feathers. Its resemblance to the

American transport plane Hercules is so striking that Egyptologists believe it can only be a model of that plane, 2,400 years old.

The Danish writer Frede Melhedegard, a specialist in ancient civilizations, has just published a study on the Egyptian hierglyphics and frescos, in which he concludes that the temples of the Nile were built with the help of very advanced machines. He also believes that the Phoenicians were very well versed in certain applications of electronics and particularly in electroplating.

According to Melhedegard, many hieroglyphics are stylized representations of electronic machines, and he supports this theory by comparing them with engines and electronic circuits, with astounding results.

Following up his investigations, he has found parallels in the drawings and frescos of Mexico, Peru, and India.

The ground plan of some temples which he has recorded really do resemble mechanical devices to such an extent that one is bound to see them as designs for some strange engine.

Without necessarily accepting this, it is nevertheless possible to accept that the architects and draftsmen of antiquity, under the influence of drugs, guided by the chromosome-memory or by some form of preknowledge, just as Jules Verne somehow delved into the 20th century for the marvels described in his books.

The elixir of youth

The events, the discoveries, the knowledge of mechanics both of the past and future are probably part of our chromosome-memories, but the Initiate who is able to find his way among these incredible archives is usually unable to orientate his discoveries in relation to time.

Five thousand years ago, according to Dr. Edwin Yale of Emory University, the aboriginal women of Australia, when they wanted to avoid pregnancy, followed a diet based on the local sweet potatoes, called yams. Now, the research of another American, Dr. Russel Maker, shows that it is possible to use this potato to synthesize the chemical which serves as the basis of contraceptive pills.

It was while studying Inca medicine that Dr. José Froimovich of Santiago, Chile, discovered the wonder drug FGF 60, which restores old people to health, vigor, and clearness of mind. This youth drug is made up of sixty ingredients, and required more than thirty years of research. Dr. Froimovich is not an amateur. He is a member of twenty-four international scientific institutions and was on the list of candidates for the Nobel Prize for medicine in 1963.

His elixir was tried out in Latin America and Europe and gave spectacular results on men between seventy and one hundred years old.

Before treatment some of them could move about only by means of wheelchairs. Some months later Dr. Froimovich arranged for them to play a short football match, which was reported by the newspapers with the help of photographs.

They had all been rejuvenated by twenty years, their memory had returned, and some of them who had been impotent gave convincing proof that they could once more produce children.

There are other ways of reaching a good old age. It appears that the Earth's magnetic field, and magnetism in general, plays an important role, by influencing the fundamental processes of life.

Mice, for instance, when exposed to a strong magnetic field have their lives extended by 20 percent. Magnetism acts at the level of enzymes, that is to say, at the very initial stages in the process of cell formation.

Adolf Unmüssig, of Freiburg, has informed us that in Germany they have experimented with subjecting the stomach of a pregnant woman to atmospheric decompression, by encircling it with a device filled only with rarefied air. The experiment was carried out for one hour each day, and resulted in an unusually vigorous irrigation of the fetal tissue.

The child proved to be a veritable genius and was much reported by the press. At three years old he had an incredible memory, could talk fluently about world geography, recognized all the different makes of cars, etc.

It is thought that this system of decompression applied to the organic tissue of old people could be very beneficial, leading to the regeneration of cells and prolongation of life.

A 16th century two-stage rocket

The very respectable French journal *Archeologia* carried details in its forty-second issue of reports coming out of Russia which clearly demonstrated that our so-called barbaric ancestors were considerably less so than we have imagined.

An archaeological discovery has shown that 2,300 years ago, in the area of central Kazakhstan, a surgeon amputated the left foot of a young woman and replaced it with an artificial foot. This is shown beyond doubt by a skeleton found in a tomb.

The operation was successful, for the patient lived for several years with the artifical foot, which had been made from the bones of a ram.

There will, of course, always be "rationalists" who refuse to believe such reports, just as they would not believe in the heart operations carried out 100,000 years ago in Turkmenistan; facts vouched for by the Marmiadjaijan expedition and the Moscow Academy of Science. But every year such doubters become fewer in the face of undoubted facts.

In the same way the doubters had to retreat when we reminded the world that seventy-four years before the Montgolfier brothers, the Jesuit Gusmao demonstrated a heavier-than-air machine before the royal court of Portugal, and when we published the drawings of a three-stage rocket which flew in Sibiu in Rumania in 1529!

Men have short memories, and they have forgotten the remarkable inventions of the Italian architect Francesco di Giorgio, who in the 16th century anticipated many of the most modern weapons of our time.

Di Giorgio designed, in particular, a rocket-cannon which fired a projectile which was mounted on wheels for the beginning of its trajectory, later rising into the air through the effect of sheer speed. Even more elaborate was the two-stage rocket, in which the first stage fired the second by means of powder charges.

Since di Giorgio had not thought of building launching pads, the rocket was loaded on a chariot, which probably rolled down a carefully calculated gradient so that it could reach a speed where the problem of weight would be overcome.

A third invention anticipated our torpedos, and if never used—at least there is no surviving report that they were ever used—they were certainly equipped with all the techniques necessary for their proper functioning.

They consist of a floating machine equipped with three rotating cylinders to diminish resistance through the water. In front they had two steel points which were to penetrate the enemy ship. The torpedo proper, placed at the back, acted initially as a means of propulsion and then exploded at the right moment.

If our modern scientists had bothered to look through the records of our ancestors' activities they would have found the V-1 recorded 400 years before von Braun! The discovery might not have exactly advanced our civilization. Thank God their curiosity was not that strong!

The past does not die

If one had knowledge of the principal events of human history and could program them into a computer, the machine would certainly be able to predict the future with some accuracy.

If it were possible to register or imprison actual pictures of the past on ferrites or in some type of television receiver, that same computer would be able, once the "film" had started, to work out the rest of the scenario and show pictures of the future.

Theoretically, following the laws of cause and effect, a computer using as its only data a really well detailed historical event could reconstitute the whole of human history in its minus sense and in its plus sense.

Recovering the waves of the past and converting them into pictures and sound, has, until recently, smacked of science fiction. But an Italian scientist, the Benedictine monk Father Pellegrino Ernetti, has achieved this scientific miracle.

Father Ernetti is no visionary or medieval sorcerer, working with magic spells and materializations: He is regarded as a genuine scientist. About fifty, he is an established authority on prepolyphonic music dating from the remotest antiquity to about the beginning of the second millennium A.D. He is professor at the Venetian Benedetto Marcello Conservatory and the Fondation Cini, and director of the Italian Secretariat of Religious Instruction for Men.

He carried out his research in collaboration with twelve physicists, whom he declines to name, in a laboratory in Venice or Rome. It is known, however, that he began as early as 1956 to investigate the possibility of resuscitating the past and viewing it on some kind of television machine. In 1957 he made contact with the Portuguese Professor de Matos, who, through his own experiments, was to give the pattern of research a new direction.

Professor de Matos was also interested in reproducing the past by some process analagous to television, and based his theories on certain Aristotalian writings concerning the disintegration of sound, writings which probably owed much to the still older theories propounded by Pythagoras.

Father Ernetti's theory was, according to his own statements, based on accepting one of the principles of classic science, which predicated that light and sound waves are not lost after emission but are transformed and remain indefinitely present.

From this it follows that it should theoretically be possible to reconstitute them by restoring to them their original energy pattern. It must be stated that this theory is not accepted by conventional physicists, because Father Ernetti claims that these waves are "inscribed on the astral sphere," a concept which is unacceptable in their eyes.

According to Father Ernetti, however, sound waves, for instance, subdivide into harmonics, ultrasonics, hypersonics, etc., and follow the usual laws of the disintegration of matter down to the atomic level and beyond, through to the farthest reaches of the infra-atomic.

With the aid of "appropriate apparatus," which includes a cathode oscillograph using the deviations of a stream of electrons, it is possible to reverse the process of disintegration and reconstitute the sound wave.

This transformation is possible, it appears, because each

constituant of the wave has its own characteristics, a kind of psychic identity, which makes possible the accurate tracing of its source.

"My invention," says Father Ernetti, "has nothing to do with parapsychology or metapsychics. It is pure science!"

The same procedure is used for the reconstitution of light waves: this being in fact the basic procedure since the basis of everything created is light, just as in the Bible!

"Every human being," declares Father Ernetti, "traces from birth to death a double furrow of light and sound. This constitutes his individual identity mark. The same applies to an event, to music, to movement. The antennae used on our laboratory enable us to 'tune in' on these furrows: picture and sound."

Physicists will perhaps be unconvinced by such theories, but it is an undeniable fact that Father Ernetti can show "photographs" of the distant past, and play back voices which have been silent for millennia.

These results are obviously difficult for many to accept, the more so since the inventor refuses to explain the processes involved, or to allow people to enter his laboratory, claiming that the publication of his methods would bring a chain of unbelievable disasters down on our civilization.

These remarkable claims rest therefore on the word of Father Ernetti and the incredible proofs which he is able to present.

He has succeeded, for instance, in reconstituting in an archaic Latin, the *Thyestes*, Quintus Ennius' tragedy, which was presented in Rome in 169 B.C.

He claims to have reconstituted the exact pronunciation of ancient languages, and the original text of the *Ten Commandments*. He has apparently recorded less distant images, which are completely convincing, of Pope Pius XII and Benito Mussolini.

Father Ernetti has not revealed a tenth of his material, but it is known that he has filmed "the presumably atomic destruction of Sodom and Gomorrah."

A portrait of Christ

Undoubtedly the most sensational achievement of this machine for filming the past are the photographs of Jesus Christ on the cross during His agony.

One can picture Father Ernetti following on his magic screen the remarkable scenes of the Passion, from the carrying of the cross to the cry at the ninth hour: *Eli, Eli, lamma sabacthani,* (according to Matthew), or *Eloi, Eloi, lamma sabacthani* (according to Mark) or (it is presumed in Aramaic): *Father, into thy hands I commend my spirit* (according to Luke).

What really were the last words of Christ?

This mystery has been studied over many years by theologians who were unable to agree either on the words or the exact meaning of them. Now Father Ernetti, *if he is to be believed* has *heard* the last words of the crucified Christ!

Questioned on the subject, he refused to comment, claiming that it was not for him to make revelations of this importance.

The pictures obtained lack more in clarity than in character. Jesus appears to have a black beard, his hair is long and straight, his mustache forms a downward-curving crescent, and his mouth is partly open, as if in soundless agony.

The eyes, large, very beautiful, full of suffering, are raised to heaven, in no way sentimentally, but full of moving sincerity. An attractive person, arousing intense emotion, but . . . Christ?

The key to the mystery

In 1950 the English engineer George Delawar was experimenting along lines parallel to those of Father Ernetti, with the collaboration of a group of Oxford physicists. He claimed to have photographed the past and supported this claim with a somewhat unconvincing photograph of his marriage, which had taken place in Nottingham some twenty-three years earlier. Then his invention seems to have been forgotten.

We ourselves, in collaboration with the astronomer-engineer Emile Drouet, examined the perilous subject of time travel and our integration with waves of the past, not by delving into the cosmos, but by following a theory concerning the wavelength at source.

It seems that Father Ernetti was partially inspired by this theory, which as far as we were concerned was offered as a form of mental recreation.

Father Ernetti defends his secret with arguments which would certainly have validity if one were certain of the authenticity of his claims: "If I published the details of my apparatus," he claims, "people would make use of it to read minds, since thought itself is a form of wave."

This would be an invasion of privacy and conscience and a criminal aggression against the essential ego of man.

Nevertheless it is said that he intends to look into the mystery of the Man in the Iron Mask, to interview Saint John concerning the date of the end of the world, to discover the treasure of the Incas, to film the death of Joan of Arc, and to reconstitute some of the precious manuscripts of the Library of Alexandria.

His first undertaking, however, will be to consult the wise men of antiquity: Solon, Thales, Anaximander, Leucippus,

Phercydes, Pythagoras, Anaxagoras, Socrates. . . . a constellation of great minds.

Fortunately the inventor of this machine has no personal ambition, not even that of becoming Pope, which should fall to him by right!

"When will you lift the wraps from your machine?" asked a journalist for the *Domenica del Corriere*.

"When man has learned to act for the good of mankind," replied Father Ernetti. "Only then."

It looks as if we shall have to wait some time. . . .

PART IV

The Mythology of France

CHAPTER NINETEEN

WHEN THE GODS WERE MEN

Mythology is history transformed by time and the faulty transmission of events which happened at the dawn of civilization.

Generally speaking, mythology tells of the creation of the world by a God-Mother or by a Supreme Being, then the creation of the lesser gods, one of which gives the gifts of writing, agriculture, arts, and science.

Still speaking in general terms, mythology points to certain individual gods who appeared about 5,000 years ago and who were identified or had connections with the planet Venus; it speaks too of the fertilizing water and relates legends of heroes and flying animals.

To these themes may be added stories of floods, hybrid monsters, of wars between men and monsters, all this described in a context which includes the classic archetypes: the Initiate, a man or woman come from another world, carried by a flying object such as a snake, a ram, a dragon, a bull, a ship, or "*vimana,*" and also the Mater, the grotto, the fountain, the spiral, and the treasure.

All civilizations borrow to a greater or lesser extent from this common stock of myths.

The Christian countries

As it happens, the principal Western nations—France is the one which concerns us here—have been stripped of their legendary histories by the invasion of an alien religion, Christianity; by an alien god, Jesus; and dogmas which are sectarian, offensive, and sacriligious.

The most intensely Christian countries—France, Spain, and Italy—which should have the richest and most colorful mythologies, have none at all and view the distant past through the legends and traditions of Greece, Scandinavia, and Ireland.

In the state schools Greek mythology is taught: in the religious schools that of the Hebrews is favored.

To rebel, to claim that the French are Celts, and that the names of their ancient gods were Teutatès, Esus, Lugh, Cernunos, etc., is an abominable heresy, which in the old days led straight to the stake.

At Ephesus, Saint Paul burned a whole library of scientific books, in which, contrary to the word of God, it was written that the Earth is round and revolves round the sun.

In the 7th century ignorant Irish monks burned 2,000 precious runic manuscripts dealing with Celtic civilization.

The Christians in 490 burned the library at Alexandria, and in 789 Charlemagne abolished the pagan cult and ordered the destruction of all objects and documents connected with it.

Almost all human history has foundered amidst such incidents, more fatal than barbarian invasions or wars of conquest.

It was in this way that the Christianized peoples, French, Spanish, and Italian, were cut off from their ancestors and lost their national mythologies.

But the past is trying to re-emerge, and the time has come for the truth to step naked out of the depths, if only to provoke cries of horror from hypocrites of all kinds.

Although it has escaped the attention of historians, the legend of Melusine is today claiming its right of entry into the Celtic mythology.

More important, this legend proves to be the very essence of Celto-Gallic mythology, or to be more accurate, of the people who lived in France 5,000 years ago.

The dreaming time

The period when mythologies were created, those of the Great Ancestors and the Initiates who brought with them the secrets of science—this period is almost completely ignored by pre-historians.

The more loyal, more intelligent primitive peoples regard myth as sacred, the attitude which one still finds among the English, Germans, and Greeks.

To ignore or forget this ancestral tradition is to break with nature, with the vital essence of the past; it is the equivalent of cutting the umbilical cord which connects us to primordial life. Then, isolated in an alien universe, men lose their qualities, their character, and their sense of life.

Dreaming the past is a custom held in common by the American Indians and the natives of Australia and Polynesia. They believe, with good reason, that in dreaming they learn traditional truths in the most effective way. For these peoples the first period of their civilizations, of their unknown history, is called *the time of dreaming.*

There is little doubt that this system offers a firmer base for speculation than the aberrant guesses of many pre-historians.

Without knowing it, these primitives are making use of a fact accepted by some biologists: that children when still in their mother's womb may dream facts, events, and phenomena from the distant past, imprinted in their chromosome-memories.

"To know is to remember," said Plato. "To think," wrote Maeterlinck, "is not only to observe . . . it is also to seek out from one's personal depths one's sorrows, hopes, and dreams." To dream, we would add, is sometimes to regress to the thoughts of the *being-matter*, which we once were.

The genius, the innovator, the star

The Samaritans (the tribe of Judah and Benjamin) claimed that man was not created in the image of God, but in that of the angels, because the *Sephir Bereschit* used the word *Eloim*: the gods.

It is possible to interpret these angels from heaven as beings coming from another planet to create human life on the Earth.

The *angels* were the originators of polytheism; these "strangers to the Earth" have become the Initiates, the ancient heroes; gods, in fact.

We should emphasize that it was 2,400 years before our feeble writings that an Initiate, the Greek philosopher Euhemerus (4th century B.C.) wrote that the gods of mythology were simply human beings who had been deified by their admiring peoples.

This was the case at Athens and Rome for Sapho and Plato, for many emperors and exceptional men.

Even in our days this same phenomenon can apply to those who become stars, or to really eminent men.

The actress Greta Garbo, as well as many other stars, was

called "the divine"; a cult was established around the person of Rudolph Valentino; the beautiful nude dancer Colette Andris was literally adored by her admirers.

In certain temples in Dahomey, in 1950, divine honors were paid to photographs of Lydie Bastien, the French heroine.

From his death in 1970, General de Gaulle was treated as a divinity in the same region.

The racing cyclist Fausto Coppi even in his lifetime had followers who were nothing less than fanatical believers.

At the beginning of the third century of our era, the geometrist, astronomer, and doctor, Sextus Empiricus,* who was no believer of idle tales, claimed that Euhemerus had in his possession some authentic and very ancient documents, which, he wrote: "Stemmed from an era when those of superior strength and ability forced the less gifted to submit to their will, and then, aspiring still higher, claimed supernatural powers, so that men came to regard them as objects of adoration."

Euhemerus the atheist

The converted pagan Arnobe claimed that "Euhemerus set out to show that the ancient gods were really men: from this stemmed the extreme care with which he identified the place of birth and death of the gods, taking careful note of their graves, and considering them simply as men who had been particularly useful to the human race."

We know from Sextus Empiricus that Euhemerus was called "the Atheist" by those who believed that Venus, Jupiter, and

*Sextus Empiricus, a Greek, was born about the beginning of the 3rd century B.C. in Mytilene. He set out the theories of the skeptics in three works, the most important of which was called *Hypotyposes Pyrrhoniennes*.

Mercury were actual gods, and creators of the universe. (Right up to our own day the real deist, who knows that Jesus was not a god, is called an atheist. The age of superstition is not past!)

This "atheist" in fact believed that the real Creator was some sort of Superior Intelligence, cosmic and indefinable.

In the same way the Hebrews believe in Yahweh, which was the name of a mountain region, or a hero of Arabian antiquity, and the Christians believe in a god, a third of which was a sort of hero called Jesus, who lived in the first century.

Euhemerus explained his views in a book: *Sacred Inscriptions,* in which he made use of numerous epigraphs, etc., from temples and tombs and other monuments which he had visited in the course of his travels.

The floating islands

Diodorus of Sicily reports that Euhemerus, who was charged by Cassandro, king of Macedonia, with a mission to India and the Near East, discovered to the south of Arabia three islands called Panchaea, of which the main temple was covered with Egyptian hieroglyphics.

One of these islands produced enough incense to satisfy the demand from all the churches in the world.

Panchaea was the country where the phoenix was born and reborn (the country of Cousch, or Ethiopia, or south Arabia, according to Herodotus).

It has never been possible to identify these three islands, and it is thought that Euhemerus simply retold this tale, copying "the book of the Egyptian priests, who had misconstrued the mythical *Tri-Cuta* of the Hindus, believing that it treated of real things.*

*Tri-Cuta is a triple town belonging to Hindu legend. Cutha,

"In much the same way that Hecataeus placed the Hyperboreans in Briton, facing Gaul, the Egyptians seem to have found a place for the Floating Islands of the Orient, and to have added to it a dogma concerning a triple Elysium and other properties, derived from their own culture."

We are now much less certain that the Floating Islands of the Indian Ocean, rivals of the Fortunate Islands of the Atlantic, never existed, for we are aware of the submarine geological eruptions which can swallow whole islands.

Hesiod brings the legends down to earth

In the writings of Euhemerus, the god Uranus, the oldest of all, was a traveler, an Initiate, who became King of Crete. In order to bolster his prestige with his subjects he claimed that he and his wife were children of heaven and earth.

The kings of Egypt, Peru, and Mexico used the same means of acquiring divinity: They too claimed to be descended from divine kings who came from heaven, through the air; often from another planet, as with the "Venusians" Viracocha and Quetzalcoatl.†

Saturn, Jupiter, and Uranus were, in fact, most probably ancient kings or heroes.

These ideas were not new in Greece, where long before

---

or Cuta, or Kute, was a mysterious Asian town whose inhabitants, according to the Bible, worshiped the god Nergal, who represented the planet Mars.

We should regard the *Panchaea* of Euhemerus as having to do with the original land mass (if not identical with it) which contained according to some geologists all the continents, about 100 million years ago. This original, single continent is called *Pangea*: ("*Pan*": "everything" and "*gaea*": "the earth").

†In Peru, Manco Capac, the first Inca, claimed to be the son of the sun and moon.

Euhemerus, in the 6th century B.C., the historian and geographer Hecatee of Miletus claimed that Geryon of Erithye, who figures in the Twelve Labors of Hercules, was in reality a king of Epirus, and owner of huge flocks, and that Cerberus, the dog of Hades, the god of hell, was in reality a snake which lived in a cave in Laconia, where the ancients believed the entrance to the infernal kingdom to be.

Even earlier, Hesiod, in the 8th century B.C., was writing that Geryon was simply a man of unusual power, or perhaps a powerful king.

The Greek historian Ephore, in 400 B.C., regarded the giant Titye** as simply some sort of brigand, and the serpent Python as being in fact a particularly unpleasant character called Python or Dracon, who killed the hero Apollo.

It so happens that the Athenian legislator Dracon (c. 624 B.C.) was a reformer of integrity and genius, but of absolutely inflexible severity, who punished all infringements of the law with death. (Hence the term "Draconian laws.")

According to Strabo this Titye was the tyrant of Panope or Phocide.

Herodotus, basing his narrative on the revelations of Egyptian priests, tells the strange story of the origin of the oracles at Libya and Dodona.

The oracles of Dodona and Epirus were the most ancient in Greece, and the only ones known to the Pelasges, the ancestors of the Greeks.

Their traditions state that two black doves from Egypt

**Titye or Tityos, son of Gaea, had raped Latone, and was killed by arrows shot by Apollo and Diana. Then he was thrown into Hell where two vultures picked at his liver through all eternity.

stopped, one at Dodona and the other at Libya, where they ordered the establishment of a cult of Jupiter.

Herodotus, like Euhemerus, removed the mythical element from this legend and concluded, after careful investigation, that it in fact related to two priestesses from Thebes, Egypt, who had been sold as slaves to Epirus and Libya, and who set about founding a religion with ceremonies based on those of their native land.

Homer concluded that these creatures, also known as Pythons, were in fact men: Later, in the 16th century B.C., Strabo and Scalinger came to the same conclusion.

In spite of all this, the most probable explanation is that the priestess of Dodona was a Druidess from Gaul, as this would explain the use of the name "dove," remembered by tradition. The ancient pythons of the gods were called *pelaiades*, which also means doves.

The oaks of Dodona

The god's temple was deep in a forest, which was why Homer said that the oaks of Dodona acted as oracles.

It is possible that the priestesses claimed the noise of the wind in the leaves to be the voice of Jupiter, but Strabo denounced this superstition.

A more probable explanation is as follows: Two pillars had been erected in the temple, very close together. On one stood a copper caldron; on the other was a statuette of a child holding in its hand a whip with very flexible bronze lashes.

When the wind blew, the lashes struck the caldron, which gave out a very eerie sound, calculated to impress the credulous. In addition, the temple, instead of having walls, was surrounded by bronze caldrons, standing on tripods, and carefully placed so that they touched each other. If one caldron was struck, the vibrations carried from it to another, giving a mysterious wave of sound, well designed to resemble the somber voice of a god.

Those who came to consult the oracle were thus filled with a religious terror which helped to make them particularly amenable to suggestion.

Much the same effects—the tolling of bells, the colored windowglass, the smell of incense, the theatrical disposition of the altar, lit by huge candles, the priest in sumptuous clothes—precondition the Christians of our day, who feel God to be particularly close to them in such a dwelling, consecrated in His name.

False gods

Superstitious, credulous people are obviously more easily impressed by crude stage effects than by the miracle of a flowering rose, the birth of a child, or a germinating seed.

All religions have made use of apparently mysterious forces which strike the imagination and the subconscious of the common man, and convince him of the authenticity of their gods.

In all ages attempts have been made to show the true nature of mythology and to fight superstition.

The marvelous, the fantastic temples of Mexico, India, or Egypt, whose religions once dominated large parts of the globe, were, for the Initiate and men of commonsense, nothing more than the decayed shadow of a once valid truth, conjured up by the ignorant priests of false gods.

In the same way, we have to accept that our thousands of churches and cathedrals, our thousands of priests and crowned archbishops, our mitred Popes with their golden thrones, are simply manifestations of a religion, which while more sophisticated than those of old, is nonetheless subject to error and falsification.

The legend of Montmartre

One of the least-known and most typical instances of the corruption of words and facts due to the Christianization of France is the legend of Montmarte, the sacred hill in Paris, famous throughout the world under its false name, Montmarte.

Etymologists confess to not knowing the origin of the word, and suggest *mons Mercurii* (Hill of Mercury) or *mons Martis* (Hill of Mars), hill of martyrs, in memory of Saint Denis.

The latter suggestion doesn't bare examination, of course: mont Marte as a name being in use well before Saint Denis (272 A.D.). Still, it tends to be more generally accepted than the others.

It has also been suggested that this Parisian hill is connected with the marten, a carnivore rarely found in France, and which prefers woods and forests rich in birds and small mammals. (It seems possible that there is some connection between the bloodthirsty marten and the *martes* of pre-Celtic mythology.)

The true origin is much more remarkable and fascinating than those suggested by the so-called experts.

The *martes* of pre-Celtic mythology shared something of the attributes of Amazons, or bacchantes—some say they were priestesses of even demons—who haunted the countryside.

They were said to be big, beautiful women, with thick brown tresses, and went naked, their breasts carried proudly, "like shields of love."

Later peoples, on the other hand, described them as ugly, with long, slack, drooping breasts.

According to the writings of S. de Beaufort, the peasants

went in terror ot the *martes*, who chased them, their breasts thrust back over their shoulders, calling, "Suck on this, man of the soil!"

The descriptions of these women and the fact that they lived near the ancient dolmens, which were known by the same name, inclines one to assume that the *martes* were priestesses who carried out bloody and erotic sacrifices, of which the docile peasants were no doubt often the victims.

In Poitou-Charentes, where the old traditions are still very much alive, the *martes* were thought to be at one and the same time, Bachantes, Dryads, and skillful sorcerers, with the gift of healing wounds and curing illness.

In fact, they seem to have been warrior priestesses, active sometimes in the woods, sometimes among the dolmens or menhirs, which were usually built on the summits of hills. In addition, on appropriate sacred dates, they gathered medicinal herbs, whose properties they well understood, and rendered to the telluric currents, the forces of nature and the phallic menhirs, a form of worship as shameless as that rendered by the Armenians and Lydians to Anaitis.

The *martes*, who were expert in the arts of love, are believed by some to be the originators of the powers attributed to the fertility stones and holed menhirs.

At night, in some sort of trance brought on by the use of hallucinating and no doubt aphrodisiac drugs, which they were expert in preparing, they searched the countryside for some male capable of satisfying their devouring appetites.

It would seem that to associate with them at such times was not without its dangers, since they have left a legend of being cruel and insatiable Bacchantes.

To the little that we know of them legend adds reports of their ability to change into terrifying animals, or take their terrible forms.

It appears too that they may have forced their victims to drink the aphrodisiac mixtures that they knew so well how to prepare.

Albert Goursaud sees them as "demon-females" of the lower order, which Germanic mythology calls *Mahr*, of which the best-known manifestation is the nightmare (German *Nachtmahr*).

He sees a connection between them and the *Chaucho-vieilho* of Limousin, the very name of which indicates creatures which would enter by night into the bedroom of a sleeping person, "and stretch themselves out so as to cover him completely and suffocate him to the point where he became defenseless."

Predestination of places

This is the true story of how the hill situated to the north of Lutece received its name Mont des Martes, then Montmarte. How strange and yet inevitable is the predestination of certain places: The Parisian Montmartre has always been the center of illicit pleasures and doubtful activities.

It is at Montmarte that *la vie galante* has its domain, where the prostitutes flock, where nightclubs and striptease joints prosper, and where the drug-pushers and peddlers of erotic books and pictures are to be found.

This irreversible geological predestination has lasted since the time of the pre-Celtic *martes*, and is as inescapable as that which planted commerce in the Marais, and intellectual life in the Latin Quarter of Paris.

In the same way the Subure district of Rome, on the slope of the Esquilin, has been the haunt since time immemorial of barbers, actors, athletes, gladiators, and courtesans.

The nuns of the order of Saint Benoit, who lived in Montmartre at the abbey founded in the 12th century, had at first a reputation, according to the *Dictionnaire Universel*, "of the utmost sanctity, but wealth gradually led to a weakening of their moral fibre, and eventually even the repressions of the Parisian archbishops could not control their excesses."

During the Revolution Montmarte was named Montmarat, in honor of that bloodthirsty "friend of the people," Marat.

In exactly the same way as Montmartre, Subure was the district of ancient Rome, where popular wit, and eloquent, colorful slang was to be found.

It was at Subure, as at Montmartre, that vice flourished, the *lupanaria*, the displays of stolen goods, and where the gangsters of the period could always find shelter.

The Empress Messalina used to go to Subure to wear out her amorous appetites with the gladiators and other likely lads. In our day, in much the same way, suburban ladies go to Montmartre for the low company and to drink beverages fully as aphrodisiacal as those concocted by the *martes*.

The Americans call Pigalle "pig alley," and even while admiring its charming young ladies, feel some of the apprehension which the peasants of old felt for the insatiable *martes* of Limousin and Poitou-Charentes.

The divine falcon and Ouraios

The falcon of Egypt—there were in fact several—was the winged symbol of the sky, the stars, and the most royal of gods. It is a member of the most ancient of pantheons, dating back to the Thinite dynasty of Menes, 6,000 years ago, and is so important that it was carved on every pediment of the temple, immediately under the most important symbol, the sacred uraeus.

It is interesting to note that this uraeus, or *ouraios*, was a representation of the goddess Mertseger, who was a serpent, or if one prefers, a snake-woman, like Messalina.

Egyptologists, or those claiming to be such, are very reticent, not to say completely silent, when it comes to discussing the significance of the falcon and the winged serpent: "They protect the king," they say, somewhat unconvincingly.

It is quite obvious that neither the falcon (it is in fact a kite) or the winged serpent could offer protection to anyone. Even if the sacred serpent was indeed the first-born among animals: the iron snake, the issue of the primordial lotus!

Since the first Egyptian kings were "divine," it follows that the winged symbols connected with them in their role of initiators must have had to do both with aerial space and with knowledge.

Our own era, and the events which dominate the 20th century, can give us the probable explanation of this allegorical mystery of this mythological fable: Initiators, traveling in flying machines of some sort, planted the civilization of the Nile in the days following the Flood, about 10,000 years ago.

Did these Strangers come from another planet? It would appear so, when one thinks of the Egyptians' tremendous fascination with the star Sothis (Sirius) and with the sacred Uraeus.

So this governs the course of the Nile, the cultivation of rice and maize. In evoking Uraeus we are not thinking of the planet Venus, which appeared in our skies at a period which we put at 5,000 years ago: the Uraeus is a much older symbol than the Venusian bull, and seems to coincide with the arrival of the first Initiators, 10,000 years ago.

The Egyptian goddess of Venus is Athor, calles Isis—star of the Sea, the Lady of Byblos of the Phoenicians and the symbolic wife of the bull Mnevis (the god El or Baal). Her emblem, horns, is also that of the planet Venus, and spread throughout the entire world about 5,000 years ago, which we take to indicate that there was a new period of influence, which we attribute to the arrival on earth of a second group of Initiators. Hathor is the goddess of love, or of beauty, and yet she is an *orejone*, with large ears and a triangular face, like the Orejana of the Incas. The linguist Lablouski connects Athor with the Coptic Edjorh or Adjorh, which means night, and concludes from this that she was the Dark Venus or Aphrodite Scotia of the ancients.

Mythology and convergence

Marthe de Chambrun Ruspoli has written a remarkable book, stripping Egyptian mythology of its occult accretions. Remarkable not only for its arguments, but for the inclusion of many extracts from manuscripts quite unknown to the public at large.

The introduction is particularly enthralling. The author—curiously enough without reference to Atlantis—gives a résumé of the secret history of the West, with particular reference to a dramatic event said to have taken place "on a large island, surrounded by banks of reeds, at the very heart of the Vast Green Sea."

The victim (or hero) of the story was Asar, called Osiris by the Egyptians, who was crucified and dismembered by his brother, Set (or Typhon).

It is doubtful if timorous spirits and conventional religious believers will ever be prepared to see beyond the literal interpretation of mythological fables, but the fact remains that Madame de Ruspoli's *Epervier Divin* (Divine Hawk) is an Initiate document, in the true sense of the word.

There is much mention of *Amenti* (the West, the country of dead ancestors) which is not, as conventional Egyptologists believe, the west of ancient Egypt itself, Libya, but a region much farther to the west: the country of Asar and the Aryan peoples of the Asia of antiquity, in other words, Central Europe.*

Not unnaturally we find ourselves at this point drawn towards Thulis, Thule, Tula, or Tulan-Zuiva (where the Mayas believed their gods to reside) since Egyptian mythology is directly and fundamentally related to those of the Celts and Mayas.

Mythology cannot be really understood unless one is familiar with the underlying principles and the archetypes of all mythology.

This *Knowledge* is a strange phenomenon, requiring the ability to synthesize, working on the basis of culture, experience, commonsense, honesty, careful research, and sheer inspiration.

As far as Egypt is concerned, and her marvelous myths, a synthesis can be achieved by studying the work of de Chambrun Ruspoli, Marcelle Weissen-Szumlanska (a most erudite Initiate) and, above all, the work of Eugene Beauvois, who, more than any other historian, has succeeded in resuscitating the ancient past of the West in books which are, unfortunately,

*It should be remembered that a regrettable inversion of names completely falsified some aspects of the history of the West. Originally, Asia was the heartland of Europe: The Caucasus, Transcaucasia, the Asov Sea, Astrakhan, etc. (the country of the most beautiful among white women). By a strange reversal of terminology the continent of the white races has become that of the yellow races! Asia derives from the Phoenician "Asir," which comes in turn from the Scandinavian "*Ase*": god.

nowadays practically impossible to find.

We mention these authors in particular, because we believe that they are the only ones to have found the true way through the labyrinth of mythology and history.

Osiris, god of the recent past

And yet, de Chambrun Ruspoli is writing of a very late mythology. Osiris and Isis came onto the scene no more than 4,000 years ago, at a time when the early Truths were already faded.

Egyptian civilization dates back at least 8,000 years, and anyone who wants to penetrate its mystery must sweep Osiris and Isis out of his mind along with King Farouk and President Nasser.

On the other hand, the myth is rich in significance once cleaned of mystification and seen as the transmission of Initiatic traditions, which are the very backbone and essence of history.

There is no mention of Osiris or Isis in Egyptian prehistory, either at the time of the semi-divine kings of Menes or at the time of the Ancient Abydos.

"Osiris was a very late comer to Abydos," writes Jean Yoyotte, "identified with the local god, Khentamentiou, under the Fifth dynasty, about the year 2,300 B.C. But his followers grew steadily in numbers until from about the 2nd millenium his personality obliterated forever the memory of his obscure predecessor."

Jesus was an Egyptian god

L'Epervier Divin sheds much light on the borrowings made by the Bible and Gospels from this late arrival among the gods. Particularly from the story of the Flood, described in the texts found at the pyramids of Saqqare (Third Dynasty) and in relation to the Garden of Eden, the Chosen Land of Amente, and the tree of life of King Peipi (Sixth Dynasty—2280 B.C.)

The Papyrus of Ani and Hunefer call Osiris "The Lord of Justice (Maat), Holy Lord," and speak of the human serpent, Sata, Son of Darkness, of the Passion of Osiris, after a supper during which "the King distributed the bread and meat consecrated in the name of the Lord of Divine Sustenance. This Lord then passed his cup to each in turn.

"Osiris knew that his hour had come and that he had lived out his life. . . . Osiris is afraid. Osiris is terrified of walking in the shadows. . . . Those who wish to undo me and harm me are the sons of darkness, he says.

"Father of Osiris! Ha Tum in the shadows! Take Osiris to your side."

Then, when the Enemy comes to catch the Egyptian Messiah, Osiris says, "I am your Lord. Come join my ranks. I am the son of your Lord, and you are part of me through my divine Father who made you. I am the Lord of Life."

This was exactly what Jesus, son of God the Father was to say 2,300 years later!

The same common source provides the theme of the Bhagavod-Gita, given to the world more than two thousand years ago by a god-made man: Krishna.

"Krishna came on Earth to wipe away the sins of the Age of Kali (Age of Iron), to take up the burden of the sins which crush humanity. His mission once accomplished, he returned to heaven, thus showing the way to his followers."

The crucifixion of Osiris

Madame de Ruspoli's work has the merit of having extracted

from the Egyptian manuscripts and papyrus the essential outlines which were to serve, 2,000 years later, as the prototype for Operation Jesus.

- *Papyrus of Hunefer*, Chapter 52: "Let not my flesh and my limbs be torn by knives! Let me not be scourged!"(Jesus was scourged.)
- *Papyrus of Nu:* "O fortify me against the murderers of my Holy Father! None shall drag me by the arms! None shall seize me violently by the hands!" (Jesus was to implore his Father for help, and to be treated in this way.)
- *Papyrus of Any*, p. 32: "The hands of Osiris (Ani) are the hands of Ba-neb-Tatu." (The Ram, the Lord of the Gallows: Jesus is the Pascal Lamb.)

And exactly as was to happen to Jesus, Osiris was crucified on a gallows made from the trunk of a sycamore onto which a beam had been fixed horizontally. The cross of Osiris was called *tat*.

- *Papyrus of Paris*, Chapter 180: "Oh, do not chain me to your gallows of death! Do not drag me to the place where my enemies make sacrifice!"
- *Papyrus of Kerasher,* Chapters 4-9: "Let not my arms be garrotted! Let not my hands be bound!"
- *Man: Pyramid of Peip 2*: "Hommage to you, O Sycamore, mighty gallows, companion of god. Thy chest touches the shoulder of Osiris."

His hands and feet are tied to the tree. *Man of Pyramids*: "I am he who tied his feet and hands and caused his death."

- *Papyrus of Any*: "I am he who came and took away that offensive thing which was on Osiris (the crown of Ureret). I put the crown of *Atef* (crown of his Father?) in place of the crown of Ureret. I relieved the suffering of Osiris. I held firm his foot support."

• *Text of the Pyramids*, line 954: "May Pepi come to you, Osiris! May he wipe your face!" (repeated four times)

• *Papyrus of Amenhotep*, Chapter 130: "My heart! My Mother! My heart! My Mother!"

It is difficult indeed to avoid comparing the crucifixion of Osiris with that of Jesus and to claim the first as model for the second.

Jesus and the Myths

Juris Baltrusaitis, in his essay on the legend of a myth, *In Search of Isis,* underlines that the Celts and the Egyptians confused Isis with Jesus.

"The words of Isis and Jesus were essentially the same in their origin, and each talked of the little gods *born in the vessel*, in other words the natural children of the gods of Egypt."

The author also draws attention to the resemblance between "Is-is," "Es-es," "Esos," "Hesus" and "Jesus."

Thus, at all levels it is possible to establish obvious connections between the different mythologies, a fact always known to the Initiates.

Osiris (papyrus of Any) was symbolized by the sacrificial ram, just as Jesus was symbolized by the lamb!

Osiris did not walk upon the waters, but in death he sailed in his coffin-ship. On the other hand the Christians attributed this miracle to Jesus, drawing inspiration from the Vedic cosmogony of the Hindus, in which *Nara*, the divine spirit, was called Narayana: He who moves on the water.

One finds then, in the myth of Jesus, the fundamentals of more ancient traditions, which is why we repeat that none of the myths can be properly studied without a profound knowledge of all of them.

Vishnu, Siva, Zoroaster, Osiris, Marduk, Viracocha, Quetzalcoatl, Jesus, etc., were gods for the people of antiquity, it and would have been pointless—and considered sacrilege—to try in those days to deny their divinity or to compare them with other symbols and myths.

The Emperor Julian

This was the view of a great, misunderstood philosopher, the Roman Emperor who reined from 361 to 363 of our era: Julian. History has never known a ruler more knowledgeable, humble, more full of integrity,

Raised in the Christian religion, he later espoused the cult of Mithras, absurd fancies of the Bible, for which he was given the name Apostat.

An emperor without fear, irreproachable, leading the life of an ascetic and wise man, he tried during his short reign to reestablish a pagan cult based on a philosophy borrowed from Pythagoras and Plato.

His god was the universe, symbolized by a mystic triple sun. The first was the Essence, the first cause, pre-existing all others: the second, born of the first, was reason, the word, the intelligent world: the third was the visible sun, sharing the intelligence of the first and receiving its beneficial influence. He wrote:

> The Greeks, I Admit, invented incredible, monstrous fables about the gods. They claimed that Saturn had swallowed his own children then vomited them out.
>
> There are incestuous marriages. Jupiter slept with his mother and had children by her. He married his daughter, having first slept with her, then he gave her to another. . . . These are the fables given to us by the Greeks.
>
> In the Judaic doctrine the Serpent speaks with Eve! What

> language did he use? That of man? In what are these fables different from those of the Greeks? The Lord of the Hebrews says: "Let us build a tower, the top of which shall reach unto heaven!" (The tower of Babel) You are ready to believe that, but are not prepared to believe what Homer says of the Aloades, who decided to put three mountains, one on top of the other, in order to climb up into heaven. As far as I am concerned the one story is just as much a fable as the other.

Julian goes on to explain that mythology must not be taken in its literal sense:

> Nevertheless here are cases when the allegorical form can be used with a practical end in view, in order that men may have no need of strange explanations, but instead, learning from the fable itself, may penetrate its hidden meaning as they wish, guided by the gods, and pursue their research with vigor.

Chapter Twenty

When Men Dream of Venus

The phrase "French Mythology" is incorrect, but we will not rectify it simply in order to impress the reader. But our essay is unquestionably more about Gallic or Celtic mythology. There are no written documents to help us with this task. The Celts never really achieved a writing as such and the Gauls only left traditions and mysterious monuments.

Nevertheless, from their almost unknown civilization certain legends have been handed down to us which we now have to interpret from certain signs, taking into account the wear and tear of centuries, the nature of the "dreams" and the images of desire which inspired them.

Return to the source of knowledge

Professor André Bourguenec points out that the etymology of the word *rêve* (dream) is almost unknown, and is in a way extraordinary. In Old French, *resver*, "to dream," not only described a phenomenon of ideas and pictures, but was also physical and material. The phrase "*resveur de nuit*" (night dreamers) was applied to vagabonds or men of doubtful morals, who ran about the countryside or towns at night. From there, figuratively, we have moved on to the spiritual meaning, in the sense of a disturbed mind which we still find now in the expression "*vous rêvez*"—"you are raving!"

Other possible etymologies: from the old word *desver* (Latin *deviare*) to stray; or from the Latin *repuerare*, to revert to childhood; or from the Greek *rembein*, to turn, to wander, to look for adventure; or from the Welsh *rabhde*, to talk nonsense.

Bouguenec suggests an explanation which can only be applied to the French language, but which has a curious empathy with the mysterious and unknown nature of this phenomenon. "*Rêver*," to dream, is a palindrome—a word that can be read backward or forward—and he implies that if dreams have no direction it is because they conjugate the time present, past, and future. In the center of the word is "Eve:" R-EVE-R, symbolizing the return to Eve, to the Source, to the Fountain of See (of knowledge).

The dream the word "slumber" (*somme*) suggests (*memos*) memory, remembrance. Dreamers, poets, and thinkers would therefore be "*sommites*," slumberers of knowledge, makers of slumbers of every kind, as "remember" or "memorize" means: to replace (*membres*) limbs, reconstitute. This is the meaning that natives of Australia gave to dreams: the ability to reconstitute and rediscover truths of the past.

The Celts, says Jean Markale, have always excelled in legends . . . which are of course neither true nor false, real or unreal. But when a legend exists there is behind it, of necessity, a complex cultural truth.

"Mythology is a later interpretation of visions seen by primeval man," said Rudolf Steiner. The legends of France, without claiming to revise Genesis, enlighten us on how our ancestors' minds worked, ancestors who "dreamed up" both their wonderful past and the images of their desire.

"They take inspiration from a rich and spectacular setting, from the exploits of outstanding heroes, from great deeds, where dreams, magic, the impossible, voyage into time and into the Other World themselves to transform reality, with an underlying preoccupation with expressing that which is at the very core of the Celtic soul: self-sacrifice, service, and chivalry. And always in the background, the yearning for a wonderful land, outside our world, a land where miracles come true."*

Seen from this angle, if the ancient French have "dreamed up" the legend of Melusine, it is because her story was engraved in the chromosomes of their memory and marked with the seal of a wonderful reality.

*We have often researched into this other world of the Celts. It refers to the "country of small hills" or hillocks situated in North America and Mexico, where lived the Tuatha De Nanann.

This American paradise, which one could reach by crossing the dense fogs around the Fortunate Islands, was the Amenti of the Egyptians, the Tir Nan Og (land of youth) of the Irish, the Sikhavati or paradise of Amitabba of the Hindus, the paradise of Cutanapishtim which Gilgamesh the Assyro-Babylonian wished to find; the western paradise of Amourrou of the Phoenicians . . . and, finally, the country of the chosen few! The town of Ys, submerged in the bay of Douarnenez, and the Island of Avalon, buried in English Somerset, have perhaps reappeared from the Other World of the Celts which we ourselves definitely identify with ancient Atlanta, or country of the Superior Ancestors killed in the Universal Flood. The Atlantis flood gave rise to the legend of the submerged towns and continents.

A story of extraterrestrial beings

The old Poitou legend finds its roots in the time of the Celts and of French national gods.

Lugh, "the prodigious child," hero of Tuatha De Danann,* presided over the birth of French and European towns which bear his name: Lusignem (Lusignan), Loudun, Lyon, Lugano, Lund, etc. He was the son of the Mother Goddess of the Celts: Danu, Donu, or Don (who gave her name to the rivers Danube and Don) and we must also certainly identify him with the gods of civilization, Gwydion, Ogmios, and Odin, whose mysterious origins lead us to believe that they came from a land alien to the planet Earth. Although they were not the Gods of Creation, they acted like biologists who had played at trying to make human beings from vegetable matter. A sort of scientific experiment!

Lugh—Apollo of the Welsh and Irish—is the son of Arianrod, the only daughter of the Mother Goddess, and it is interesting to note that "Arianrod" means "silver wheel" or, according to some people, "Aryan wheel." A wheel which conjures up the wheel of Ezekiel and flying machines in the shape of a disk, or the wheel which, according to Hindu mythology, brought our first ancestors from Heaven to Earth by "way of Aryaman."

*Tuatha De Danann: Celtic tribe which came from a "country of hills situated beyond the country of mists and of the large Ocean River" and settled in Ireland about 5,000 years ago.

Lugh, etymologically, could mean light (*lux*) or be taken from the Greek word *logos*: word, speech. He was the Initiator who brought light into the world with his words, the alchemist who could operate a real transmutation, that of barbaric facts into golden knowledge, with the magic of his words.

The word of the Initiated is gold.

Without believing in the present theory of flying saucers, we must acknowledge that extraterrestrial machines of a similar shape and appearance, have, in antiquity, in every country, had an important role, one might even say a pre-eminent role, as these strange machines are always linked with the arrival of an Initiator or with the birth of a far more advanced civilization.

The dark and stormy cloud of te flying god

''God,'' who received Moses on Mount Sinai to tell him that the Hebrews would be the Chosen People, said to him (Exodus 19, Verse 9): ''Lo, I come unto thee in a thick cloud.''

At first they witnessed thunder and lightning, a very thick dark cloud covered the mountain, the trumpet sounded loudly, and the people in the camp were seized with fright.

In Exodus 23, Verse 11, God spoke to Moses face to face as a man accustomed to speaking to a friend. When Moses descended from Mount Sinai (Exodus 24, Verse 29), ''the skin of his face shone when he talked with him'' so that seeing this irradiating being the Hebrews are scared to approach him. Then Moses puts a veil over his face, either to protect it or to protect those who approach him.

According to Bible exegetes of today, this account, which is not very clear, seems to describe sulphur or some kind of irradiation, and God's dark cloud seems to throb like a jet-propelled aircraft. For in the 20th century we no longer believe in a God chatting face to face with a human being and coming down from Heaven in a big black cloud. Faced with this restricted image, our more sophisticated minds react either by denying that this phenomenon ever happened, or by substituting a cosmonaut for God; a space rocket for his dark and throbbing cloud. And, Welsh and Irish mythology state:''We know of

Lugh, that the irradiation from his face was such that no mortal could bear to look at it."

The similarity between the God Yahweh-Jehovah, Initiator of the Hebrews, and Lugh, Initiator of the Celts, is accentuated by the fact that one brings a law engraved on stone tablets, and the other the understanding of oghamic writing. Both their mysterious adventures are related to a celestial phenomenon, either because they come from outer space, or because they have received instructions or have been sent on a mission by Masters, strangers to our planet.

The truth has a smell of sulphur

History has never dared approach this problem, has never explained why Incas, Mexicans, Phoenicians, and Assyro-Babylonians had Gods who represented Venus or who were from Venus. Without a doubt it is beyond historians to explain this, and they are afraid, as they might throw a light on the past altogether too sulphurous and bright for their orthodox taste.

To put it more clearly, History as we know it is always corrupted for the benefit of religions, for above all it is important for people to be ignorant that the true gods, the true Initiators, were not an uncertain Yahweh, a Moses, or a Jesus, but superior men whom we have good reason to suppose came from another planet. And this planet, Venus, is particularly abhorred by Hebrews and Christians. It is forbidden to name God . . . particularly if it is the right one!

The luminous ones and Venus

The history of civilization has been falsified by flagrant errors, and historians, conditioned, blinded, and fascinated by these lies, have embarked, sometimes in good faith, on many a lost cause.

Such was for many the mirage of Eldorado and the belief in Jupiter, Osiris, and Jesus, as real gods, almighty creators of heaven and Earth. The dates on your calendar, the myth of the symbols of the French Revolution: Liberty, Equality, Fraternity (!), of the resurrection of the body, etc., all belong to the same phenomenon of mass mental aberration.

Another enormous error—if one can call it that—was to call "Asia" a continent which was not at all Asiatic, and to name "Europe" a continent which was in fact Asia! But the wine is drawn, we must drink it!

Also, Apollo was made to be the Sun God, whereas he in fact symbolizes the bright star: Venus. No one knows the etymology of "Apollo" and "historians" cannot find an answer to explain its origin, but its appearance in the solar system is only recent and dubious. According to Greek tradition—the richest, the most muddled, and the most false—the godly hero would be the son of Latone, Goddess of Night, of the Night Sky; and yet he impersonates the image of light. Not the sun, as is too often said, but "something shiny."

Tradition tells us that Apollo, each year at the end of autumn, departed over the hills of Riphee, kingdom of the impetuous Boreas, toward the mysterious country of the Hyperboreans. There, where the sky is always bright, lived in complete contentment a race of virtuous men, dedicated to the cult of Apollo. His mother, Latone, or Leto, was also a native of the Valley of "Tempe" in Hyperborea.

These traditions are not just a more or less believable version, but the very essence of the traditions of all races of the world as we know it, who usually called Apollo "the Hyperborean," or "the Nordic."

So how could anyone ever have identified this god with the Sun (Helios) when he really symbolizes the opposite, retiring in winter not to the South but to the North, "Where it does not shine in winter?"* So it is really senseless to talk of "Hyperborean Sun." Who then is Apollo?

His name, we have said, evokes an image of light, "from which he gets the names of Phoibos, the Brilliant; of Xanthos, the Fair; of Chrysocomes, with the golden hair. In fact he closely resembles—if he is not identical with—Belisama (flamelike), Venus "with the burning mane"! Could he not be the Star, so hated by the Hebrews?

On the Danube he was called Belenus, the Splendid; and in Great Britain, Balan, Balin, Belinus. He was the Belin of the Gauls, probably the Granus, too; the Bala (Bala Rama) of the Hindus; and the Osiris of the Egyptians.

Henri Dontenville remarks: "Apollo's identity is to be found at Aquilee in the province of Venice, where according to the "Corpsus de Mommsen" five different inscriptions can be found bearing the name Apollini Beleno. . . ." We can therefore consider this as a fact: Apollo was Belenos, husband, father, brother, or companion of Belisama, the "flamelike" Initiator from Venus. And this Brilliant one, this golden-haired being, is the Baal of the Phoenicians, the Bel of the Assyro-Babylonians, and the "Great Star" or "Shining Star" of the American Indians.

In brief, and to put this idea in concrete form, Apollo represented the planet Venus, which is in perfect keeping with

*We refer to the apparent movements of the sun, which in reality stays almost exactly in the center of our system. Because the earth is tilted, the North Pole is plunged in darkness in winter over a period of six months. During this time, the South Pole enjoys six months of sun (the midnight sun).

the theme of other mythologies. With Apollo as the Sun, Western mythology is nothing but contradictions and errors. With Apollo as Venus everything explains itself, fits, and becomes logical.

Handsome as a god

After considerable study one realizes that although gods seem to be as numerous as stars in the sky, in fact a great many names often covered the identity of a single god.

"Researching the story of Gargantua, in 1868," writes Dontenville, "Gaidoz had the good fortune to find in the Welsh chronicles one essential piece of information: the Gurgunt with the terrifying beard mentioned by Geoffrey of Monmouth is the son of Belen, Belinas, that is to say the same name as the Belenos of the Celts, equivalent to the Apollo of the Greeks. After these events, Belinus Gurgian (the Giant) was succeeded by his son (writes Geoffrey and Giraud de Barry) known also as the Cambrian or the Welsh: Gurguntius, *filius nobilis illius Beleni.*"

The same author adds that Belisama—the one who resembles Belen—"is recognisable beyond doubt first at St. Lizier (Ariège), where she is identified as Minerva, and secondly by the ancient inhabitants of Vocones, at Vaisons, and by Ptolemy when he speaks of Great Britain."

Arbois of Jubainville translated Belen, Belinus, as "brilliant," "resplendent," and while we are on this subject we note that "*Belen*," "*Belin*" signifies in Old French and colloquial French "little beauty, nice-looking little man or little woman," just as "*bellot*," "*bellotte*" mean: "beautiful," "sweet."

We do not know the etymology of *beau* (beautiful) which the English have taken from us: "beau," "beauteous," "beautifier," "beautiful," "beauty," etc. but perhaps by assimilation of ideas, just as one says of a nice person: she's a *chou* (cabbage), she's a *coeur* (heart) this word, *beau*, may have described a person, a thing, or a god very pleasing to look at. And we think of the beautiful Apollo, of Bel, or of Belin. This conjecture is all the more acceptable as in Old French, the word *beau* was *bel* masculine: *bel Sire roi* (*beau Sire roi*) *bels fut li vespres* (*beau fut l'apres midi*) (the afternoon was beautiful.

Another fact that supports our assumption is that the Hebrews and the Christians desperately tried to discredit the Star (Venus) and its radiant representatives: Bel, Baal, Belus, and even the pseudo-demon Belaam, "who whispered dishonest thoughts to honest women," which they very willingly listened to, as Belaam was irresistibly beautiful. All Venus people from time immemorial have the gift of beauty and it is not a coincidence that Venus is pre-eminent in this respect.

Lucifer, incarnation of the shepherds' star, was also superhumanly beautiful, and Roman shepherds, at the ritual date in May, paid him homage in the "Palilies," calling him "Pales" or "Bal."

We therefore feel we can take up Dontenville's remark and add to it: "Gods have always been represented as bigger and more beautiful than men." And we do not fear to add, Because they were of Venus or represented the planet Venus.

In this light, Gargantua, Belen's son, was a good and benevolent giant of divine Venusian descent, whose grave at Mount Tomb still attracted pilgrims at the time of Charlemagne.*

*The ending "tua" of the word "Gargantua" reminds us of the mysterious Initiators who arrived in Ireland one 1st of May and who were called Tuatha De Danann. Gargan, the Celtic hero was perhaps a Tuatha? From which comes "Garganthua" if we accept this theory.

Water fairies and serpents

Belisama, Astart, Astarte, Ishtar were all goddesses who represented the planet Venus, with the recurring idea of water, rain, the cave birthplace of the spring. Melusine, related to Lugh, was a fairy of superhuman beauty. She was always associated with the theme of water, of the cave, of eternal youth, and was undoubtedly closely related to Venus, Goddess of Beauty, born of the foam of the sea.

Morgan, the fairy so bright, loved to roam along the streams and rivers, to float above the surface in a skiff pulled by marine mammals; her dwelling was a palace at the bottom of the sea, for she was also a water nymph. D'Arbois of Jubainville said she was "born of the sea," she attracted Breton fishermen down to her grotto at the bottom of the sea.

The "fata Morgana" of the Straights of Messina, writes Henri Dontenville, shows in the middle of summer reversed images of invisible objects, she is certainly of the sea . . . and exercises her powers just before sunrise. That is to say, when the last star of the night sky still shines: Venue Lucifer. The same author reports, so Leo Desaine tells us, a legend in which one can find combined the myths of Melusine, of Water, and of Venus.

A lord had brought with him from a distant country a being of wondrous beauty, and he had made her his wife. Everyone praised her beautiful face, her graceful figure, her good manners, her elegance—but they thought it strange that she always wore a long dress, very costly, but which utterly concealed her feet and legs. Just as with Remondin of the Romaunt of Melusine, her husband had made a solemn oath that he would never try to see her feet and, just as with Remondin, his curiosity overcame him.

Her lord spread around the nuptial bed a layer of cinders,

hoping thus to obtain an imprint which would give him a clue. His beautiful wife undressed, and wearing only a long nightgown, walked towards her bed. Suddenly she cried out in pain and anguish, as she had stepped on a burning ember and had cruelly burned herself. She at once ran away in the guise of a fairy, casting a spell, and her spouse discovered in the ashes the marks of a webbed foot. Since that time, the castle has sunk under water and is replaced by a large lake.

The legend of Melusine comes partly from this fairy story but mostly from the contents at the Libraries of Mehun-sur-Yevres and the Louvre.

In Gervais de Tilbury one reads this anecdote: "On the banks of the river Arc, upriver from Aix-en-Provence, the knight Rousset met perchance, one night, a fairy who consented to become his wife, and from then on, his prosperity never ceased to increase. But one day, having promised not to, he looked at his lady in her bath; she had a serpent's tail. She left for ever this disloyal man, and from then on his prosperity declined.

These Morgans, these fairies, these water nymphs, these extraordinary serpents, have certain common denominators: beauty, the grotto, and certain physical formations linked with water: the webbed foot or the serpent's tail.

According to writers in the past, Elinas, Melusine's father, was named Belinas, which is to say: Belin of Venus. We therefore always come back to the Initiators descended from the planet Venus, to physical abnormalities which we presume are caused by unsuccessful attempts at cross-breeding between different races, and also mysteries which seem to have a link with Eleusis, whose present name, Levsina, is not unlike Melusine. And these mysteries could well be concealing the secret which leaks out of every pore of tradition, legends, and sacred writings: the extraterrestrial origin of our civilization.

The myth of the flying serpent

We must, in the legend of Melusine, discriminate between accounts which are impossible to believe and those that are possible.

After close examination it seems that the hero, Remondin, only incidentally takes part in the events and could very well be replaced by Percival, Roland, or Huon of Bordeaux. The story thus stripped can be summarized as follows: A woman of exceptional beauty sits beside a fountain in the forest of Poitou in the middle of the night, hoping for an amorous adventure. She is the possessor of a secret, something to do with water, a treasure, and a cave. She will later give birth to monstrous children, and one day will fly away in the guise of a winged serpent.

These are the essentials, which are credible, save the ending: We find it difficult to believe that a beautiful woman, bewitching as she may be, could change herself into a flying serpent!

Neither do we believe in all the other flying serpents which abound in mythology: Quetzalcoatl, the feathered serpent, god of the Mayas; Mertseger, goddess and serpent-vulture of the Egyptians; Karnak's so-called solar boat, the hull of which is a serpent and which flies from one horizon to the other; the sacred "*uraeus*" inscribed on the façade of the temples, represented by two winged serpents; Mardouk, the flying dragon with a serpent's head of the Assyro-Babylonians; the propellered serpent of the Phoenicians, described by Sanchoniathon; the Nagas, famous serpents of Indian mythology, and the innumerable magic serpents, mermaids, and flying dragons which haunt most mythologies.

Magic serpents, mermaids, flying dragons are generally

associated with water: fountain, river, or marsh. Dragons, in the very old days, called up floods and drownings, and abided in marshes and deltas. These serpents always represent the flying machine which transported the Initiators who came from Heaven to our Earth, and are usually identified with the Initiator.

The myth of the woman changed into a serpent belongs to every race. In the folklore of the Marind-anim in New Guinea, the hero, Teimbre, married a serpent who changed into a beautiful young girl. The Papous of Kiwai island tell how a serpent girl who lived in the water married a fisherman who had to conceal the extraordinary union. The couple gave birth to "purely human" children. The Nez-Percés of North America have legends of girls who change into serpents.

There are also the winged "angels" of the Bible. One is tempted to believe that the flying serpent of Lusignan also belongs to this extraterrestrial race, who in the very distant past came to cross-breed with us and to lavish its learning on us. If we accept this theory, Melusine takes on other dimensions, and the mysteries that surround her become instantly clear.

What was she doing beside the fountain of Coulombiers where Remondin first saw her? As water plays a vital part in her secret, just as it plays an essential role with all serpent-goddesses, we conclude that Melusine was in the water, which could well have been an indispensible elixir to preserve, even after eight children, this wonderful and eternal beauty which was her prerogative.

Following this idea, the water running from the Fountain of See was a rejuvenating water. Melusine could there recharge her life potential, just as Orejona in Lake Titicaca and as all the fascinatingly beautiful mermaids in the sea. And these suppositions, in which the Serpent-Queen is an Initiator come from another planet identify themselves remarkably with the cycle of known mythologies.*

In this concept, the Lugh-Melusine adventure happened 5,000 years ago, at the time when civilizations such as the Phoenicians, Assyro-Babylonians, Incas, and Mayas flourished, under the symbols of serpents, rams, or winged bulls and of the planet Venus.

We cannot be absolutely sure that the Initiation of mankind was undertaken by extraterrestrial travelers, but everything points to it. In this day and age, when Americans and Russians land on the moon and are launching their assaults on Mars and Venus, we cannot in a logical and rational study ignore the possibility.

The mythology of the Celts and Gauls

Lugh, the most popular of all Celtic gods, strangely intermingles the letters of his name with those of Lusignan (Lugsignem) and Melusigne, Jehan d'Arras' heroine. It would have been pointless to unfold an adventure centered on Melusigne without remembering in what way Lugh was related to Lusignan.

In 1387, this relation was difficult to establish: Jehan d'Arras, who came from the North of France, could hardly assimilate the whole essence of Poitou traditions and point to a group of coincidences only perceptible to a historian. When the Iberian Lugh died, his adopted mother, Tailtiu, built a superb monument for him and started festivities in his honor called

*As in other mythologies this planet would be Venus, whose nature may be oceanic, and whose arrival in our solar system started rain and floods (the flood of "Deucalion") according to many different testimonies.

"*lugnusades,*" which were celebrated in the month of August.

It is very curious coincidence (yet another) that Lusignan has preserved these traditions with fairs or festivities on the first of August, where servants can be hired. "And," Marcel Moreau writes, "these *lugnusades,* which were in antiquity consecrated to Lugh and his mother Tailtiu, symbol of Mother Earth, conjure up the image of the sacred serpent linked with the cult of the *virgo pariturae* serpent with a ram's head synonymous with learning."

Melusine, whether she is the Mother of Light or a serpent forming circular waves upon the surface of the water* of the Fountain of See, or guardian serpent of the treasure, is the very prototype of Initiation at its highest level: the cosmogenesis (or cosmic origins).

In this theory, which we entirely accept, we rediscover an important aspect of French mythology which is missing from the general history of the Celts because it has been smothered, disfigured, and Christianized.

Besides Orejona, Quetzalcoatl, Astarte, Ishtar,† etc.,

*Circular waves, or better still, the serpent swimming and thereby producing circles of waves is, in Druidical teaching, the symbol of the first vibration of the expanding universe.

†Orejona: Eve of the people of the high plain of Peru, Mother of Men. According to tradition from the Andes, at the beginning of humanity a flying boat, shining like gold, landed near the Island of the Sun in Lake Titicaca (Bolivia-Peru). From this alighted a very beautiful woman, but whose skull was in the shape of a sugar loaf, and whose feet and hands had only four digits. She had very large ears like the gods of Asia. This is how she got her name: *Orejona* ("Big Ears"). She came from the planet Venus and gave birth to the first men, the father being a tapir. One day Orejona departed on her flying boat and was never seen again.

Quetzalcoatl: God and Initiator of Ancient Mexico, identified with the planet Venus.

Melusine the beautiful, the "Miraculous Unicorn," as Remondin called her, is therefore the Initiator come from another planet (Venus) and identifies herself with Venus. This identification will not shock any historian familiar with mythology.

Already, in the 18th century, innovators, pioneers of true human history, those who were mockingly called "Celtomaniacs" had tried to enlighten their contemporaries on the probable existence of a national mythology which until then had been linked with Irish and Welsh mythology.

Lusignan, capital of the Celts

Against this background Jehan d'Arras' narration takes on unexpected and logical proportions, and it is with this in mind that we have studied and rewritten it and have added to it from certain documents and local variants which the author in the 14th century could never have found or analyzed.

The legend of Melusine now becomes the primohistory* of French civilization, or, rather, Western and Celtic, and a myth similar to those of America and the Near and Far East. It is important to note that this essential ingredient is closely connected with Poitiers, where thousands of years ago the most ancient migrant Celtic tribe settled, the Picts. We remind you of the coincidences which force us to include this legend in our national mythology.

Astarte: Phoenician goddess, the ancient Aphrodite, born from the foam of the sea. She represented the planet Venus.

Ishtar: Assyro-Babylonian goddess, representing the planet Venus.

*"Primohistory": a neologism meaning prehistory based on a different theory from that of the classical prehistorians. In primohistory man does not descend from the ape, has not lived in caves, or only incidentally, and had Superior Ancestors.

Lusignan, hometown of Lugh; Poitou, fief of the most ancient western Celts; Lugh, the bright-faced Initiator, a descendant of a mysterious tribe issued from "the Earthly Countries" confused in the Graal tradition with the "Country of the Other World"; the very beautiful Melusine, similar to the Orejona Venuses, Astarte and Ishtar; a winged serpent similar to the flying Initiators of the Middle East, of Egypt, of Peru, and of Mexico, knowing everything in every science and choosing to appear at the Fountain of See (Knowledge). Just as the Biblical "angels," just as Orejona, Melusine travels by air and attempts to bear children on earth. Finally, her adventure is closely related to universal symbols such as the fountain, the cave, the serpent, and the treasure.

It was inevitable that one day a historian would see that all these facts add up to a remarkable story, fantastic yet infinitely probable.

A Celtic-French Academy is about to be formed. Aims: Research into French identity, to give back to France its own mythology, to search for the remains of our national heritage, to list them and rekindle the very essence and spirit of Gaul-France.

For information write to M. Philippe Vidal, 13 rue Fernet, 94700 Maisons-Alfort, France. Correspondents are required in all French *departements*, in all French-speaking countries, and also in Celtic countries: England, Ireland, Spain, Portugal, Italy, etc.

Chapter Twenty-One

Melusine, the Winged Serpent

The following theories are largely derived from the manuscript of Jehan d'Arras, held at the Arsenal Library, Paris, with a few amendments from manuscripts kept at the National Library, Paris, and from translations or interpretations by Louis Stouff, André Lebey, Jean Marchand and Louis Naneix.

They were also inspired by local Poitou traditions retained in the towns of Poitiers, Lusignan, Civray, and Charroux, which modify the end of the story as told by Jehan d'Arras "in this modest essay taken from the chronicles collected by the Duc de Berry, Count of Poitou and Auvergne, Lord of the Marches, also from the Count of Salsbery (*sic*) in England and also according to certain books which were found on the subject."

Preliminary

To avoid any misunderstanding we wish to stipulate that this attempt to reconstruct a French mythology from the Melusine legend is mainly based on a synthesized study of facts and happenings and their relationship with identical traditions found in the mythology of Peru, Mexico, and the Near East.

In addition we felt that Jehan d'Arras' book, written and inspired by accounts gathered from the court of the Duc de Berry or from manuscripts long since disappeared, should now be updated from local unprinted traditions and additions suggested by the study of esoteric and modern beliefs. Was this story complete fiction or was it based on sound historical facts?

Certainly, many legends are born in the minds of poets, moralists, or quite simply imaginative storytellers, but the Legend of Melusine borrows so much from history, from the esoteric, from the science of biology and the supernatural, and coincides on so many points with foreign mythologies, that it is difficult to accept that this very essence of the knowledge contained therein, the remarkable parallels are just the result of happy coincidence.

Our interpretation keeps as close as possible to the archaic style and wording, the repetition of certain words ("supernatural," "false," "high," "large," "lord," etc.) and even the variation of spelling for the same name (Melusine, Melusigne), but it does sometimes stray from Jehan d'Arras' account, to come back to the original texts completely unknown to 14th century authors. . . .

We must thank our Lord for everything

Before starting, we must thank our Creator, who is master of all things made and in the making, which strive toward perfection despite the vices of the world. Here I pray to our Lord to look favorably on this story and on its readers.

Listen, good people, to this story, neither true nor false, but the most wonderful ever told at the hearth of French homes. It is the Legend of Melusine of Poitou, of the Fountain of See; it tells of love spells, and of the fabulous treasures forgotten and waiting in the hills of Lusignan. Whosoever discovers these treasures bequeathed by the Serpent-Queen will be richer and more famous than kings, but pray the Heavens may protect him from the fate which goes with their possession.

So tradition warns us: Melusine's magic jewels, her rubies, her diamonds, emeralds, and golden necklaces are hidden in an underground chamber in the hillside overlooking the Vonne, but reckless would be the man who attempted to carry them away!

Poitou is above all the land of treasures, legends, and of the supernatural. It is a truly wonderful land, with caves in the hillsides, rivers, an almost unexplored marshland—known as Green Venice—vast beaches edged with pine trees, fabulous legendary castles associated with names such as Melusine, Blue Beard of Tiffauges, the Unicorn. . . .

It is also the home of Norman cathedrals, of the "Belator"—the largest piece of the True Cross—of flowering mimosas which grow in the forest of Oleron, a place of bright sunshine, and most sunlit of all, the privileged isle of Yeu, last remaining trace of Atlanta lost in the Ocean. It is the land of sunsets, of witches and sleepwalkers who have the power to cast or remove evil spells.

The great hunt of Count Aimery

On this day, some time before the Great Fear of the year 1000, took place a great hunt on the land of the Count of Aimery of Poitiers, the powerful and just Lord of Poitou and the lower Marches.

The day before, one of his keepers had told him that there was to be found in the forest of Colombiers the most wonderful pig [wild boar] ever seen, and at dawn servants, squires, barons, and other noblemen of the court set off to hunt the beast.

The two most eager, the Count and his nephew, Remondin, a handsome boy, loyal, full of charm, an expert in the handling of weapons, led the hunt at great speed over hills and dales. The beast had ten times been surrounded, ten times wounded, had torn open four hounds, eight mastiffs, and two Great Danes, had sprung all the traps going from here to there with a sort of massive ease and strength as if possessed by the vigor of youth.

At dusk no one had strength left for the intolerable pursuit: The horses were exhausted, the dogs lay licking their wounds, and the tired barons decided to give up the chase. Only the Count of Aimery and his nephew persevered, but the wild boar kept going faster and the old lord was losing ground. At last he called out in annoyance. "Good Nephew, this son of a sow will drive us mad, let us end this accursed hunt! And a curse on the person who sent us on this adventure."

They had galloped and tracked so long that night had fallen, so that on finding a suitable clearing both men dismounted.

"Good nephew," sighed the exhausted Count, "we will remain here under this great tree as long as the moon is up. Tomorrow we will make further plans."

"As you wish, my Lord," replied Remondin, as he dismounted. He then collected dried wood, struck a flint, and lit a fire.

Far, far away over the hills one could hear the hundreds of bells, large and small of the thirty-five churches of Poitiers, ringing the angelus.

Written in the stars

Then the moon rose, strange, as it shone so close, a thin crescent, clear-cut against the dark expanse of night, making the night blue round its pale light. The stars soon responded, exactly as if they had been there forever, flawless, so clear that they appeared undefinably evil. Added to this was the hooting of an owl, so close that it seemed that this bird, flying softly, made of feathered cemetery soil, could see those he wished to warn. . . . The Count and Remondin remained silent.

With a last night cry the owl, with heavy and laborious flight, passed them, swooping down beside Aimery's horse, and disappeared. Three modulated whistles were heard in the distance. Then the two men and the horses breathed again and the former, who had bowed their heads at the accursed sound, lifted them up to the sky.

Aimery, lying on his back, his head resting on a tuft of moss, was studying the position of the stars, calculating their relationship and deducing their influence. He was an expert not only in grammar, logic, and physics, but most of all he was a great and knowledgeable astronomer and knew how to read the stars, as clearly as a parchment, thanks to the science of Arbatel the magician, his Court Astrologer.

Now, what he read was dramatic and made him sigh deeply:

"True gods, how wonderful is all that exists here on Earth in your servant, nature, and how varied in its purpose, when you pour upon it your divine grace! And how wonderful is this adventure which I read in the stars you have set there in the sky at the beginning of time, by the great science of astronomy, which you have imparted to me, and for this I must thank you with all my heart.

"But how would it be possible, unless we are subject to your invisible judgment, for a man to acquire wealth and high honors by doing evil? And yet I see by the high science and art of astronomy and by your heavenly grace that it is so." He then sighed still more heavily.

Remondin, who had attended the fire listening to these thoughts, replied with deference.

"My Lord, the fire is burning bright, come and warm yourself." As his uncle sighed deeper than ever, he added: "Ha! My Lord, may God chase away your visions! It is not right for so high a Prince to torment himself with such things, as, thanks be to God, he has provided you with high and mighty baronies and good lands. It is in your power to forget these doubtful reveries which can neither help nor hinder."

The Count smiled, a smile distant, imperceptible but great, superior to fate.

"Ha, foolish one," he said. "If you knew of the great, rich and wonderful adventure I read for you in the heavens, you would be quite amazed!"

Remondin, thinking no evil, replied:

"My most dreaded Lord, let it be your pleasure to reveal this secret, if it is sought I should know."

"By God, you will know it! Know for certain that I hope neither God nor men will ask you reasons for it, but that this adventure could happen because of me as I am now old. I have enough heirs to manage my domains, and I love you so much that I would be glad for such an honor to be bestowed upon you. Learn therefore what I have read in the stars: Should at this very hour a vassal kill his Lord, he would become the richest, most powerful, most respected man in his family and his descendants would be of such noble birth that they would be talked of and remembered until the end of the world. And know that this is true!"

"In this case," replied Remondin, "I cannot believe that this prophesy can come true, as there would be no justification for a man to gain such honors as a result of deadly treason. Also, at this place and time only you and I stand here; you are my Lord and uncle, more revered and loved than even my father. How could I be the cause of your misfortune?''

''It is written in the sky!''

The prediction becomes reality

The Count and his nephew were plunged in their thoughts when they heard deep in the wood a great thrashing of branches and brambles. Remondin picked up his stake and his uncle drew his sword. After a brief wait they were faced with ''a wild boar large and wonderful, coming straight at them foaming and gnashing his teeth in the most dreadful way.''

''My lord,'' said Remondin, ''climb this tree so that the wild boar cannot reach you and let me deal with this.''

''By my faith, I could not for Jesus Christ leave you in this predicament.'' And Aimery, seeing that the boar was coming straight for him, sheathed his sword, and with his stake low, wedged against his foot to impale the beast, he waited for the attack.

But he was knocked over and in such a desperate plight that Remondin had to administer a fearful blow, which unfortunately slipped down the boar's bristles and stabbed his uncle. Another blow, better aimed, killed the boar, and now, on the grassy glade, lay helpless two lifeless bodies.

''Alac, alas,'' cried Remondin, ''what ill and treacherous fate made me kill the one who loved me so and did so much for me! Almighty Father, after such a crime what country will now accept me? All who will hear of this will condemn me to a shameful death and torture, for never was such false and base treason committed.

''Earth, why do you not open? If you should swallow me up with the darkest and ugliest angel who in another life was the most beautiful, I would well deserve it.''

And addressing himself to the Count, who lay dead, he said bitterly:

"My Lord, you told me that if such a thing happened to me I would be the most honored man of my kind. But I can only see the contrary, as I will be the most unhappy, disgraced, and this certainly is as it should be."

Then he stepped towards his lord, kissed him, sadly crying, and picking up his hunting horn, he laid it at his feet. Then, springing onto his horse, he entered the forest where he rode aimlessly until midnight, feeling downcast and miserable.

The three maidens at the well

And so he found himself beside the Fountain of See* which some people called the Fairy Fountain because many wondrous adventures had taken place there in the past. The white and bluish light from the brilliant moon lit the fountain and played across the great rocks above. Three maidens paddled in the water or played about on the edge. One of them was so beautiful that no planet or star in the firmament had ever seen anyone so wonderfully ethereal.

Immersed in sorrow, Remondin passed by without seeing them, so that the Queen said to her female companions:

*One generally translates this passage as "Fountain of Thirst," which has no great meaning. If we take into account the logic, and the symbolical and Initiating aspect of the Romaunt of Melusine, the importance of Lusignan, the town of Lugh, who introduced these rites to the Celts, it most probably refers to the Fountain of Knowledge, of Science, of "See" in Poitou dialect.

Melusine is the Fairy of Knowledge, the Initiated Serpent-Guardian of the treasure hidden in the cave. The grotto represents esoterically the inner sanctum of Initiation, the serpent is the person who possesses the knowledge, and the treasure is the knowledge.

"By my faith, this horseman may be a gentleman, but he conceals it well, for it is very discourteous to pass before ladies or maidens without saluting them as he ought."

Then, taking the bridle of the horse she firmly said:

"Vassal, it is very arrogant and artless of you not to salute these maidens."

And as Remondin seemed still to be lost in his dreams she added:

"Pensive Sire, are you so preoccupied that you do not deign to answer? By my faith, I do believe this man is asleep on his horse, or else he is deaf and dumb. *Sire vassal, are you asleep*?"

Remondin jumped up, gathered his wits, and saw a maiden of incomparable purity and beauty.

"Dear lady," he answered, "please forgive this unintentional insult, but let me tell you that I was thinking of something dreadful that means much to me, and I was praying to God to help me."

"This is well said! In all things we should appeal to God but after our Lord I am the one who can help you most in this mortal world, and change adversity and evil into good fortune. I know, Remondin, that you have killed your lord, but it was an accident, and you have not sinned."

When the valiant knight heard his name he was so astounded, he did not know what to think. He eventually replied:

"Dear Lady, what you tell me is the absolute truth, but I wonder how you could possibly have known such things or who could have told you! Are you a witch to read so into my heart? Are you a creature of Satan?"

"I know that my acts and words seem to you ghostly or the work of Satan but I promise you that I am of God and believe everything a good Catholic should believe. If you will hear me, I will steer you out of your difficulties and will render you such services as will make you rich, powerful, and honored, and from you will be born descendants so noble that this will be remembered till the end of the world."

Remondin, much troubled, was reminded of his uncle's prophesy, and already under the spell of this beautiful creature, he asked what he should do.

"First of all you must love me!" she said. "Do I please you, handsome squire?"

Giving himself the pleasure of looking at her, he was struck with admiration.

She was wearing a dress the color of daffodils and violets, gracefully arranged; her hair was of gold, her eyes were emeralds, her flesh of honey and milk. He particularly noticed her bare feet, more beautifully chiseled than a jewel of Araby, of such enchanting and delicate shape more perfect than rose petals.

"My Lady," he murmured, struck with amazement, "I have never dreamed of anyone as beautiful as you. How could I not love you?"

"Well, you will have to marry me."

"It would be a great honor."

"And furthermore, handsome Squire, you will have to pledge your word never to doubt my honest and Christian behavior, free of any spell."

"My Lady, I will loyally do all I can. I will take you for my wife before God in a chapel, as soon as you desire, but I beg you to tell me your name."

Every Saturday night to Sunday morning

There was then complete silence in the forest and the fountain ceased to play; after a few seconds outside time, the birds seemed to sing more sweetly, the flowers exhaled the most subtle perfume, the water of the fountain took up its sweet music over the pebbles and the mint, and in this paradise was heard the music of a voice of love and magic.

"My name is Melusine!" said the beautiful creature. And already the breezes, the visions, the sounds and perfumes repeated this name in Remondin's living dream.

"I am at your mercy," he found the strength to say, but his mind reeled as if he had drunk too much wine under the shade of a lime tree.

"Listen to my last request," said Melusine. "You will swear to me by all that is holy for a good Christian that each Saturday night, from sunset to dawn on Sunday, you will neither try to see me, nor seek to find out where I shall be."

Charmed and captivated by the Enchantress, Remondin swore at his peril that he would never on the evening and night of that day do aught that could harm her and in all honor would never want to discover her whereabouts. And now the die was cast.

There was no escape from a magic web for the following characters: Remondin, impulsive and upright, a hero of the Middle Ages; Melusine, loving, cunning, yet sincere, more beautiful than day, more beautiful than stars reflected on the dark oceanic seas, an expert in wonderful and benevolent witchcraft, the fairy of another world; the Count of Forez, Remondin's brother, a wily fellow appointed by fate to shape the course of this adventure towards the diabolical.

Melusine's secret

Melusine was a fairy but she wished to become mortal to know of love and the good, appeasing death, so sacred, which concludes the life of every mortal on earth. But she had committed a sin with the help of her two sisters: She had imprisoned her perjured father (in the mountain of Northumberland, England), and her mother, the fairy Presine, condemned her to come under a spell every Saturday night to Sunday. But she would be able to live a human life if she met a man who was capable of loving her and of never trying to uncover the mystery which would always link her, one night a week, to her nymph and fairy life. If the secret were to be known, Melusine would then become a fairy again, forever.

Perhaps she withheld from men of this planet a deeper and more inaccessible secret, for her origin is quite unknown, and in a century conditioned by superstition, it would have been unwise to claim an extraterrestrial origin. (Melusine came at the very time when people claimed they could see ships sailing in the skies and cavalry troops swooping out of the clouds to fight for Christ.)

Nevertheless, just as with the Venus Orejona of the Incas, who aboard a celestial vessel landed on the shores of Lake Titicaca in the Andes, so Melusine appears in the Middle Ages as an Initiator, come from another world to educate terrestrial beings and, perhaps, to attempt an integration of her race.

Contrary to the "sons of God" of Genesis,* she united herself to a terrestrial knight with the intention of bearing children, not giants, but a new species of humanity. In the Bible this attempt resulted in the Flood and the end of the world.

In the traditional and generally known story as reported by the

*Genesis, Chap. 6, Verse 2: That the sons of God saw the daughters of men that they were fair; and they took them wives of all which they chose . . . and also after that, when the sons of God came in unto the daughters of men, and they bore children to them the same became mighty men which were of old, men of renown.

chroniclers, Melusine was apparently a fairy, and she proved it when she gave Remondin two golden rods, one preserving him from death by means of weapons, the other insuring victory in all conflicts. Then she gave advice on how best to conduct their lives, to serve their now mutual interests.

Remondin remounted and returned to Poitiers, the beautiful town, strong, subtle, and lovely inside its long, thick-set walls, dominated by a fortified castle, with superstructures and battlements one above the other.

Enchantments in the forest

The Count's death was attributed to a blow from the boar's snout and his son, Bertrand, who succeeded him, wished to reward his most deserving and devoted subjects, among them his cousin, the gallant knight Remondin.

"Sire, the only gift I ask of you is that above the Fountain of See, in the rocks and dense woods, you should let me have as much land as can be covered by a deerskin."

"So please God," said Count Bertrand, "let my cousin enjoy the gift I bestow on him!"

But it so happened that a mysterious stranger sold to Remondin a deerskin cut out in such thin strips that it surrounded the mountain near the Fountain of See for over two leagues. As if by magic, a torrent sprang up the domain and in less than one hour several windmills appeared on the hillside with humming sails.

When these wonders were reported to the court, they caused a great sensation and the Dowager Countess spoke for everyone when she said to her son Bertrand:

"Never believe anything I say again if this time Remondin has not met with some adventure in the forest of Colombiers, for it is enchanted and many adventures have taken place there."

"I think you are right," added the Count of Forez, (Remondin's older brother), "and I have heard that at the Fountain of See many have been witnessed."

To the valiant knight's amazement strange happenings continued: First it was a great house which sprang up on the domain, with a vast and magnificent hall "larger than the hall in the castle of Poitiers, and a court of numerous noblemen, and young maidens richly clad, their beautiful hair covered by graceful hennins and accompanied by squires." In another room "larger still," a sumptuous supper was served, by an army of well-trained servants; an orchestra composed of mandoras, lyres, cellos, viols, and lutes played skillful music.

"Where do all these people come from, my beloved?" asked Remondin.

"These knights and ladies are at your command," replied Melusine with a bewitching smile.

"Will you not tell me how you achieve these marvels?"

She looked at him solemnly, and smiling strangely, said: "If, one day, you want to know, and I do not advise it by my faith in God, go and drink three times the water of the Fountain of See which will open your eyes and widen the boundaries of your mind. For it is miraculous water, made for the strong who wish to defy fate, but for our love I beg of you control your manly curiosity."

Melusine's wedding

At last it was the nuptial day and never in memory of man, lord, king, or emperor was such ostentation seen.

A very ancient-looking knight richly clad in clothes well worn but of splendid cut, held in at the waist by a belt of precious stones and pearls, received the Count of Poitiers as if he were the master of the house.

"Powerful and noble Sire, Damsel Melusine of Albion presents her respects and thanks you for the great honor you do to your cousin Remondin and herself by being present at their wedding."

Each guest had at his disposal magnificent rooms, jesters dressed in scarlet to amuse him, and pretty girls to please his eyes. The Dowager Countess' pavilion was hung with cloth of gold hemmed with pearls, emeralds, and amethysts and the old lady was so filled with admiration that she declared that in all the world no queen, or king, or emperor could be found who could display so many riches or possess half the jewels Melusine wore on her person.

To anyone who wondered about so much display of riches, such lavishness, and wonders so sudden and multiplied, the Knight replied:

"My Damsel could do better still; she only has to wish, to receive!"

The marriage was solemnized in a chapel whose long and slender spire was as lightly worked as lace. It had sprung up by magic on the rocky point of the Fountain of See, embodied in it as if born of the rock to project it and throw it up to the sky. The banquets, the festivities, the entertainments surpassed in splendor anything seen to this day.

At the tournament, the Count of Poitiers, the Count of Forez, and the Poitiers Knights excelled themselves, but the most skillful were Melusine's knights and above all Remondin, dressed all in white and mounted on a superb dappled gray.

When night came, after being undressed by the Countess and her daughter, Melusine slipped between the nuptial sheets where Remondin joined her without delay. That night their first son was conceived, the brave Urian, who became King of Cyprus. . . .

The fairy builder

A few months after these events saw the arrival at the Fountain of See of an abundance of workmen, landworkers, and woodcutters, and Melusine had the ground cleared and the great trees uprooted until the rock was bare and clean.

She then called on a multitude of masons and stoneworkers to build foundations so strong that it was wonderful to see. And the workmen worked so fast and hard that all who passed by were astonished. And Melusine paid them each Saturday night so that she never so much as owed them one penny. And no one knew where these workmen came from or who they were. And in a very short time the fortress was built, with not one but two strongpoints guarding the keep.

"And I must tell you that all three walls were turreted and the vaults of the tower were in Gothic ribbed style, and the battlements very high. And there were three double fences, high and strong. And there were also some heavy and wonderful postern gates.

"When the fortress was finished the workmen departed as they had arrived, on foot, on horseback, and in elongated wagons, resembling strangely shaped vessels unknown in this country.

"There never existed a stronger fortress nor one more beautiful, even much later one at Coucy; for this was the fortress of Lusignan."

The days went by happily, filled with delights for Remondin and his wonderful bride. She seemed to grow in fairness and his love increased.

This was the time when Melusine erected the churches of Poitou: Saint-Pierre-de-Melle, Limalonges, Chamdeniers, Saint-Pompain, Fronteny-l'Abattu, Clussay, Saint-Jouin-des-Marnes, Civray, Genouillé and the marvelous abbey of

Charroux, where in only one night the forest was cut down, the site surrounded by walls, and towers, belfries, and bell turrets.

At the same time she built the two perfect keeps of Niort fortress and the castles of Latour at La Mothe-de-Méré, Fontaine-Epinette, Cremault, Barbeziere, Saint-Maxire, Sainte-Pezenne, Souche, Prahecq, Saint-Hilaire-la-Palud, Charriere, Benet, Moutiers-sur-le-Coy, Brulain, Aiffres, Echire, Chef-Boutonne, and many others.

Melusine's apron

To Remondin, who wondered how so many buildings had sprung up so suddenly, a beggar disclosed the secret.

"It is the work of Melusine, Sire. She came one night on horseback, and set herself to work, she worked so fast that the church seemed to grow of its own accord. Ah! If only you had seen her. She carried in her "*dorne*"* the building bricks and the earth for the ditches. And the work advanced prodigiously."

At Saint-Pierre de Parthenay-le-Vieux, a monk told him that the façade, the vaults, and the belfry were built in three nights by Melusine.

"She worked by the light of the stars, without a pause."

Taken by surprise at dawn, just as she was finishing her work, she fled, leaving behind her on the last stone the imprint of her horse's shoe, which is still to be seen there. (The space where this stone should have been has never yet been filled, any stone which is placed there inevitably drops out.)

Then Remondin went to Armorica to claim his father's inheritance. His father was Hervy de Leon, Lord of Lower Brittany, and of French Brittany, and the King's Seneschal.

The Gallant Knight proved himself strong, brave, and loyal,

*An apron which is held up with the hands to carry a load.

but soon came back to his beautiful wife, as he could not be parted from her for very long.

She had given him many children: Urian, the first-born, good-looking and masculine, with a short face, one eye red and the other green: Odon the next, well-built, but his ears did not match; Guyon had one eye above the other; Antony had a lion's clawmark on his cheek; Regnault had only one eye but a very good one; Geoffroy had a fang; Florimond had a birthmark. The eighth boy, Oruble, the strangest, his three eyes forming a triangle, was cruel and killed two wet nurses in four years. Only the last two sons, Raimonnet and Thierry, seemed quite normal.

Three signs of destiny

As her family grew, Melusine took care to add to her lands and domains. So she took ownership of castles and hamlets at Parthenay, La Rochelle, Saintes, Pons, Tallemont and further afield toward Brittany, Gascony, and Guionne.

The happiness of this couple would have been cloudless if Count Forez, a disloyal and evil man if ever there was one, had not taken a malicious pleasure in teasing the valiant knight's curiosity on the absences of his wife. With insinuations, hints, and malicious remarks, he succeeded in arousing doubts in his mind.

One Saturday, when they were in Lusignan, or according to Jehan d'Arras, in Mervent, he told him:*

*Jehan d'Arras' account places this important event at the Castle of Mervent (Vendée), but Poitou tradition states that the scene took place at Lusignan, where people still show you on a stone the footprint that the fairy is supposed to have left before changing into a serpent. We choose to think it was Lusignan where Melusine's retreat and treasure were, and where she returned on certain occasions as a winged serpent.

"Dear brother, bid Melusine come, as I would very much like to see her and embrace her."

"You will see her tomorrow, at the moment she is in retreat and cannot come out for anyone."

Forez replied, stressing each word: "You are the only one not to know what everyone else knows! You are my brother and I must not seal your disgrace. . . ."

Then Remondin could contain himself no longer, an irresistible and fatal force drove him to the small low door in the tower leading to Melusine's mysterious retreat.

He simply had to know, and remembering his fairy wife's warning, he ran towards the Fountain of See and three times he drank of the miraculous water which unveils the eyes and grants knowledge. But he was so distraught that no sobering thought could appease his angry excitement. His blood was up and drove him toward a desperate act, even at the peril of his life.

However, Melusine had prepared three magic obstacles which could give Remondin a chance and divert him from his fatal plan.

First of all, although he strove to walk in the direction of the tower he was searching for, three times he trod the same ground, as if he had strayed upon walking on this witch's grass which, we are told in Poitou, makes you always return to the place whence you came.

The second was better still, and should have made him recover his senses.

As he noiselessly climbed the tower stairs, he saw each step growing as he advanced, even until the last one, so high that it was a good six or seven feet tall.* This staircase was certainly

*This account, told in the story of Melusine by André Lebey, does not appear in Jehan d'Arras' manuscript, but we have put it

not one which would lead to a shameful retreat in which to commit adultery or other misdeed, but Remondin had become madly jealous.

He managed the ascent and found himself before a door of incredibly good wood cased with huge ironwork fittings across the whole width and with no lock. Remondin forced open this third magic obstacle: With his knife he managed to pry apart the wide wooden panels, and setting off by chance a mysterious mechanism, he found himself thrown inside a vast room.

The secret of the tower

The floor was covered with golden sand, the walls lined with madrepores, coral, shells, and thousands of precious stones which sent out a soft blue light. Here and there, on the sand, he saw strange stones which fell from the skies, black and circular, which Arbatel the astrologer called meteorites.

Lit by a moon ray and reflecting it, it seemed to have an inner life. A large *abbadir* [moonstone] softly shone, polished like a fruit from another world, mysterious, and suddenly it disappeared as if it had only been a dream.

The sound of running water made him look at a patio with glass walls; he moved nearer still, until he came upon a sight his eyes should never have seen. Alas, alac, he grieved and his brave heart and soul were tortured with remorse! He knew the

---

in as we think it conforms with the fundamentals of the story. Also, André Lebey, who was a great poet, has visions of the past that are a better reflection of the truth than is orally transmitted to us by the ordinary folk.

Thus he often emphasizes this supernatural and extraterrestrial adventure: "the elongated carts like strange-shaped vessels, unknown in this country," the possibility of an extramarital affair between Melusine and a lover "come from the faraway atmosphere."

whole truth now, and it was both comforting and terrible. . . .

In a large ornamental lake covered with black irises and violets, Melusine, naked, fair, and still fairer than when he first saw her, occupied herself innocently: She combed her long gold mass of hair, holding her breasts out and looking at her reflection in a mirror of crystal, her charms and perfection were distracting. But below these breasts which he had so cherished and caressed, Remondin preceived the secret of his beloved wife's voluntary retirement: a long serpent's tail, covered with green scales prolonged her belly and back in undulating form. . . .

The wonderful unicorn

Panicstricken, he ran out and escaped her notice, and on his return to the castle, he almost killed Count Forez, whose calumnies had so utterly broken his happiness.

Remondin shouted at him:

"Flee from here, false traitor. Because of your false and treacherous words, I have perjured myself against the best and most loyal lady ever born except for Our Lady the Mother of Christ. You have brought me only pain and have taken away my joy. . . . Alas, alas, my sweet companion, I am the false and cruel asp and you are the precious unicorn, for I have betrayed you with my venom. . . ."

Distraught by grief, he even cursed her who had given him so much happiness but also so much suffering and disappointment.

"By the faith I owe to God I think this woman is only a spirit, not one seed that I have planted in her has come to perfect fruition; she has never carried a child who was not born with some strange sign. Do I not see Oruble here, who is not yet seven and who has already killed two my my squires, and before he was three two of his nurses died from bites on their breasts?

And did I not see their mother, the Saturday my brother Forez told me the bad news, in the shape of a serpent from the navel down?

"This is true, by God. She is some spirit, phantom, or chimera who has thus deceived me; the first time I saw her, was she not able to tell me of my sad adventure?*

"Oh, you false snake, by God, you and your deeds are nothing but uncanny illusions, and you could never produce a normal heir!"

Then as his feelings toward her took their accustomed bent, the Gallant Knight admitted that he had failed to keep his word and acknowledged his sins:

"My beloved, my beautiful unicorn, my own true one, my

*We are reminded once more of the theme of the esoteric story with a mixture of unearthly myth. Remondin reproaches his strange wife for bearing children tainted and abnormal (there is a certain amount of doubt about the last two). In short the cross-breeding between a human and her does not give good results, just as in the case of the marriages of the "angels" (sons of God) of the Bible, with earthly women.

In Jehan d'Arras' narration Melusine strongly advises before she leaves that her son Oruble be killed; in Genesis God kills, by means of the Flood, all the men born of the marriages between "angels" and earthly women.

We can only assume this, but we find enough signs to link this adventure of the Serpent Fairy to that of the "angels," to Orejona in Peru, to Quetzalcoatl with the Mayas, to Astarte in the Middle East. Following this train of thought, Melusine would be a foreigner, like Mersteger (or Marit Sakro), the Serpent Queen of Egyptian mythology, whose name, curiously like that of Remondin, means "the beloved of he who kept silent." These coincidences added to the myth of the flying serpent, which, in all mythology, represents the flying device of another world, makes us look into the legend of Melusine to find the tale distorted over the centuries, of a very ancient adventure of Initiators come from another planet.

hope, for the sake of Jesus Christ's Holy Passion the Holy forgiveness he showed Mary Magdalene as true Son of God, I beg of you to forgive me and to stay with me."

And at dawn, Melusine returned to the room where Remondin had come to cry with grief. When he heard her, he pretended to be asleep, and Melusine undressed and lay beside him.

She was back to her normal body, and her womanly beauty, but she remained dumb and as if stiff with cold. As a fairy she knew all and perhaps she had seen him in her mirror when she was a serpent.

Time went by and seemed never to end as they stayed in bed all morning, silently aware of the drama and of the last few fragments of pleasure that they could live to enjoy. They were determined to savor them to the bitter end. For they knew their love was shattered, forever.

Here and now Melusine began her penance until the end of the world. Oh, if only they could turn back in time . . . recapture the paradise of days gone by! Now and then, Remondin wondered whether this had all really happened. Could this not just be another mirage such as his beloved Serpent used to bring up before his eyes for his delight?

And if he really did see her, could she not by magic blot out his dreadful misdoing, conjure up the influence of a fairy more powerful than herself?

It was now late, very late, the bells of the Chapel of the Fountain of See had long ago announced the time of the Sunday mass.

She was the first to free herself from this terrible numbness.

"My Lord, you will be late, it is time you dressed for mass."

"Melusine, my sweet, beloved unicorn, do you promise never to leave me in this world or the next?"

"In this world, I cannot promise, my dear friend, but in the next I faithfully promise that you will always be close to my heart and loved."

"Oh, I do see fate is against me and I should not have forgotten my solemn promise, but false words weakened my resolution, and because all our children were born with some strange sign I began to think there was a spell."

Melusine drew a deep breath and replied in a sweetly sad tone: "Oh my sweet love, these afflictions our children have suffered are not the evil work of the Devil, but the natural result of heredity, for I came from another world where life is different from life here on Earth. And nature will not allow a birth to contravene her primeval law."

And they both sunk from then on in deep and bitter thoughts, she understanding what the words meant and he suspecting an unjust curse. Melusine once again beseeched him not to miss the service and at last they both arose.

The flight of the serpent

Hand in hand they walked along the long passages of the castle, trying to belong to each other with all their heart and soul.

"My beloved," she murmured, "if only I could die now!"

He held the little trembling hand in his and with a faltering voice he grieved:

"Poor beloved Serpent, sweet unhappy Siren . . . you have never been so dear to me. Oh, Melusine, I beg of you, stay! If you will not, I shall never be happy again."

She burst into floods of tears and spoke in such desperate terms that their hearts ached.

"My sweet lover, destiny wills it so and I am powerless. Beautiful and dear country, I must also leave you and, from now on, those who will see me will recoil as from a poisonous beast.''

Just then they heard from the chapel the elevation bell inviting them to receive the Holy Spirit.

''My lord, time runs short. Let us kneel here, in this very spot, and ask God to absolve us at the Day of Judgment.''

They knelt, bowed down, and heard the last crystal-clear chimes of the bell. When Remodin looked up, Melusine was standing in the window recess of the passage, looking out over the beautiful sunny valley, and cried out from a broken heart.

''Farewell! Farewell to you all! Farewell my husband, my beloved, my lover, devoutly pray to God to relieve my suffering.''

Then, as if tearing herself apart, wounded and undone by this self-inflicted violence, she straightaway soared out the window in the shape of a winged serpent at least fifteen feet long.

And nothing was left of her, save the small mark of her foot molded on the window sill which had been the stepping stone of her speedy and unbelievable flight.

God gives his glory to the deceased,
and strength and victory to the living!
Allow them to achieve this!
If you wish me to finish this story
Thanks be to God.

Many centuries have passed, but in Poitou people still firmly believe that when a member of the Lusignan family is in danger of dying, Melusine returns to this world in the form of a winged serpent to give the alarm.

''Then,'' people say, ''she flies three times round the castle, cries pitifully, and suddenly crashes down in a horrible way on the postern gate, creating such turmoil and terror that it seems as if the whole castle will fall down and all the stones loosen.''

In the 14th century an English officer named Sersuelle was commanding the garrison in the Castle of Lusignan which was being besieged by the Duc de Berry, brother of Charles V.

One night, the officer saw in the fireplace the shape of the winged serpent dancing in the flames. ''This is Melusine's signal,'' he was told next morning. ''You can prepare yourself to leave.'' And they were right!

Melusine still appears to the inhabitants of Lusignan, but at longer intervals. She will return, it is said, to show where her treasure is buried in an underground passage linking the Castle to the St. Hilaire church in Poitiers. If the finder of the treasure gives it to charity, he will break the spell at once, and Melusine could once again become a real woman. Otherwise, he will be under a spell, and the Lusignan ghost will continue to haunt the dark nights of this ancient town.

Commentary

One copy of the manuscript written in Old French is at the Arsenal Library, others are at the National Library.

The original text, although exceptionally good for its time—1387—can neither be fully published nor even condensed chapter by chapter, for it contains such a rich abundance of detail that the main thread is often smothered and lost. Thus, the author sometimes leaves Lusignan and its fairy to take us to the Middle East, to Britanny, to England, and we become spectators of long and heroic adventures that have little or nothing in common with the main theme.

This process was often used in the Middle Ages by the troubadors, minstrels, and court poets who told their tales at night around the fire with endless digressions. It was usual, to please the lord of the manor and a few distinguished guests, to tell of their great deeds, not as part of the story but as an addition often colorless and boring. Moreover, storytellers, sometimes at the request of their listeners, liked to enrich their own accounts with the wonderful epics of famous knights.

Thus, during the marriage celebrations at Lusignan the author cannot resist the temptation of quoting a stanza by Pierre de Corbie, verses by Rutebeuf: la Grische d'Yver, and of telling about the incredible game of chess of Garin de Montglave, quotations by Huon de Bordeaux, Andréle Chapelain, and a long story by the bard of Penhoel telling of Remondin's adventures in Brittany which proves that the story of Melusine is older than Jehan d'Arras.

These long passages, which make the original book so difficult to read, have been cut in later versions and it is our opinion that the book, thus simplified, becomes a masterpiece of French literature and the most fascinating romance of chivalry.

Certain writers have thought that Jehan d'Arras had based his theories on historical facts, and there are great differences of opinion as to who Melusine really was.

She could have been Melisende, widow of a King of Jerusalem, or the lady of Mervent, wife of Geoffrey of Lusignan, or again the "Mater Lucina" goddess to whom Roman women in labor prayed for a safe deliverance. Some people have also pointed out that Melusine is (more or less) an anagram of the old name of Lusignan, Lusignem.

According to André Lebey, the fairy lady of Albion, was an English allegory, just as Remondin was a French one. At the time of Jehan d'Arras we were, after all, right in the middle of the Hundred Years' War.

Or did the author simply write to please his master, the Duc de Berry, whose private secretary he was? This is a possibility, as the Duke valued art and literature.

Count Aimery, Jehan Arras tells us, was the grandfather of King William the Saint, ''who became Count and gave up all his worldly possessions to serve Our Lord and Creator, and became a monk of the religious order of the White Fathers'. William the Saint, or William the Great, Duke of Aquitaine, lived in the 8th and early 9th centuries. He died in 812. He was the son of Count Thierry, who is thought to have been related to Charlemagne.

In 806, with his wife's agreement, William withdrew from worldly things and returned to the Valley of Gellene, near Lodeve, where he built the Monastery of Saint-Ghilhelm-du-Desert. A medieval verse chronicle, called the *Romance of William the Short-Nosed*, was written to tell of these heroic deeds at the beginning of the 10th century, and in it we find the legend of Aimery of Narbonne.

The William of the chronicle went to defend Paris, besieged by the Infidels, and killed Isore the Giant at a place now called the Tombe of Issoire. There are many other Williams, Counts or Dukes of Aquitaine, known in history:

William III, Tête d'Etoupe, born in Poitiers around 900, died in 965, was robbed of his vast duchy by the King of France.

William IV, Fier à bras (proud of his strong arms), son of the previous one, lost Loudun to the Count of Anjou, but victoriously defended Poitiers against Hugues Capet in 988. He retired to a monastery.

William V, the Great (960-1030) was a patron of the arts, founded several monasteries, and rebuilt the Cathedral of Poitiers.

The first Count of Lusignan was Hugues I, known as le

Veneur (the huntsman), who lived in the reign of Louis IV d'Outremer (Louis from overseas) son of Charles III, le Simple, between 921 and 954.

This chronology is not necessarily historically accurate, but what is quite certain is that the Legend of the Serpent-Queen is far older than the 14th century and that none of the proposed explanations have a sound basis.

To anyone who has the smallest understanding of Celtic esoterics and history, Melusine is beyond doubt the slightly modified image of a great Western myth. In it we find all the main elements of symbolic introductory rites: Lusignan, an inner sanctum dedicated to the God Lugh; the fairy possessing knowledge; the cave, or retreat, which is her chosen haunt; the serpent, symbol of learning, as the Fountain (of See or of Knowledge) is the symbol of knowledge; and last of all the treasure which is outwardly represented as rubies, diamonds, and gold but esoterically speaking is the Initiation itself. The Vouivre (symbolic word for "Guivre": fantastic serpent), the dragon, the *naja* (or cobra) of the Egyptians, the Serpent of A thena, the *nwywre*, or flying serpent, of the Druids, all belong to the same basic myth.

All these elements seem to us to clarify and authenticate the basic character of Melusine and of her story as seen in the imaginative tales of Jehan d'Arras and the writers of the Middle Ages who had a cult of the supernatural.

Part V

Witchcraft

Chapter Twenty-Two

Demons and Wonders

Witchcraft was the first thing men believed in; civilized and stripped of its savageness it became the art of magic; organized, spiritualized, and more skillfully exploited, it took the name of religion; subjected to controls, to experiments, and to reasoned studies, it became science.

Through all its ups and downs it always bore a hallmark—perhaps that of the Devil—and common denominators: holocausts, bloody sacrifices, physical and mental tortures, and the will to dominate. From the prehistoric sorcerer to the maker of atom bombs, all had the same fundamental objectives—a will to power and the wish for a better world.

The Grand Master of the Rosicrucians, in his book, *Message du Sanctum Celeste*, maintains that witchcraft has no power whatsoever over those who do not believe in its cures. This is undoubtedly true, and we can apply this maxim to the art of magic, to religion, and to science.

But if we put our faith in these overpowering beliefs, everything can alter and results become tangible: Sorcerers walk on fire, magi can read thoughts, saints accomplish miracles, and learned scientists invent machines to sail to the stars.

Solomon's clavicles

There are three famous books which are the authorities for empirics on sorcery and magic: *Albert the Great, Solomon's Clavicle*, and the *Enchyridion.* The first is an uninteresting collection of impossible recipes and refers to the very basic witchcraft of the Middle Ages. The second, much more technical, is for the benefit of magicians, and claims to give them clues (clavicles = small keys = clues) to science which conjures up "spirits."

There are thirty-six main clues or talismans which are Hebrew hieroglyphics and we can state with certainty that they have no virtues whatsoever. Even if we *do* believe in their power! The learned and sympathetic Eliphas Levi, Master of Magic, does not fear, however, to answer for their effectiveness.

The Enchyridion

The *Enchyridion* is the book of magic talked about above all others in occult societies, although most people have never seen it, as it is a very rare book. (We only know of one copy (publ. 1633) which belongs to Jacques Tacher, 17 Avenue Julien, 63000 Clermont-Ferrand, France.)

It is a collection of mystical orations and prayers, attributed without proof to Pope Leo III, and published in the 17th Century under the following title: *Papoe Leonis Enchyridion, serenissimo imperatori Carolo Magno in manus pretosium datum.*

His Serene Highness, Charles the Great, to whom the Pope addresses himself, is really Charlemagne, who would owe the prosperity of his reign entirely to the almighty secrets revealed to him in this book.

> One reads on page 2 of this work: The Emperor Charlemagne, to whom this work is dedicated as a very precious token and treasure, was the first person who experienced its surprising and wonderful effects—with great veneration, he recited prayers from it, his face turned towards the rising sun and has vowed to carry these prayers with him written in letters of gold. All the signs which adorn this precious book are taken from the most valuable manuscripts handed down to us from antiquity and they are always related to the prayer they illustrate: They only work if they are continually in the person's possession. We can consult about them the Magic Calendar and Occult Phylosophy of the celebrated and wise Aggripa.

According to the editor, Charlemagne sent the Pope a letter of thanks, and this letter is held by the Vatican. The text of the letter is reproduced in the 1633 edition.

Empirical researchers speak with immense respect of the *Enchyridion* and attribute magic powers to it with disarming naïveté, and bad faith. We give here a brief analysis of this magic and all-powerful book, which will enable the reader to draw his own opinions.

To be invincible . . .
and the garter for walking

Page 19: "A prayer to shield one from all sorts of charms,

enchantments, spells, writings, visions, illusions, possessions, obsessions, obstacles, the evil spells of marriage and all that can befall us through the evil work of sorcerers, or by interventions of devils; also very useful to fight all sorts of illnesses that can befall horses, mares, oxen, sheep, and other kinds of animals . . .'

After calling upon the cross, the Savior, the Father, the Holy Ghost, all the Saints, and other such affectations, the incantation continues in the same disappointing way: By the great living God +, by the real God + by the holy God, + by God the Father + by God the Son + and by the Holy Ghost, also God + but mainly by the one + who was sacrificed in Isaac, etc. . . .

One is stupefied by such platitudes and ineptitudes. Even in the 9th century it would have required a very strong and simple-minded faith to take the *Enchyridion* seriously!

Page 83: "Charlemagne used it in war and thus he became invincible; in those days people had such faith in prayers of the Holy Church that one deflected cannonballs by saying prayers such as . . . etc."

In the contents one can again find: "'For love; to cure colic; garter for walking (prayer written on a piece of paper folded in the shape of a garter . . .) and that is how the marathon world record is broken; to remove any curse or enchantment; against wolves, etc. . . ."

One prayer reproduces the words used by Adam when he entered into hell, and his prayer to make his wife faithful!

When your house is burning

A "mystical secret" which is useful, even essential to know, figures on page 146:

To avoid the spreading of the fire burning a house. "Say: Let it stop, let it stop—I have placed my hope in you, Lord, whose glory merges with eternity." And this of course will work much better than a fire extinguisher or than a call to the fire brigade!

Otherwise the magic powers of the *Enchyridion* tend to be simple mystifications.

The finest subtlety, the crowning piece, seems to appear on page 71, describing a peculiar drawing: "This figure, forty times enlarged, represents the height of Jesus Christ." (This is the title.)

"It was found in Constantinople inside a golden cross; whoever wears it can have no better protection; he will never die from sudden death, nor from fire, nor from water, nor from an arrow, nor from tempest, nor from thunder, nor from poison, nor from evil spirits, nor from misjudgment, nor from false witnesses. . . ."

And as if by chance this unexpected prayer comes before "a copy of Abagarre's letter written and sent to Jesus Christ in Jerusalem by the messenger Ananas"!

Denise de la Caille, possessed of the Devil

In 1972 A.D., the "very solemn Biship Robert Mortimer, Bishop of Exeter, leading an English ecclesiastical commission, asked the Church to strengthen her fight against Black Magic. "The presence and power of evil spirits has become greater," said Robert Mortimer. "We must create special schools to train priests capable of exorcising people possessed of the Devil."

In fact ever since the period of armor, palfreys (royal parade horses of the Middle Ages), and enchanters, this superstition has remained alive in the Western Christian world, nearly as lively in 1612, when demons possessed the body of Denise de la Caille, the possessed girl of Beauvais!

The story is told in a book of that time which is called: *A True Story, which happened in our days in the town of Beauvais about the incantation and exorcisms enacted on Denise de la Caille, possessed of the Devil, with the actions and evidence instituted on the very spot by order of the Bishop, a profitable and religious account, full of the Devil's wonderfully strange deeds.*

The possession of Denise de la Caille is the very case in point, with the happy characteristic that the poor woman was not burned as a witch, but taken care of, although somewhat empirically, with charity and simple kindness.

According to the official report, the possessed was filled with horrible torments "particularly when she went to church to pray." She then remained unable to walk, blind, "sometimes crying and howling." The parish priest took her to see his Bishop, René Potier, who advised a visit to "a doctor or someone who knew." Jean Cheron, theologian, recognized that the illness was not merely physical, a fact agreed by the medical expert. "Exaggerated agitations, an unnaturally fast pulse, also he admits that such strength could not come from a human being, he now decides with the advice of others that this must be the work of evil spirits. . . ."

Doctor and priests now agree that Denise de la Caille is possessed of the devil and they decide to send her to an exorciser of the order of St. Dominque, named Laurent le Pot.

She bellows and departs

On August 1, in the little church of Saint-Gilles, the priest begins his exorcism in public: He bids the evil spirit, cause of these agitations and convulsions, to appear before him. He questions him in Latin, asks his nam, , and whether he is acting on his own or with other devils. The answer to these questions is a series of grimaces and a name "Beelzebub."

On August 9, during the Mass of the Holy Sacrament, "he asks him whether some sorcerer or spell was preventing him from coming out, he refused to do anything but howl, lifting himself into the air with such incredible strength that those who were holding him down could not stop him." (This must be read knowing that the author now identifies the patient with the Devil. In a sense, it is the Devil who bellows and not Denise.)

Two days later the exorcist "burnt the name of the Demon with blessed fire and sulphur; he then asked him why he had entered the body at which the devil howled and bellowed at nine intervals: *Nolo.*"

At each seance the devil is questioned; he is asked his name, which is Lisis, they also want to find out who are the other devils possessing the body of this wretched girl. The answers are quite absurd: "Brissolo, Brissilula, Brulu, Campala. This burden will torment Denise; I will dig her teeth into the earth; I hold her; I will torment her in front, sideways, internally and externally."

Then, looking at the two priests, he adds: "Dirty beards, you are two against one. Yes, I have lead many people a dance, for I have broken Moses' tablets, while the people were made to dance round a statue. I also threw Daniel in the lions' den. . . ."

When she is in a trance, Denise takes the opportunity, consciously or unconsciously, to take revenge on the Christian religion, which oppresses her, and on the neighbors she wishes to harm: She bellows in the church, throws her church candle, insults the priests, refuses blessed water, and says of her neighbor, Griphon, "He is a villain and a rogue and that he is not worthy of kissing her backside."

She tries to compromise several other girls at Beauvais,

saying that they have dealings with Beelzebub but Father Le Pot is an enlightened priest and he does not let her influence him.

Satan, in danger of excommunication!

Sentence given against the devils by the Father Exorcist:

> On December 12 the Devil appeared at the beginning of the incantation, seeing this the priest ordered him to hear his sentence of arrest: We, vicars-general of his Lordship the Bishop and Count of Beauvais, command, wish, ask, and order the devil Lisis to descend to hell, and to leave the body of the aforesaid Denise de la Caille forever.
>
> We command, wish, and order that Beelzubub, Satan, Matelu, and Briffault, the four leaders and the four legions which are in their charge and under their power and also that all other devils, whether they be in the air, in the water, in iron, on earth, or other places, which have other powers over the body and in the body of the aforesaid Denise de la Caille to appear now and without delay on pain of excommunication, and hell, and if they do not appear now in this body I throw them into the power of hell to be more crucified and tormented even than is usual, and this will happen as they do not answer the third summons.
>
> We command, wish, ask, and order that the aforesaid sentence should last three thousand years from this day of judgment. We forbid the same Lisis, and all others who have possessed the body of the aforesaid Denise, ever to enter a body again, be it of an animal or human, on pain of suffering extra sentences, on possession.

One fully understands how when threatened with excommunication and hell Beelzebub and Satan, terrified, preferred to admit defeat!

Beelzebub, Satan, Lisis, Matelu, and Briffault sign their su   !er

> The hearing proceeds:
>
> Following this, the aforesaid Lisis, the evil one, ready to depart, has signed; Beelzebub comes forward, Lisis retires to the right arm, then Beelzebub also signs, then Beelzebub having retired, Satan comes forward and signs for all his legion and retires to the left arm, then Matelu appears, signs for all his legion, and retires to the right ear, straight away Briffault comes forward and also signs for his legion and all five abandon the creature, leaving her as if she was dead for six hours or more. [It is quite clear that here also the patient is identified with demons, but one wonders how far the inquisitors believed in this farce].
>
> Signed: LISIS; Signed: BEELZEBUB; Signed: SATAN; Signed: MATELU; Signed: BRIFFAULT.

As everyone knows, devils respect their pledge, and the inquiry certifies that Denise de la Caille, from that day forward, was never again plagued by them! The document moreover was authenticated by a host of prelates and witnesses who signed "the present document on the twentieth day of April of the year one thousand six hundred and thirt ..

We must be grateful to the Bishop of Beauvais and to the good father Le Pot for having shown such humanity in dealing with this woman, but already in the 16th century, and long before, right back to Greek antiquity, certain enlightened thinkers knew that the Devil and all his legions were mere fantasy! Today we know that most trances, raptures, and convulsions, which were once called "furies of the womb," are hysterical.

The curse that killed Papus

Pierre Mariel, in a remarkable study of legends and anecdotes connected with Parisian cemeteries, retells a story of Doctor Philippe Encausse, son of Gerard Papus, occult writer.

"Fifteen days before his death," writes P. Encausse, "my father was the victim of a hoodoo which he admitted himself was a fine piece of work.

During the night, pins had been planted on the front door of our flat. Cleverly arranged, they formed a cross and a coffin. . . ."

"They must come twice more," Papus was supposed to have said, "but I will probably be gone before that. I am not allowed to defend myself." Nevertheless he drew a protective triangle.

The following week the same image was drawn on the door. A few days later coming up the stairs, Papus staggered, spat out blood, and collapsed, smitten by the curse—which was most probably pulmonary tuberculosis.

The death of Fabre d'Olivet

Fabre d'Olivet, who is the much-appreciated author of the book, *Les Grands Initiés*, was a talented writer, a magician, whose exaggerated spiritualism had somewhat deranged his mind.

In 1800, writes Pierre Mariel, he married his first wife, who remained in spiritual communication with him after her death so much so that she made him believe that he was a high priest whose mission was "to reveal the most profound mysteries of mankind, of the Universe, and of God."

In 1805, he married a second time, a sensible wife who divorced him rather than engage herself further in the diabolical course her "high priest" husband wished to lead her into.

Fabre d'Olivet did nonetheless find another wife who was a medium, which enabled him to indulge in insane and preposterous psychic speculation.

He died "a magician, struck at the foot of the secret altar which he had consecrated in his Parisian abode, 35 rue des Vieilles Tuileries (now rue du Cherche-Midi)." According to certain chroniclers, he had an apoplectic seizure just as he was about to solemnize his mass; Saint-Yves d'Alveydre believes that he committed suicide.

The magician was found clad in a linen robe, a dagger planted in his breast, victim of his own hoodoo or of unknown forces which he had unwisely invoked.

Sacrilege at Raivavae

At the beginning of the 19th century Christian missionaries in Polynesia achieved the conversion of Variatoa, or Pomare II, King of Tahiti. It was the start of a campaign of vandalism and destruction of the stone idols the natives had held sacred for centuries.

In 1820, of all the hundreds of statues on Raivavae Island, there were only three left; two were later taken to Papeete; the third has remained on the island. This idol, or *tiki*, represents the god Tetuaranui and is only 8 centimeters high, which seems incredible when one knows that the ancient Polynesians believed themselves to be descended from a race of giants.

The Chief of Raivavae was always chosen from the tallest among the natives, and he had to pass the test of being measured at the *marae* of Rangura. (A *marae* is a kind of altar or platform made of stone. It is the *ahu* of the Easter Islands.) At the center of the *marae* stands a menhir (or standing stone) 2 meters high: This the measuring stone of the chiefs.

"The candidate taking the test, to succeed had to be of sufficient height to rest his armpit on the stone. King Maha-otoa's tomb, three meters long, gives an idea of his impressive stature."

According to local belief, the *tikis* are inhabited for a time by the spirit of the dead. Only members of the family may touch them, but woe betide the stranger or ill-disposed person who disobeys this rule: Instant death is the penalty.

On the other hand some *tikis* grow fond of their owner if they feel he is sincere, honest, and reliable; then they have a good influence.

Moana, the evil statue

On November 12, 1933, the captain of a schooner, Steven Higgins, and his first mate, Tetua Mervin, brought to Papeete the two large *tikis* from Raivavae and they were placed first at the entrance of the law courts, then in front of the old Museum of Mama'o. Shortly afterwards, Higgins' schooner was wrecked. The captain escaped, but a few days later he died of an unknown illness. As for the workmen who put up the *tikis*, they nearly all died from accidents or strange causes.

Each statue has a name: Heiata is the man and Moanaheiata is his companion, and she is called Moana for short. Heiata is "dead"; his height is 2.17 meters, he weighs 900 kilograms, and he is castrated—as he is "dead" that is to say not inhabited by a spirit, he does not need sexual attributes. This is why he was castrated.

Moana is alive. She is 2.02 meters tall and weighs 2,110 kilograms, she is the one who is "charged" and throws evil spells. Particularities: She originally had six fingers on each hand and undecipherable inscriptions engraved on her back.

These statues are carved out of fairly soft stone, a sort of red basalt, just like the giants of the Easter Islands. When they were in Raivavae, they were placed facing north, and they were considered as genii of the sand and shore, which they protected from the encroaching sea.

When plans were made for the building of the Mama'o Hospital, the taboo which surrounded these statues became a great source of worry: No private firm would take on the task of dislodging them to transport them elsewhere. The French Navy was called in and were about to do the work, when a Commander, who had retired to Tahiti, where members of the armed forces were seldom admitted, advised the naval authorities not to act against local belief. Finally, the Public Works Department was made responsible for this operation, which took place in June, 1965, with the men from the Marquises Islands. The *tikis* were finally installed in front of the Paul Gauguin Museum at Papeari, fifty-five kilometers from Papeete.

Again the evil spell came into play. The foreman died of a heart attack; one of his employees disappeared from his canoe while fishing on a lagoon, one young man who had gibed at the *tikis* when they were in transit (he may even have kicked Moana) killed himself on his motorcycle.

Since then, nothing more has been heard about the *tikis*, but no old Tahitian would ever dare to touch them or to come closer than six paces.

If, in Polynesia, you happen to find a cut stone of an anthropomorphous shape, the natives will tell you never to touch it. If you want to have it, you must first enquire from which family it came, then have it taken to a witch doctor to learn whether the *tiki* is still alive or not. If it is, the witch doctor will keep the statue long enough to chase away the evil spirit. Then you will be able to take delivery of it quite safely.

Bossuet, the black witch doctor

There are many more witches than witch doctors, perhaps because women still carry the original sin handed down from Eve or Lilith.

In the 17th century, the terrible and machiavellian Bossuet, "l'Aigle de Meaux," was far more diabolical than the wretched women he sent to the stake. Not only was he one of those most responsible for the revocation of the Edict of Nantes, so fatal to France, but the very week the Protestants were chased out, he plundered their homes.

"This dreadful deed," the Encyclopaedia reads, "is proved by the official despatch dated from Fontainbleau, October 19, 1685." More loathsome still: He sent to prison wretched women whose sole crime was to have stood in the way of his ambitions.

A dispatch, dated Octover 18, 1699, addressed by Pontchartrain to M. Phelypeaux, Vicar General of Meaux, contains this very significant phrase: "There are also, in the same parish of Ussy, two young girls named de Molliers whom M. de Meaux [Bossuet] deems important to lock up. . . ."

This odious man, in one of his delirious sermons, claimed to know that a conspiracy of 180,000 witches was threatening the future of Europe, and good Christian that he was, he proposed that they should all be grilled together on one huge funeral pyre!

Bossuet used the dangerous magic of his words to flatter the great, but also to bring misery, injustice, and death to the unhappy and the outcast. His black magic finally turned against him; he died of stones, after two years of deserved and cruel suffering. The Devil took his soul.

A funeral pyre for the year 2000

Nowadays witchcraft is still strong even though its image and fashions have changed.

On November 25, 1970, the Japanese writer Yukio Mishima committed harakiri in Tokyo and was at once decapitated with the stroke of a saber by his assistant, Morita, who disemboweled himself and was then decapitated in turn by Masayohsi Koga. It was to accomplish a rite in keeping with the feelings of the Samurai, a military aristocracy of Japan, still faithful to ceremonial rites centuries old, which are in fact black magic.

According to statistics there are still 10,000 sorcerers in Paris, but this includes most of the quacks: clairvoyants male and female, fortune tellers, astrologists, and water diviners, who have really nothing to do with witchcraft.

In 1971, in Saigon, sorcerers or believers in witchcraft threw some children into a tributary river of the Mekong to conjure up the evil spells of an aquatic monster who would bring devastation at the time of the monsoon.

The Cambodian French daily newspaper, *Le Courrier Phnompenhois*, announced in September, 1970, that the Vietcong had employed to fight their war, and in particular at the battle of Prek Tamaeak, amazons chosen for their beauty and their physical perfection. Naked from head to toe, these bewitching fighting women carried guns, but their mission was to distract the enemy. Cambodians are convinced that the presence of these women makes useless the talisman which the men wear on their chests to make themselves invulnerable.

The newspaper *France-Soir* of September 23, 1971, reported

at great length a self-inflicted fit of hysterical madness, whose victim was a young Swiss girl of the Universal White Brotherhood whose ''master'' is Ouraam Mikhael Aivanhov.

'' 'I mutilated myself to punish myself, and to come nearer to God,' '' said the young disciple of the ''sun worshipers,'' who had so cruelly disfigured herself, near Frejus. . . . ''During these investigations,'' continues *France-Soir*, ''the police inspector Gonzales found out that a young man had taken his own life, hanging himself in this locality. The inquest reached the conclusion that it was the suicide of a madman.''

The young girl, Diane Bontay, had inflicted cruel wounds on her eyes, her feet, and her breasts. The police found her, stark naked, on September 15, near Bagnols-du-Var, in a forest.

Witchcraft? Hysteria? Our troubled times, aggravated by unscrupulous governments and thinkers, are ripe for the total disorientation of the intellect and the senses. Satan leads the dance with his alienated youth, his drug addicts, his magicians, and his mercenary followers dedicated to gold and power. The poor witch doctors of the past were mere apprentices, the Masters are now in office and it is they who make promises to Moloch—the great universal killer of the year 2000.

PART VI

Mysteries of the sky

CHAPTER TWENTY-THREE

ADVENTURES IN THE SKY

If the origin of man is extraterrestrial, or if, once upon a time, the Earth was populated with beings from another world, it is quite logical to think that the first earthly woman, mother of our advanced human race, was a creature chosen either for her powers of survival or for her exceptional beauty.

In Chapter 3 we have studied the problems of our genesis. Either Darwin's theory is right concerning our species, and therefore there is a plurality of inhabited worlds, or else, and this is what we are trying to prove, man is an exceptional being conceived by lucky chance or by superior Intelligence, and if so, there must be, somewhere in the cosmos, a center of Initiation. This is why avant-garde writers such as Gilbert A. Bourquin and Jimmy Guieu believe in Superior Ancestors who came in days gone by to promote our development and who now return or will return—because our adventure is basically cosmic and follows the privileged destiny that is ours.

In this perspective, more rational than the prehistorian's point of view, the monkey is a natural being and man a supernatural creature. The prehistorians, to give weight to their theories, ought by now to have discovered human skulls that could relate us to monkeylike ancestors. They do not find these, either because the remains have disappeared, or because they are on another planet.

These verifications explain how well founded is the idea believed by millions of people that the conquest of space today is the echo of a distant emigration of our extraterrestrial Ancestors.

Professor Hurzeler of the University of Vienna shakes the bastions of the "rationalists" and makes a step in this direction when he declares: "There is not a chance in a thousand that man descended from the ape."

The Valley of Marvels in Mexico

The Mexican writer and archaeologist Carlos Villanueva believes he made the discovery of his life when he found a "Valley of Marvels" even more interesting than the one in the region of Tende in France. He writes:

> It is an area of pictures engraved in the rocks, which spreads over more than three kilometers between San Pedro de las Colonias and the little town of Saltillo, State of Coahuila.
>
> Near the village of San Rafael of the Miracles [de los Milagros] to the southwest, one finds a great many rocks covered with tracings, figures, and geometrical forms. A surprising detail: The bodies of human beings are engraved in the rock, but the animals are painted. The people have no eyes, no nose, no mouth and are egg-shaped or round with a sort of porthole in the center. I can only see one ex-

planation of this phenomenon: They are either deep-water divers or cosmonauts, this theory furthermore would explain why several of them seem to float or be in a state of weightlessness with hands and feet facing upward.

I also discovered in the same area spirals, squares, circles, and triangles. . . .

Message engraved by extraterrestrial beings

With his back to the wall, Villanueva finally conceded:

Several of these drawings have an extraordinary likeness to spaceships or what are called UFO's but it is wiser not to advance such thoughts in certain circles!

Nevertheless, one clearly sees domes, circular objects from which descend small ladders, triangular forms provided with what one could describe as a landing raft. One can also see circles placed on the ground and footmarks walking toward outlined mountains.

These drawings are perhaps the most tangible proof that extraplanetary cosmonauts came to our globe. The most convincing drawing is that of a man, wearing a veritable spacesuit. An aerial comes out of the center of his spacesuit helmet and on the sides tubes seem to connect the man to his vessel. This cosmonaut emerges from something that looks like an exit hatch, and his right arm touches the flank of his machine in the same way as the commander of a tank standing in the gun turret. On the same level as his head, and to the left, one can see an egg-shaped object with four lights. Perhaps this is a UFO. . . .

This is the story which one correspondent and a friend from Mexico, Mrs. M. Gaston, brought us, from the very mouth of Carlos Villanueva.

Giants and cosmonauts

The Valley of Marvels in Mexico has not yet revealed all its secrets, which another explorer, the engineer Mario J. Donde of Merida, Yucatan, is trying to uncover.

Donde has brought to light in the region of Parras, only a few miles from the "Cosmonaut," the bodies of five men standing in a vast circular tomb. The corpses, partly mummified, were wrapped in a material which seemed to be made of synthetic fiber; they were giants—at least 2.50—and as far as one could judge, they were fair-haired.*

Their human characteristics, different from ours, lead us to believe that these men did not belong to our race and that they may have been extraterrestrial beings. Moreover, other discoveries and local traditions support this theory.

A local peasant, who was exploring the mountain with some friends, tells us that in the Sierra Delicias, on the road to San Pedro and Cuatro Cienagas, he had found in a cave the skeleton of a man three or four meters long. The explorers, who had to spend the night in the cave, broke the skeleton to pieces and threw it out of their shelter.

One family still owns some large teeth which they say they took from the jaw of a gigantic man.

At Sant Eulalia, a village situated on the road to San Lorenzo, the story goes that a very long time ago the area was occupied by a tribe of genii-sorcerers who achieved miracles "more impressive than those that happen nowadays." For example, one sorcerer picked up the bones of a bull, laid them out on the

*We must link this to the divine initiator, Quetzalcoatl, who was a god from the planet Venus. Ancient Mayas describe him as tall, bearded, fair-haired, with blue eyes. A lock of his very blond hair is kept in a church in Mexico. *Quetzalcoatl, the "flying serpent," was a space traveler.*

ground, performed a certain rite, and the animal came back to life. Donde sees in this the abbreviated and mutilated transmission of an ancient scientific knowledge.

The tribe of the genii-sorcerers disappeared one day into the mountain of Santa Eulalia, which became enchanted. Since then, one can see a host of little men drawn on the rocks.

Donde has discovered other engraved drawings, much larger but which can only be seen at certain times of the day and in a certain light. At Saltillo (twelve kilometers away) they can be seen from 7 to 8 A.M. In the area of Parras, to the west, the most favorable times are between 9 and 11 A.M.; one can clearly discern a man standing and wearing a spacesuit with helmet.

Mrs. M. Gaston is of the opinion that these inscriptions, only visible at certain determined times, could be messages or signs intended for space travelers.

The flying gods of Australia

In the northwest of Australia, in the country of the Ungarinyin, the archaeologist Elkin discovered "*wondjina*" (genii galleries) where on the rocks were painted mouthless faces similar to the ones in Mexico and to the Glozel potteries. (Mouthless faces generally represent death.)

M. Lévy-Bruhl observes that *wondjina* also means: "which has the power to produce rain," which recalls the gods of Venus of Assyro-Babylonian mythology, space gods who arrived with the fertilizing rains or who had the power to produce them at their command.*

*The question of these rains, which accompanied the arrival of Venus-Gods, of Astarte, the Phoenician goddess, in particular, is not really resolved.

Symbolically, the Initiator who taught previously unknown scientific secrets brought a wealth comparable to a beneficial

These *wondjina* wear a radiant band on their heads, the "*gari,*" which, according to natives, is a very light apparatus, offering a broad surface to the wind. With the Majo, the *gari* worn by the sorcerer makes him resemble a flying man, and in fact, the apparatus, often three or four meters high, is reminiscent of the first air machines and Lilienthal's glider, which flew in 1896.

"*Wondjina*" has an equivalent: "*ungud,*" which means "rainbow serpent, flying serpent," and refers to the mythical time of the gods who knew all secrets. It is difficult not to see in this the vague recollections of contact with extraterrestrials!

The mouthless gods, and even more the San Pedro de la Colonias' cosmonaut, remind us of the gods of wealth of the ancient Hindus: Couvera, a sort of deformed monster— particularly when he wore a spacesuit—and who in place of eyes had yellow spots. Couvera traveled in a magnificent chariot called "*pouchpaka,*" which worked only at the command of its driver on land or in the air.

Moons, suns and wheels in the sky

The "wonders in the sky' overwhelmingly impressed the people of antiquity, who explained these phenomena to the best of their knowledge.

In *De Prodigiis*, Julius Obsequens, a Latin writer of the 4th century, refers to three moons which appeared in the sky of the Aegean and to the horrifying explosion which accompanied

---

rain. In a country of deserts water is more precious than gold. Besides, it is well known that rockets—those of the ancient cosmonauts—can produce clouds to rain. But it is our opinion that the real explanation is the following: The appearance of the planet Venus in our solar system started fires and torrential rain.

These torrential rains, which coincided with the arrival of the gods, or which preceded them, are the basis of this tradition.

the appearance of a globe of fire "from the North."

"In Tarquin was seen from many places a flaming torch falling from the sky in a startling and sudden flight. Across the setting sun, a spherical object exactly like a shield was seen stretching from West to East." Another time, in the middle of the night, appeared two suns, then a little later a firebrand in the shape of a torch.

"*Phenomenes spatiaux*," medium of the GEPA, revives, from *l'Histoire Naturelle de l'Air et des Meteores* by l'Abbe Richard (1771), the story of the well-known sailor, Claude de Frobin, when he was navigating by night near Cape Passaro in Sicily. He had just been told that a new sun was appearing in the sky.

"I came up on deck and I did in fact see a great fire burning in the sky, which gave enough light to read a letter. Although the wind was blowing strong, this meteor never moved; it burned for about two hours, then disappeared, fading out little by little."

Ovid, in the *Metamorphosis*, says that the Milky Way is the road the gods take to go to their palaces, and Aeschylus in *Prometheus Bound*, writes that Oceanus flew on a bridleless bird, with little wings, which in one account is called a "winged chariot."

In days gone by, just as now, people saw strange things in the sky and were not at all hostile to the idea of planets inhabited by special kinds of beings. Mexicans knew that their gods, Quetzalcoatl and Huitzilopochtli, were from Venus and that they went to their planet in a jet-propelled craft, which they have often drawn in their oldest manuscripts. When the space gods were gone, the memory faded and instead of drawing a machine with jet pipes as in the Troano Manuscript or the Dresden Codex, Perez and Cortesianus, they drew a romantic version of it: a flying serpent, with feathers and arrows symbolizing flight in space.

The Celts, also, imagined Abaris (Apollo), traveling through the air, astride an arrow. Neunins, an Irish chronicler of the 3rd century, mentions in his stories the presence of "mysterious demonlike vessels floating in the air." The Breton writer Claude Yvon speaks of a manuscript which mentions the "*roth ramarach,*" or the whirling wheel, flying over lands and oceans. "One day it crashed to the ground, attracted by the magic emanations from the stone pillar (menhir?) situated in a forest, near what is now Tipperary."

It is possible that the wheel was once revered, not because it represented the solar globe, but perhaps because golden wheels traveling through the sky had transported gods. Was that not the case of the wheel of Ezekiel, of Celtic, Basque, and Hindu wheels?

The extraterrestrial globes of Manila

The Igorots, inhabitants of the mountainous provinces of the North Philippines, built the "Eighth Wonder of the World": the vast, terraced ricefields of Ifugao, which are ten times as long as the Great Wall of China, that is to say, 30,000 kilometers.

Local tradition tells us that gods, the "Kabunians," resided for 15,000 moons in this country. They had come from the sky, on flying vessels in the shape of globes, which had landed on the terraces. Then one day the globes departed. The Igorots waited for them for than 1,000 moons, but the space gods never came back.

In Lithuanian tradition, the Milky Way is called "*Pauksciu Kelias,*" the Path of the Birds, that is to say, birds . . . made of iron, as the Eskimos would say.

A ghost island on the radar

This story, sent to us by a radio officer of a transatlantic liner, does not seem to refer properly speaking to the UFO enigma, but it throws a strange light on radar observations so valuable in detecting flying machines. The incident happened one night in October, 1971, off the Canary Islands. This is what our correspondent writes:

> I was on watch at the radio station when the bridge lieutenant sent for me. We were navigating on a busy route far from any land, but nevertheless the radar in front of us showed us, about twenty-five miles away, an island, which, of course, was not shown on our nautical map. A quick check assured us that we had not made any navigating errors, and the lieutenant, not knowing what to think, asked my advice.
>
> Could it be interference or a failure of the instruments? I was positive the radar was in perfect working order, it could perhaps have failed to indicate an echo, but it was certainly impossible for it to reflect something which was not there!
>
> We eliminated the theory of interference from other radar for, in such a case, the false sonic beams would show up as luminous trails and would not appear at the same place on the screen, after each rotation. Moreover it would quickly disappear, while this phenomenon remained and lasted for two hours at least.
>
> Visibility being poor, we couldn't see the island which, nevertheless, was coming nearer to us as we traveled on. If it was real, we would have hit it any moment. We could easily make out the details of a jagged land, with

mountains, approximately ten miles long.

As we knew our route extremely well and were perfectly sure that there couldn't be an island there, we kept on our course as if nothing had happened and without alerting the commander, but all the same we were very worried! The nearer we came to it the clearer the sonic boom sounded. We could now see a headland and a mountain range. We were very near the obstacle, and yet, in front of us, before our eyes—nothing but water!

We were ready to put the helm hard over, but to change one's course to avoid an island which was not there makes one a case for the asylum! How could one explain it later?

When we were one mile from the obstacle the picture slowly disappeared and we went over the exact spot of the echo without seeing anything out of the ordinary.

Strange Happenings in the Mediterranean

M.L., who sent us this certainly truthful observation, was in 1969 witness of another phenomenon which could this time be directly related with UFO's.

All this happened in July, 1969, in the Mediterranean. I was aboard a coaster. In the same way as in the incident in the Atlantic I was called by the lieutenant in charge of the radar: A sonic beam had just crossed the screen. I could see nothing when I approached the screen, but suddenly a great many echoes appeared moving in formation and marked out a route on the screen at an incredible speed. They turned back; went in all directions all over the radar. This activity lasting several minutes.

Making a quick and approximate calculation, they must have been moving at about 10,000 kilometers per hour!

Several times they passed close to the ship but we never caught sight of them nor heard them.

We were coming from Antibes, and were going to Lavera, traveling between the island of Levant and Cap Sicie. And, that night, at the very place where we had seen our sonic beams, two oil tankers of great tonnage met at full speed. There were several deaths, among them wives who were traveling with their husbands. Visibility was very good, the navigating apparatus in perfect order. At the inquest, this accident seemed incredible.

It was at this time, I remember very well, that the first man landed on the moon. Just within a few days, if we wish to fix the date.

We feel that these genuine accounts could prove useful to the study of the phenomenon of unidentified flying objects and strange radar observations.

Radar does not make mistakes, but. . . .

As a rule, a radar always sends back the echo of objects, but the object, in some cases, can have almost no appreciable consistence. Sometimes it is just a very close formation of electrons and ions in the atmosphere. These electric clouds, sometimes luminous, sometimes invisible, are produced by the energy sent out by some planets in the form of hertzien waves. The lightwaves and heatwaves are thus transformed by an internal mechanism and reflect on the radar waves. They can also cause reflections without one being able to distinguish on the screen whether they come from a meteorite, a rocket, a plane, or a mass of particles.

On November 24, 1960, the head of the American base

at Thule, Greenland, almost pushed the red button, which would have started an atomic war, because the radar on his set showed pictures of hundreds of intercontinental missiles coming straight at the USA.

Luckily, he had the good sense to check, and found that the emission of radio waves from the Moons, that night, on 3.2 centimeters, was particularly intense, and had appeared on the screen!

Any planet, and the Sun, under certain circumstances, can produce this phenomenon, well-known to scientists. By mere chance, the pictures on the Thule radar were in the shape of missiles!

The fuelless engine of Van den Berg

The South African engineer, Basil Van den Berg was, in 1962, so convinced of the authenticity of flying saucers, that basing his design on extraterrestrial objects and messages of somewhat doubtful authenticity, he invented and built a ''no-fuel engine'' of which the daily newspaper *Stem*, in its edition of April 29, made a long study.

It was an anitgravity machine which Van den Berg intended to take to Mexico to test for reasons he did not give.

The very day his invention was made known, he disappeared without trace. This curious incident was diversely interpreted by those who knew what the engineer was up to, and some whispered that he had been kidnapped by beings alien to our planet. Others declared that he must quite simply have been removed by a powerful industrial group, which leaves us to suppose that the UFO problem, and interplanetary travel, occupy the scientists of our globe far more than we think.

Chapter Twenty-Four

Extraterrestrial Secret Societies

Rightly or wrongly, many people think that extraterrestrials are living among us. It is a theory which is difficult to demolish, but impossible to prove.

We personally are in contact with several persons who claim to be alien to Earth, or who claim to have been to another planet. Because this phenomenon is an integral part of our times, and because to be objective we must give it exposure, we have incorporated in this report of unusual happenings the case of the mysterious Mn Y, who later became Emen Y.

The Aetherius Society

Is Emem Y really an official representative of the planet Baavi de Proxima of the Centaur Constellation? We shall probably never know! His French representative provides training, both scientific and spiritualistic, which has the advantage of being free.

At Rambouillet, René D assures us that he is the only authorized representative of the extraterrestrials on Earth, but we have good reasons for believing that he is merely the victim of a wild imagination.

He claims that "the all-powerful extraterrestrials and cosmic engineers work for our Savior Jesus Christ" and insists on the resignation of the President of France and of the two Assemblies!

At Dax, a mysterious person has become incarnate—so he says—in the body of an earthly man. He only shows himself to a very small group, to whom he reveals the magnificence of science on his own planet.

The Aetherius Society, Aetherius House, 757 Fulham Road, in London SW6, is a circle devoted to psychic research, directed by Dr. George King, yogi and master of occult science, born in 1919 in Shropshire, England. He has telepathic communication with extraterrestrials and visits other planets "in a state of suspended animation."

From his trips, Dr. King brings back scientific secrets whose nature he only divulges to his adherents: teletransportation, the use of "radioniques," the possibility of traveling at a speed four million times faster than light, the perfect control of cosmic forces, etc. The inhabitants of Venus, according to him, have the power to change the positions of planets in the solar system.

The inhabitants of Venus and of Mars, if they came to visit Earth in a condition called "third life," would measure 2.30 meters high, they would have skin the color of cinnamon, long hair, blue eyes, and wear a one-piece garmet. On Venus, animals, and probably people, have an internal temperature of 110 to 150 degrees Fahrenheit (110°F = 61° centigrade). There is no Venusian writing; as in all extremely advanced civilizations communications are not verbal or written, but telepathic.

Members of the Aetherius Society firmly believe in flying saucers and in the desire of extraterrestrials to save the inhabitants of the Earth from their errors. The Masters, Jesus, Buddha, and Shri Krishna, were intelligentsia from outer space and used bodies only to accomplish their particular mission. This is a short résumé of the program of this association.

The legend of hell

One legend which could really be a true story, according to Dr. King, but which has been distorted through repetition, gives a strange interpretation of the myth of hell.

Nearly 20,000 years ago, scientists of Atlanta are said to have reached the center of the earth in an attempt to master "the flame of eternal life" and to assert their power over the whole solar system. They failed in their mission but acquired the privilege of infinite life. On the other hand, they remained imprisoned in the central nucleus for thousands of years. Finally they were saved by certain adepts of great scientific ability, and it is said that the legend of hell is based on this adventure.

Among the Initiated also circulates information on "the flame of eternal life": about 1950 some miners in Siberia apparently became younger to a spectacular extent. Their wrinkles disappeared and they no longer needed to eat. A medium, sent by the British Government, is said to have offered Dr. King a considerable fortune if he would disclose where this youth-producing ore was to be found. The doctor was prepared to help, but Her Majesty the Queen, would not promise that she would use this secret only for peaceful ends.

Such stories and many others are publicly told at the Aetherius Society conferences.

Eugenio Siragusa

The Central Study of the Cosmic Fraternity has its headquarters in Lausanne. Address: CEFC Fracos, PB 2798, 1000 Lausanne 22, Switzerland.

This center broadcasts messages "from extraterrestrials on duty on planet Earth" and refers to the Divine Law and the Master, Jesus. The messenger of the Cosmic Fraternity is a sort of archangel, named Ashtar Sheran; the representative from Earth is Signor Eugenio Siragusa, who is a fifty-year-old Sicilian. A magic sign which appeared in the sky, when he was thirty-three, made him conscious of his mission and of his eternal soul.

From then on, a voice from inside instructed him in geology and cosmogony, and gave him a clear insight into the mysteries of creation and of his previous life. Siragusa thus learned 12,000 years ago, he was a student at Poseidon, in Atlanta, in a society founded on wisdom and love.

As with Dr. King, he is in telepathic contact with extraterrestrials, whom he met on Mount Etna, one night in 1962. Two beings, in silvery spacesuits, were waiting for him there. They were tall, athletically built, with fair hair down to their shoulders. They wore on their wrists and ankles some sort of bands shining like gold, and around the waist a luminescent belt. Strange metal plates sparkled on their chests. One of the men directed towards Siragusa a beam of green light from an object he held in his hand which gave him a wonderful feeling of well-being and confidence.

"We have been waiting for you," he said. "Record in your memory what we are about to say."

It was a message to all heads of government in the world. The two beings were the representatives of an Intergalactic Confederation gathering together innumerable planets, who had in a manner of speaking judged the civilization of Earth and found it wanting: a conspiracy of lies, crimes called acts of heroism, violence, racial hatred, distorted and fanatical religion. From a distance of many light-years, these two luminescent beings had come to help us, and our refusal to change ourselves for the better utterly perplexed them.

A reassuring conclusion: We are watched over by a superior race which will not allow us to engulf our civilization in a nuclear disaster.

Extraterrestrial base on the Black Moon

Is Siragusa a visionary, a missionary? One wonders, but certainly he is totally disinterested and it is quite clear that he is sincere, even when he publicly announces breathtaking revelations.

"There are," he tells us, "a million extraterrestrials on our planet."

The American Government is aware of this situation, which is branded, we do not know why, as Top Secret. NATO apparently has proof of the existence of these travelers from another world—the spacesuit of the pilot of a flying saucer! (After research, we are now absolutely sure that this statement is unfounded.)

Extraterrestrials have a life span of some 12,000 years; all great Initiates and particularly Jesus and Buddha were natives of another planet. As an excuse for the inhabitants of Earth, it must be noted that their average IQ is very low: 3.5 against 15 for the E-T and 60 for the inhabitants of Alpha in the Centaur Constellation.

According to the Sicilian prophet's account, flying saucers really do exist, and the landing base for these machines is on a small artificial satellite of the moon which has been placed in a certain orbit to prevent our own natural satellite from colliding with Earth. This small satellite has a name—Black Moon—which curiously coincides with the tradition of Lilith and with the observations of Cassini and of many other astronomers, who, as long ago as the 17th century, had identified this heavenly body, which is very difficult to locate.

The Black Moon, if it really is artificial, has been in existence for at least 300 years, in which case the E-T's who look after us do not seem very effective except for arranging clandestine meetings.

A Messianic phenomenon

There are many other societies or sects which assert their relationship with an "intergalactic society"; there are several other individuals who say they were born on or have traveled to planets many light-years away.

It is very important for a contemporary writer and witness to study these phenomena and record them in the archives of this century. In fact, Emen Y, Dr. King, and Signor Siragusa appear to us as the new prophets, the Jeremiah, Ezekiel, and Job of our time. Just like them, they sound the alarm, revile the rich and the powerful, the greedy merchants and the politicians, the wicked and the ignorant.

In a few centuries, perhaps, an inspired group of people will need a leader, an Initiator, and who knows whether Emen Y or Signor Siragusa might not become the new messiahs who lived through our time without being recognized! History is full of such wonderful adventures.

We must accept as fact the decrepitude and disorientation of our old and terrible Christian religion.

"By their fruits ye shall know them," said someone in Palestine, and if we pass judgment on the Jewish-Christian civilization of the 20th century, the sentence could be severe for Abraham, Moses, Jesus, and the pontifs of the Church. With the evidence of the million upon million of poor, hapless people crucified, burned, disemboweled, hung and quartered, imprisoned, exiled, laughed at, who will rise in their legions from the legend of time immemorial, condemnation to hell is inevitable.

It is no longer possible to build cathedrals, to go on Crusades, or to work for the sublime and beautiful, in the state of fear in which we live. So men look for and await help from elsewhere. Their anxieties, wishes, worries, appeals, create forces of great potentiality which will inevitably take over and subjugate the mind. This is the messianic phenomenon.

The Christs of our day are Emen Y, Dr. King, Eugenio Siragusa, and others unknown to us who have come here or will come in the course of time.

It would be sufficient to believe in one of them, no matter which, for him to become the true Messiah and to change the face of the globe.

They all come as messengers of peace and even as continuations of Christ.

Siragusa, better inspired, or more thoughtful, climbed the slopes of Etna to receive the word of the gods. Just as Moses did Sinai. If one day the Sicilian prophet should be persecuted, or even crucified, then his chances of being recognized as an anointed of the Lord would be real, particularly if this drama took place in cinemascope! There are precedents . . . !

The wonderful armor of the Celts

Apollo, the Hyperborean god, alias Abaris, who traveled on an arrow; Melusine, the winged serpent, Initiator from Venus, are in the French mythology, and are about the only indications of contact with extraterrestrials in the distant past of France.

It became the task of the Druidical writer, E. Coarer-Kalondan, to record, in the history of the Celts, the facts and signs that could logically be related to Initiators come from the sky.

His book, the *Extra-Terrestres chez les Celtes*, which he wrote with his wife, Gwezenn Dana, is truly a Bible of the teaching and great deeds of the ancient Celts, who were the heirs of the dolmen and menhir builders.

The goddess Belisama ("flamelike") Belenus ("the splendid"), and Grannus ("the brilliant one") are Celtic gods who remind one strongly of Astarte and Baal, the Phoenician Venus-gods, shining like the flame of the comet Venus.

Saint Brendan, navigating "the mysterious regions," traveled in a swift boat which took him from Ireland to the Land of the Mounts (America) in one night. The skiff owned by the magician Manannan Mac Llyr, without sails and without oars, "could go wherever his master wished."

If these reports are ture, one can conclude that these two ultrafast machines were either airplanes or vessels propelled by an energy-generating machine as yet beyond our technology. Coarer-Kalondan and Gwezenn Dana see them as flying machines and find in mythology grounds for believing that the Tuatha de Danann, who invaded Ireland, had weapons second to none, even compared with our most modern developments.

They knew of the submarine, if this is what was referred to as "silver vessels sailing in the water," which Elatha used to fetch her son after the battle of Mag Tured. One Irish poem even tells of a battle between amphibious tanks:

> One day the inhabitants of Connaught saw two huge animals fighting on the Shannon. From their mouths emerged balls of fire which reached the clouds in the sky

> [cannon fire?] They landed and took on a human form [men came out of the machines].
>
> As for the inhabitants of Munster, they saw a wonderful sight: Two large noisy birds, blackbirds, they thought, throbbed in the air and then transformed themselves into human beings. This also happened to the Goddess Badb's flying chariot, which was a rook in full flight.

We are free, in the light of what we now know, to think that these accounts referred to aircraft.

Tuatha de Danann's laser beam

In the same context, "Balor's eye," which blasted his opponents, however numerous they were, was a sort of laser which sent out death rays "when with the help of a hook the closing device which kept back these lethal radiations was lifted off."

Balor had a servant whose sole purpose in combat was to lift "this closing device whose enormous weight was due to the fact that the ordinary metal was completely lined with a lead casing to screen the radiations." Lugh's wonderful sword discharged solar-energy propelled missiles, Dagda's club was "a sort of bazooka, a sort of howitzer or a cannon so heavy that instead of being carried it was pushed on wheels." Cuchulain's "*gaebolg*," the Irish Esus, could be lengthened at will and never missed the opponent. It was a long tube from which flashed a deadly ray.

The use the Celts made of what we think is laser is therefore three times supported, in Balor's eye, Lugh's magical sword, and the *gaebolg*, and such a repetition of the same magic powe can only lead us to believe that there are certain scientific truth: in this report.

More especially as the Tuath de Dananns, famous and mysterious magicians, were really gods from a distant land to which they returned, defeated by the multitudinous races on Earth, "but who insisted on being worshiped, even in their absence, a cult respected for many years."

To prove their fantastic but fascinating theories, the co-authors mention that, traditionally, Cuchulain's sword, when not in use, had to have its point resting in water to avoid burning the surroundings.

"Now according to them, this precaution applies to certain laser ray generators, although different liquids are used."

Bearing in mind the flamethrowers which set Tara on fire, the atomic clouds which glazed the tower of Toriniz, destroyed all the houses, herds, and the whole Gorsedd Arberth countryside (a powerful weapon indeed), the ancient Celts of Ireland and the Tuathas, from a mysterious land, appear to have been people who possessed, for a time, scientific weapons which could not have originated on this planet.

This is E. Coarer-Kalondan's and Gwezenn Dana's theory, which may be mistaken in detail, but does at least link Celtic history to the great and wonderful adventure of other races where the visits of extraplanetary Initiators is more in evidence.

Flying saucers: Are they real or illusions?

The record of UFO's and of contact with supposed space travelers is certainly richer in suppositions, assumptions, and daring stories than in tangible realities, but one vital factor is beyond question: the event itself.

It is not illogical to believe that extraterrestrials visited this planet; it is quite logical to believe in the possibility of such an event; it would be wrong to ignore or deny it. To end this discussion we think it probable that ancient civilizations were the beneficiaries of knowledge given to them by aliens to our planet. According to traditional beliefs, which we judge to be genuine, these messengers, gods of antiquity, came from another world.

Mythology often insists on naming Venus as the source (before it became a planet within our solar system) and this does not seem to us at all unlikely. However, while on this subject, which could foreshadow future truths, it is interesting to have the opinion of the scientific world, which is generally hostile to our way of thinking.

To François Le Lionnais this is a collective illusion, because illusion is the misinterpretation of facts. Paul Muller, the astronomer, believes the UFO's to be lenticular clouds. Dr. René Held, psychiatrist, gives a more scientific explanation: For 3,000 years many peculiar objects have been seen in the sky but they have never added up to anything; the theory of flying saucers has never been proved. Now, in science, one drifts, one moves backward, one experiments, one sometimes misses the point but never entirely: There is always something worth retaining: Something is added.

So if there are no added facts, there are no UFO's nor are there ghosts, elves, and reincarnations.

The sky is a crystal ball

When one looks at strange objects, it is undoubtedly true that one adapts them to one's own ideas and thoughts. For example, when one sees a light in the sky, consciously or unconsciously, the idea of a flying saucer springs to mind, just as rain on the day of Corpus Christi makes us think of divine disapproval, even if we do not dwell on it. This is subjective participation at work.

For a UFO observation to be valid it would need, apart from testing the phenomenon, a study in depth of the witness. We all have emotional attitudes, and our minds are impressed with phantasms nourished since childhood. Moreover, a night sky has, more or less, the same effect as the clairvoyant's crystal ball. Whosoever perseveres in its contemplation eventually becomes hypnotized and creates in his inner self images and fantasies and a whole imaginative view of life.

Shepherds are good tellers of tales; they invent beasts, monstrous wolves, dragons, treasures, ladies, and other imaginary characters, because they contemplate the sky for hours on end. Lovers who sit on a hillside to admire the starry skies, eventually discern premonitory signs, haunting scenes, visions of the Apocalypse or of paradise.

These imaginings, which come from the contemplation of the sky, a forest, or the sea, are inherent to man's inner nature and to his inborn need of magic. Of course, these subjective considerations must be taken into account and undoubtedly many testimonies concerning UFO's are unreliable.

Nevertheless, it is also a fact that the most fantastic imaginings are tenuously but tangibly related to past or future realities, invented as a result of a projection of chromosomes or a prefiguration. It is with this in mind that we believe in the authenticity of the UFO phenomon.

Message from the inhabitants of Earth to the extraterrestrials

This view is so well based and corresponds so well to possible truth that astrophysicists have drafted a message to be sent to the inhabitants of outer space.

In March, 1972, the American satellite Pioneer 10 took with it into deep space an aluminum plate 15 × 22 centimeters giving the necessary data for an extraterrestrial intelligence to envisage the form which life takes on Earth.

Pioneer 10 will reach the vicinity of Jupiter in 1975. There can be no human life on Jupiter, which has a very strong gravity and where the cold is intense, but should the American satellite plunge on into the cosmos, it would have a chance of meeting with a more hospitable planet or of being intercepted by an advanced civilization.

The metal used for this message has been treated to resist a journey of 3,000 light-years, which is equal to 100 million terrestrial years. The sheet is screwed to the support of an aerial so that it is easily noticeable. The message is a representation of the solar system with fourteen radiating lines (or radii) representing a "radar pluse" and the fifteenth line situates the position of the Earth in relation to the center of our galaxy.

A naked man and woman give an idea of our shape: The man raises his hand to salute the possible discoverers and make them understand our wish to communicate.

It remains to be seen whether intelligent outer-space inhabitants, of unknown nature, shape, or consistency, could decipher this Sybiline message. The men of this Earth do not lack cerebral qualities and yet they are disinclined to interpret as possible attempts at communication with these UFO's, these phantom images which appear on their radar, or the signs in the skies which could perhaps be signals sent out by an outer-space civilization.

But we can always hope that the extraterrestrials of distant stars are more intelligent than we are. . . .